To Become an Investment Banker

Girl Banker®'s Bullet Point Guide to Highflying Success

Heather Katsonga-Woodward

a.k.a. Girl Banker®

This book was proofread by the following outstanding professionals. I am extremely grateful for the time and attention they gave to my book.

Alma Donohoe	• 2002-05: Economics, BA, University of Cambridge • 2005-07: Consumer and Retail Team, UBS Investment Bank • 2007-11: Davidson Kempner Partners • 2011-13: MBA, Harvard Business School
Dominic Legg	• 2002-06: Economics & Management, BA, University of Cambridge • 2006+: Equity Trading, Lehman Brothers, now Nomura • 2011: Completed CFA qualification within 18 months
IIM Goldmanite (Anon.)	• Some of the best feedback came from an individual who graduated from India's best business school, the Indian Institute of Management (IIM), and who has worked at Goldman Sachs for several years
Sydney Chuka	• 2005-08: Medical Physics, BSc, University College London • 2008-09: Computer Science, AA Montgomery College, USA • 2009-11: CDH: Business Development Officer, Malawi • 2011-12: Banking & I. Finance, MSc, Cass Business School
Dr Harry Woodward	• 2001-06: Medicine, MB BChir, University of Cambridge • 2007-09: Medical Intern, Addenbrooke's Hospital, Cambridge • 2009+: Pediatrician, London

Thanks also to Sola Jagun and all friends and family who encouraged me, especially my husband, Harry. And of course, a big thank you to my eagle-eyed editor, Debi Alper. This book would not have been the same without her.

First published in Great Britain & the United States in 2012 by Zumex Press. Girl Banker® is a registered trademark of Zumex Trading Company Ltd.

Website: www.girlbanker.com

Facebook.com/GirlBankerPage, Twitter: @GirlBanker, YouTube: GirlBanker

Phone: +1 646 233 3220 (US) / +44 20 3286 4625 (UK)

Grateful acknowledgement is made to the following for permission to use their work or data: Bloomberg, British Geological Survey, Paul G. Mattiuzzi Ph.D and Private Equity International (PEI).

ISBN 978-1475169614

Images on the cover, the second page and the last page by Bob D'Amico of Millennium Design Group, cartoonbob.com

For my dad,

who taught me that money isn't the most important thing in the world.

He said, "Only chase work and money will start chasing you."

For my mum,

who taught me confidence. As she dashed off to an interview she said,

"Even if they only wanted one person, it would definitely be me."

Give yourself the best chance. Subscribe, like and follow Girl Banker® on:

Get coaching from Girl Banker®; see girlbanker.com for details

Avoid weight gain with a weight tracker designed by Girl Banker®

You're competing against hundreds of people. If you prepare adequately,
"Even if they only wanted one person, it should definitely be you!"

Contents

Introduction

I knew jack squat about investment banking before 2003. My plan was to finish my Economics Degree at the University of Cambridge then go back to Malawi, establish a profitable enterprise and work my way to financial freedom. Then in October 2003, when I walked into the first economics lecture of the second year, I was taken aback to find over half of the now familiar faces stuck in an FT (the Financial Times). I raised my eyebrows and asked whoever was with me at that time, probably Rahul, perhaps it was Dom (two of my best friends), why it had all of a sudden become fashionable to read the FT.

"They're getting ready for banking interviews," was the answer. I didn't get why everyone wanted to work in the same industry but I soon found out that the pay and the status was a big lure. Don't get me wrong, there was intrinsic interest, too, but of the many industries that an economics degree gives one access to, banking is probably the most challenging to get into and the highest paid. We all love a good challenge.

I decided that I too would give this investment banking thing a shot and from that point on the learning curve was steep.

A lot of people hear about bankers and their multi-billion dollar bonus pools and think of it as a world mutually exclusive to theirs. Indeed, a fair number of bankers may think they're really quite 'special', a cut above the rest in intelligence, but this is not necessarily true. Intelligence is not the key factor that will get you in; it's grit, perseverance and having the right information. You will have to take care of the first two elements but information, I provide in this book. I would suggest you read it more than once because some things will make more sense after you start to penetrate the world of investment banking. You don't have to do a business or economics related degree to get into banking; it is open to many disciplines.

Why might banking as a career suit you?

A genuine interest in seeing economic principles at play

When you're learning economics at school or university, the material tends to be highly theoretical. By working in front-line banking you actually see all that book stuff at play: announcements from the Government or companies quickly feed into data that you have been monitoring; rumors (good and bad) immediately impact the price of a share you've been keeping an eye on; you advise a company on its financial strategy and you see the impact of your advice being put into practice - it's really quite exciting stuff.

A desire to learn more about the world of business and finance

You will very quickly learn how companies raise money, how to pitch for business, negotiation skills, financial modeling, the financial products available to companies to help smooth their cash flows, the varied funding costs that different companies and industries face, the things banks worry about when lending money, the factors that drive companies to raise money in one way rather than another. The list is pretty endless.

If this is your primary goal then classic investment banking (corporate finance) may be for you.

Personally, I found the intellectual content thoroughly stimulating. I have a deep interest in finance, both investment banking and personal finance, and this factor had major appeal for me.

Experience working with others, especially those from different cultures

Financial knowledge is not the only desirable skill one picks up from the world of banking. Especially at Goldman Sachs, I personally encountered a lot of different cultures and learnt a little about different ways of life. This is one industry where you will definitely meet a wide range of interesting people.

2

I now have friends and acquaintances from India, Italy, France, Senegal, China, Kenya, Australia, Côte d'Ivoire, Norway, Sweden, Belgium, Lebanon, Nigeria, Ghana, Pakistan, Iran, Morocco, Greece, Cyprus, Malaysia, the UK (obviously) and, of course, the US of A. What was particularly exciting was that all these people had actually been born and bred in these respective countries. There are very few jobs in this world that would have given me this sort of exposure.

As a kid growing up, I always wanted to be my own boss. I didn't want to work for ANYBODY, not my dad, not anybody – well, maybe for Richard Branson. Over time, however, I decided it was probably a good idea to have experience of working with others and I stand by that. If you want an intense course on learning how to work with others – banking!

Meritocracy

There are many metrics by which performance can be measured in front line banking. As such, if you perform well it will be evident and you will get rewarded for outstanding performance.

Influence and social responsibility

Some of us have grand hopes and desires for the world. The most direct way to contribute is with money. You can follow in the footsteps of Warren Buffet and Bill Gates who have earned large fortunes and have chosen to donate much of that to good causes. Your contribution can extend beyond donating money. You can use the financial skills that you develop to devise a lasting solution to poverty.

Get that start-up capital

Some people are fortunate enough to find backers for their world-changing idea from the get go. Many others have to start off by themselves before they're recognized enough to get any capital. A lot of people go into banking just for that reason, to save enough to start their own business. An example that I know of is Nick Jenkins, a former commodities trader who started Moonpig, the online greetings card company.

Indeed, some people know they want to do something entrepreneurial but they're not sure what they should do; so they work in banking whilst they figure this out. It's not a bad thing to do. Having to work as hard as you will in investment banking really has a way of forcing ideas out of you.

Want an early retirement

"If I had it my way, I wouldn't work," one guy said to me. "I figured I could work my butt off in banking for a few years and retire by 40." Not the best reason but whatever floats his boat. There are a fair few that fall into this camp.

Those are the reasons for, and you may have more of your own, but what can be said to those that are thinking: *"I hate bankers. Why would I want to work with them?"*

Investment bankers have received a lot of negative press, especially over the 2007-2009 credit crunch, and in some cases this was deserved. I wouldn't let the negative press stop you from potentially working in the industry. Go for it. You may find there are indeed things you don't like, but you will also find a lot that you do enjoy and relate to.

If you decide not to go into the industry, you're leaving a gap that might be taken up by a less responsible gambling type. As you get more senior, you'll find that you have the power to change things that you don't like. You can even be the catalyst for the change you want to see in banking. It's obviously easier to change things from the inside than from the outside.

1

FIGURING OUT WHAT'S WHAT

Is investment banking for you? Read this book to help you decide that.

If by the end of this book you think the good pay is the only attractive aspect of this career, you should probably look at doing something else. I don't think you can survive any career if you're doing it just for the money.

COMMERCIAL / RETAIL BANKING

To help you understand investment banking, it's best to differentiate it from the type of banking that you have experience with: commercial or retail banking – the banks that you see on the street.

The bank where you maintain your current (UK), checking (USA) or savings account is a commercial or retail bank. Some investment banks have a commercial banking unit, others do not.

Table 1.1: Investment Banking versus Commercial/Retail Banking

Investment Bank	Commercial /Retail Bank
Don't take deposits	Take deposits
Don't provide loans	Provide a lending service to their customers
Have a few hundred core customers or less	May have millions of customers

Investment Bank	Commercial /Retail Bank
Provide a very bespoke service	Provide a very standardized service
Don't provide transactional day-to-day services	Provide transactional day-to-day services • Current / checking / savings accounts • Credit and debit cards • Mortgages and personal loans • Insurance
Provide strategic advice to companies, e.g. on their structure, acquisitions, divestments and capital markets products such as debts and equity instruments	Don't provide strategic advice to companies. A retail bank will explain **all** the services available to a company but it's not usually within their remit to provide strategic advice on what the company should do

Example

A Loan Structuring team in an investment bank can give a company advice on how to structure a loan; however, even if the investment bank has a commercial banking unit, it does not necessarily follow that they will *provide* that loan.

When the loan is fully structured (i.e. the most achievable terms are determined) the borrowing company can show it to a variety of banks and select the bank that commits to the best terms. This may not be the structuring bank. The structuring bank gets a fee for their advice and the loan provider receives whatever fees they are due for actually providing the loan.

Of course, the lending arm of the structuring bank is likely to provide the best lending terms in many cases as they can account for the fees received by their structuring team. That is, a bank providing several products to a client can afford to charge a little less for each product than would be the case if they were selling just one.

WHAT IS INVESTMENT BANKING AND WHAT DO INVESTMENT BANKERS DO?

Many investment banks are composed of two key divisions:

1. Corporate Finance. Frequently referred to as the (Classic) Investment Banking Division or simply (Classic) IBD in many banks.
2. Debt and Equity Capital Markets. This frequently includes Sales, Trading and Research functions.

Many investment banks now also have large asset management divisions including private wealth management; however, this book focuses only on corporate finance and capital markets.

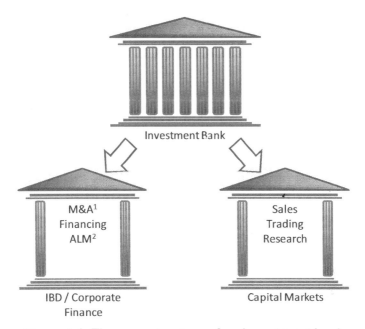

Figure 1.1: The core structure of an investment bank

1 M&A = Mergers and Acquisitions; 2 ALM = Asset and Liability Management

Throughout this book the term 'investment banking' will be used as a catch-all for both corporate finance and the capital markets (sales and trading jobs). However, keep in mind that when you hear the term 'investment banking' it could either be referring to the industry as a whole or the corporate finance division within an investment bank.

Chinese walls

Have nothing to do with China. Certain divisions of an investment bank are legally forbidden to interact to avoid conflicts of interest; this information barrier is the Chinese wall. Engaging in any financial transaction based on non-public information is illegal.

For example, corporate finance regularly receives private customer information but traders, on the other hand, trade based on public information. If traders had access to privileged information, they could trade in a way that causes harm to a corporate finance customer. Every bank will have its own written rules and documentation process regarding Chinese walls and how different classes of information should be handled.

What does the Chinese wall mean for your day-to-day life in banking?

- If you're in corporate finance, your work pass will be barred from trading floor access and vice versa if you work on the trading floor.
- Whenever you receive private client information you'll probably have to fill in a form to declare this.
- Your Compliance Division will hold a list of all the companies for whom your bank is holding confidential information.
- You'll need to ask your Compliance Division for permission every time you want to buy or sell a financial instrument, especially shares for your personal account. If you're planning on privately buying or selling a significant number of shares in a company listed as one for which your bank has private information, you will probably be told that you *cannot* transact.

Google 'Raj Rajaratnam' for an example of the consequences of dealing based on private information.

Corporate Finance or the Investment Banking Division (IBD)

Within corporate finance, you will find two key categories of bankers:

- **Mergers & Acquisitions (M&A) bankers**: provide strategic and valuation advice on mergers, acquisitions and company restructurings:
    - Buy-side: advise a company that wants to buy another company
    - Sell-side: advise a company on selling its assets or its entire operation (**divestments**)
    - Defense advisory: advise a company on how it can protect itself from a hostile takeover
- **Financing bankers**: provide advice on raising money (using equity, debt or some combination thereof); they also provide advice on managing any risks associated with these instruments.

Corporate finance tends to be very hierarchical compared to the capital markets. Why?

- Experience counts for a lot in corporate finance. Revenue goals are given to senior management and it is ultimately their responsibility to bring in profitable transactions.
- Analysts and associates do not have revenue goals (generally) and are evaluated according to how hard they work on allocated projects, so to get recognized you need to work extremely hard,
    - Hard work is difficult to measure. Different people measure it in different ways: it could be according to face-time (i.e. the number of hours you're 'seen' to be working), the complexity of the financial models you can manage, the quality of the presentations you produce or some random mixture thereof.

People working in corporate finance normally specialize according to a country team or sector:

- It's important to have country teams because local, country specific knowledge, including language, may be necessary to do business, e.g. people working on a 'German Team' normally speak German and have good knowledge of German culture and regulations.
  - o It is common for London offices to have a lot of country teams because of its central geographic location and its relatively friendly business environment compared to Europe.
  - o Economies of scale also mean it's cheaper to service some European clients from London because the client base in that country is too small for a dedicated office.

Table 1.2: Common COUNTRY team desks in a large investment bank

UK	Germany	France	Nether-lands	Iberia: Spain/Portugal	Nordic region	Emerging Market

  - o Regional teams that may be found in a US based corporate finance team:

Table 1.3: Common REGIONAL team desks in a US corporate finance team

Latin America	East	Midwest	Southwest	West	Canada

- It's important to have sector teams because some industries have so much sector-specific knowledge that it would be difficult or confusing for someone to work across too many different sectors.

Table 1.4: Common SECTOR team desks in a large investment bank

Consumer & Retail / Healthcare	Energy / Power	Financial Institutions Group (FIG)	Mining and Metals	Sovereigns & Supra-nationals	TMT*	Transport & Infrastructure

* Technology, Media & Telecoms

Different banks will have a slightly different variation on the above sector themes, e.g. Mining and Metals in one bank may be called Natural Resources in another. Boutique investment banks may focus only on one sector.

10

Sales and Trading a.k.a. the Capital Markets

The purpose of a capital markets division is to provide a range of **financial products** to investors and companies. The sales force specializes by product and will be the first point of contact for clients. Any buy or sell orders are passed on from sales to a trader, who executes and manages the risk associated with such a purchase or sale.

Many traditionally advice-only investment banks have incorporated capital markets activities to their offering because they wanted to offer a fuller suite of products to their clients.

Table 1.5: Summary of Sales versus Trading

Sales	Trading
• Give clients trading ideas • Give clients market activity updates • Price financial instruments • Take orders from clients to buy or sell a given financial instrument Note that some sales positions are more technical than others. In some banks structurers come up with ideas and salespeople market them; in other banks the sales desk is expected to come up with their own trading ideas	• Give salespeople updates on market activity • Execute the client orders collected by sales • Sales can give indicative pricing to clients but a market price from a trader is needed to execute a buy or sell order • Prop (proprietary) traders[1] make speculative trades on behalf of their bank (with bank money not customers' money)
Research	
• Many sales and trading decisions are based on research • Some banks have their own research departments whilst others will subscribe to a third-party research company • Research analysts may cover specific companies or a specific industry or may carry out macro-economic research covering a country or group of countries	

---

[1] Following the credit crunch there are proposals to ban prop trading in investment banks due to possible conflicts of interest. For example, if a bank has insider information it may be tempting to tip off their proprietary traders.

The capital markets tend to be less hierarchical than corporate finance. Why?

- Salespeople and traders are given individual revenue targets quite early in their career, possibly within 12 to 24 months of starting out.
- It is possible for a junior to earn more money for the firm than someone senior to them so there is limited room for overbearing seniors – one minute the guy or gal is your analyst, the next they're raking in more money than you.

Some view capital markets as more meritocratic than corporate finance. Why?

- The primary goal is to earn revenue by trading or selling. It's easy to measure revenue goals and hence reward performers accordingly.
- Nonetheless, it's possible to land oneself on a team where the existing sales people or traders won't give you access to the good clients; they keep them for themselves and you have to wait until someone leaves before you can get profitable accounts.

Origination versus Execution

You may hear people working in sales refer to themselves as 'origination' or 'execution'. Originators bring in the client along with whatever the client's problem is and executers structure the solutions.

Table 1.6: Summary of Origination versus Execution

Origination	Execution
Are essentially marketers	Come up with creative solutions to client problems
Pitch for new business	Price up various solutions to work out which one is optimal
Propose financing solutions to clients	Monitor and manage bank's risk position
Maintain client relationships	Execute mandated deals

Flow Sales versus Structured Sales

I've done both: over four years in structured sales and a few months in flow. With structured sales the products are more complex; they take time to price and to analyze. The transactions will by nature be more profitable, and also larger. A team dealing in structured products will do fewer transactions in a year than a flow team.

Flow is pretty much the opposite: less complex products in large numbers. The products are simpler and quicker to price. Each transaction is less profitable and usually smaller but, due to sheer volumes, it can be a good business.

Banks will frequently deal small 'flow' deals at no margin (or even a slight loss) in order to have access to larger transactions. Many companies will only award their bigger more structured transactions to those banks that handle a larger volume of their day-to-day flows. They develop trust via the flow.

Is Structured Sales harder than Flow Sales or vice versa?

There can be some snobbery between 'flow' versus 'structured' salespeople with the structured guys thinking they are smarter. However, having experienced both, I can confirm that a day in flow is much more intense. If you are doing flow at an established bank, the phone will never stop ringing. A less established bank will have fewer clients calling in but you need to be constantly on the phone nonetheless, calling clients and trying to direct more business your bank's way.

Work in structured sales is indeed more analytical and complex. However, since you have more time before the point of trading, you will know your transaction's details inside out so you are less likely to make errors. In this sense, it is less stressful than flow.

For flow, you trade several times every hour hence you are taking small risks on a very regular basis. If you're taking your sweet time to get a price, the client might hang up on you; you pretty much need to have your wits about you ALWAYS!

Is a big bank better because they already have more customers?

The above makes it sound like it's a lot tougher, and perhaps less desirable to work for a less well established bank, but that is not necessarily so. Frequently, because it is recognized that the money is hard earned, there is likely to be a stronger correlation between the revenue you manage to pull in at a small shop and your own compensation. At an established bank there may be a discount to compensation if most of your contribution is as a result of long-standing clients calling in and doing the same thing they have always done. If you want recognition in a big bank you need to amplify things: either bring in new clients or significantly increase volumes dealt with established clients.

How's a day in 'flow' different to a day in 'structuring'?

If you're doing multiproduct flow sales, like I did, over the course of the day you will go from executing an interest rate product to FX transactions in a multitude of currencies and then to commodities; it all depends on the products you are mandated to deal with. Different products will require you to think in different ways and will likely all be priced in different systems that you'll need to learn how to use. Structured salespeople will tend to deal in one product because they need to have in depth knowledge on that single instrument in order to produce a properly structured product.

Flow teams will tend to end their day sooner than structured sales and I never used to understand why. It's because of the intensity of the day. Your brain is toast by 5-6 p.m. and you need to recover.

Is performance in 'flow' measured in the same way as in 'structuring'?

There are probably more performance metrics for flow sales than structured sales, e.g. management may have numbers showing how many deals you executed each month; how many executed deals you had to amend (and hence how conscientious you are); how constantly you are on business calls.

If these metrics vary widely across people on a team, management can use them to allege underperformance. A structured sales team transacts fewer deals; the number of deals completed and time spent on the phone are not useful metrics because a lot of time needs to be dedicated to devising bespoke solutions that solve a unique customer problem. A top structurer may execute only a handful of deals in a year but their uniqueness may mean high revenues.

To summarize:

Table 1.7: Summary of Flow versus Structured Sales

Structured Product Sales	Flow Product Sales
Complex, more detailed products	Simpler, more standardized products
Products take longer to price and analyze	Products quicker to price and analyze
Fewer transactions per year (low volume)	Many transactions per day (high volume)
Higher profit per transaction	Lower profit per transaction
Sporadically intense	Intense every day
Cover fewer products to a more in-depth level	May cover many products in less detail
Fewer performance metrics	Likely more performance metrics
May be required to work longer hours as the structuring process is less driven by markets	More standard (shorter) day as the day is very market-movement driven

What is the difference between cash equities and equity derivatives?

Cash equity specialists are essentially equity brokers. They are in touch with the equity research of companies in a certain sector. They act for companies and investors that want to buy and sell shares. If a customer asks them why one share is better than another, or what the growth prospects are of one compared to another, they will have this knowledge.

On the other hand, equity derivative specialists are more product-orientated; they have in-depth knowledge of instruments whose value varies according to changes in the price of specific shares. These include, but are not limited to, equity futures, equity options e.g. put and call options, equity swaps e.g. total return swaps, and convertible products e.g. convertible bonds. For instance, an equity derivatives specialist will be able to explain why call option prices are rising or falling and how pricing might evolve.

Broad Product Categories in the Capital Markets

People who work in sales and trading will normally work with products that broadly fall into one of the below categories.

Table 1.8: Capital markets products overview

Equity	• Primary issuance (initial public offering, IPO) • Secondary trading including block trades
Debt	• Loans • Bonds (investment grade and high yield) • Structured bonds or loans
Currency	• Vanilla foreign exchange (FX): spot, forwards, FX swaps • Structured FX including FX options
Commodities	• Energy • Precious metals (gold, silver, platinum etc.) • Agricultural produce (wheat, grain, pork bellies)
Hybrids	• Products with features of both debt and equity, e.g. convertible debt
Hedging	• Equity derivatives • Fixed income derivatives • Asset and liability management, e.g. pension solutions

What does the career ladder look like in investment banking?

The table below sets out the different career stages in an investment bank; the terminology used in European banks is slightly different to that used in American banks. You may find further differentiation in specific banks, e.g. splitting the VP category into junior VP and senior VP, but broadly speaking the below applies.

Table 1.9: The investment banking *'food chain'*

European Bank	American Bank
• Analyst	• Analyst
• Associate	• Associate
• Associate Director (AD)	• Vice President (VP)
• Director	• Senior Vice President*
• Managing Director (MD)	• Managing Director (MD)
	• Partner Managing Director** (PMD)

* Some banks do not have a Senior VP tier

** Most investment banks do not have this level; Goldman Sachs is one example that does.

Corporate finance roles are more structured compared to the markets. Analysts do most of the analysis and 'grunt work' on a project. Associates own the analytics (i.e. they manage the analyst) and the process. VPs lead projects. MDs are the client's trusted advisor.

In the capital markets, analysts write market summaries and much of the number crunching that is required. However, job function can be very similar between a third year analyst, an associate and a VP. Differentiation comes along when you receive management responsibilities, e.g. managing people, heading up a team's strategy and so on.

A TYPICAL DAY IN THE LIFE OF AN INVESTMENT BANKING ANALYST

It's no secret that bankers work very long hours. On average, an analyst in IBD is in from 8:00 / 9:30 a.m. and will work through to 10:00 p.m., midnight and beyond. If you are working on a 'live' project (i.e. one where there is a meeting coming up or which is close to final execution) the hours will tend to be longer than if you're not. Analysts in the capital markets will generally have shorter more intense working hours say 6:00 / 7:00 a.m. to 6:00 / 7:00 p.m. The day can be very varied so the below is just a guide and not a fixed timeline of one's day as an analyst.

Domenico, the London-based IBD Analyst (Telecoms, Media and Technology Team)

Time	Action
Morning	
6-8	<ul><li>Got up at 7:15 a.m. after a rare seven hours of shut eye. Was showered, suited and at my desk by 7:50 a.m. I live a 15 minute walk away.</li><li>My bed gets made once a week on Fridays when a cleaner changes the sheets and sorts out my laundry; the room is quite neat otherwise.</li><li>Grabbed some milk and cereal from the café on my floor and ate whilst I read through the Project Rhino[2] comments which my MD had already left on my desk. He was in by 7:00 a.m. as usual.</li></ul>
8-10	<ul><li>Worked through the project comments:<ul><li>Corrected a few typos and grammatical errors</li><li>Added a new slide with the multiples of</li></ul></li></ul>

---

[2] Corporate finance transactions are normally referred to by a project name to protect the client or deal's confidentiality before it is publicly announced.

	comparable companies (covered in Chapter 7)
	o Added a deal team slide which I got off Amanda, my colleague
	o Included a couple of new charts
	o He's deleted the industry slides which took me half of yesterday to complete. I'll save a new version of the presentation because no doubt he'll want to reinsert some of them later
	• I take the slides up to the Presentation Team so they can make the more mechanical changes. I could do this myself but it will take ages and I need to do some work on Project Gecko so I'll save myself the time.
10-12	• Before jumping into Project Gecko again I surf the net for major news (FT.com, wsj.com, hereisthecity.com).
	• The VP on Project Gecko has emailed me a bunch of changes that she wants made to the financial model. Amongst many things she thinks my growth assumptions are far too conservative.
	• I love modeling so I completely forget about the time until an email from the Presentation Team pops into my inbox at 11:30 a.m. with the updated presentation for Project Rhino.
	• I print it off and leave it on my MD's desk.
	• It's nearly lunch time. I'm famished so I decide to have a break and finish the model after that – food always boosts my creativity levels.
	• Jane and Amanda join me for a canteen lunch. We're early so we've skipped the lunch time lines and can afford to sit down for longer.

Afternoon

12-2	• At 12:10 my Blackberry vibrates. It's the MD on Project Rhino: "Left some minor comments on your desk, we're almost there. Can you turn around by 2:00 p.m. please? I'm leaving at 4:00 p.m. for another meeting and I want to have a look before I go." • I say goodbye to Jane and Amanda and rush back to my desk. The Project Gecko Model will have to wait. • The comments are not that "minor". The waiting list in the Presentation Room is ridiculous so I have to do everything myself. • At 1:40 the VP on Project Gecko comes round to ask about the model. I tell her I need another hour.
2-4	• I finish the Project Rhino slides at 2:00 p.m. on the dot, hit print and drop them on my MD's desk a few minutes after 2:00 but he's not at his desk anyway so it doesn't matter. • It takes just 20 minutes to finish the Project Gecko Model. I promptly email it to the VP; I got it to her before an hour was up: 'under-promise, over-deliver', that's my motto. • I'm starving again. I leave my desk and walk to a small park 5 minutes away from the office grabbing a Coke, a bag of crisps and a bar of chocolate en route. • I stay in the park for half an hour before returning to my desk. • I read a few news articles then clear my inbox.
4-6	• The Project Gecko VP tells me the model results are good, now we need to build a presentation around the

	model for a meeting in two days' time.
	• The VP has scribbled a framework for the presentation on paper which she explains to me. I start to work on this right away.
6-8	• I manage 30 minutes on the treadmill, have a quick shower then return to my desk. The dinner I ordered before going to the gym is already at my desk.
	• I continue to work on the Project Gecko presentation until around 8:00 p.m. when the MD on project Rhino sends through his final comments which he's scanned in from home.
8-10	• By 10:00 p.m. the slides are done.
	• I print them off, check them, then send them off to the Print Room to get client meeting pitch books printed.
	• The pitch books will be on my desk by 8:00 a.m. tomorrow ready for the 10:00 a.m. meeting.
	• Project Gecko can wait until tomorrow; I walk home and watch 30 minutes of TV before hitting the sack. Looks like I might just get 8 hours tonight, result!

Ultimately, what does a career in corporate finance mean for you?

At the junior level, you will have long unpredictable hours, some weekend work, presentation making, number crunching, exposure to very interesting transactions. You will gain highly detailed knowledge of the companies and sectors that your team covers.

As you gain experience and become more familiar with modeling, your hours will improve and you will gain more power and control over the type of work you do.

Fiona, the New York-based Market Analyst (Derivatives Desk)

Time	Action
Morning	
6-7	• Three months in, I still need an alarm clock to wake me up at 6:00 a.m. • Bed made, showered and dressed, I leave my immaculate flat at 6:30 a.m. on the dot for the ten minute walk to my desk – the analyst commute, any further would be hell. • I pick up a porridge en route. • By 7:00 a.m. I have scanned through my inbox and added three new things to my to-do list, more 'urgent' items will be thrown at me throughout the course of the day.
7-8	• I read through the news and market data updates from Hong Kong and London and pick out the important stuff for the 'New York Open' market commentary that I send out every day between 7:30 and 8:00 a.m. • I'm done by 7:30 a.m. and allow myself 15 extra minutes to read more news before I start responding to some pricing queries.
8-9	• I price a rollercoaster swap for a potential project financing in Hawaii. • My manager wants to know the risk to the bank of executing the swap, the revenue potential and the swap price the customer would get if they execute today. • I email the required details to him.

9-10	• I calculate the risk and return numbers for a strip of forwards and send them to another manager to check before they're sent to the client.
10-11	• I start working on a client presentation for a meeting tomorrow afternoon. • We're seeing a large Texan private equity fund that is about to buy a chain of supermarkets in New York City. We're showing a variety of hedging solutions that might interest them: a variety of cross-currency swaps, interest rate swaps as well as options. • Before 30 minutes have passed, I'm asked to run some quick and urgent numbers (risk and returns) for swapping a bond from a fixed to a floating interest rate. A retail conglomerate is taking advantage of an unexpected dip in government bond yields and wants to issue as soon as possible.
11-12	• The 'quick' bond swap analysis takes over three hours to complete. The company's undecided with regards to whether to issue a USD or a EUR bond and is also debating maturity: five, seven or ten years.
Afternoon 12-2	• I run credit risk and return numbers for every scenario being contemplated and by the time I'm done it's almost 2:00.
2-4	• My manager needs a draft of the Private Equity presentation by 4:00 p.m. so I grab a sandwich from the café on my floor and continue with the draft.

	• Whilst I'm writing the presentation, two different customers ask for 'live' swap pricing. I compete for the two swaps; I win one. I'm officially running late now.
4-6	• The presentation is done just shy of 4:30 p.m. and I email the slides to the VP that will be presenting them. He knows it's been a busy day for me so he doesn't fuss over the delay.
	• Although I would kill for a coffee, two more urgent pricing tasks have hit my inbox so I get on with them.
6-8	• By 6:30 p.m. my brain is toast. I've been working on overdrive since 6:45 a.m. and I can barely think.
	• I still have the end of day market commentary to write but I need a break, so I take a ten minute timeout and walk across the street to buy a frozen yoghurt.
	• I return refreshed and write a comprehensive summary on the performance of the swap market during New York business hours that day.
	• This commentary used to take me two hours initially but now I can produce a good piece within 30 minutes so I'm out the door by 7:30 p.m.
	• I call Louis who works on the swaps desk at a neighboring bank and we eat out at a top restaurant before heading home. We both have early starts so we save our late night outings for Thursday, Friday and Saturday. It's still only Monday.

Ultimately, what does a career in the capital markets mean for you?

An early start, sometimes you're at your desk as early as 6:00 / 6:30 a.m. However, you will rarely have to work on weekends because much of your work is dependent on the capital markets being open.

At the junior level, you will be heavily involved in writing market summaries and market commentary related to the product your team specializes in. You will have to do some presentation writing but more time will be spent using product pricing software that is specific to your bank.

You will gain highly detailed knowledge of a product. Whilst your knowledge of companies and certain sectors will improve, it won't be as detailed as would be the case in corporate finance.

As you gain experience and become more familiar with your product, your hours won't change by much; they will be slightly shorter when you pass the end of day commentary onto someone else. You will gain more power and control over the clients you cover and how you cover them.

What is investment banking pay like?

Table 1.10: Investment banking pre-bonus pretax annual pay

Year	London (GBP)	New York (USD)
Analyst		
Year 1	45,000 – 50,000	72,000 – 80,000
Year 2	50,000 – 55,000	80,000 – 88,000
Year 3	55,000 – 60,000	88,000 – 96,000
Associate		
Year 1	60,000 – 65,000	95,000 – 105,000
Year 2	75,000 – 85,000	120,000 – 135,000
Year 3	90,000 – 98,000	140,000 – 160,000
Year 4	93,000 – 115,000	150,000 – 180,000

Survey by an international recruitment firm

What about the bonus?

Bonuses are very variable especially during a recession. The bonus is more fixed at junior levels with larger differences between people at more senior levels. Bonuses can range from 0% to several hundred percent of base pay.

What does the structure of bonuses mean for you?

- Don't spend it until you get it.

What does the structure of bonuses mean for your bank?

- In challenging years, they can cut costs significantly by chopping the bonus pool.
- In profitable years, they can share the success with their most valuable asset: the people.

ASSET MANAGEMENT

What do Asset Managers do?

It pretty much says it all in the name – they manage assets! There are two key categories in asset management:

1. **Institutional asset managers**: manage the assets of a large spectrum of individuals with whom they do not interact, e.g. Pension Funds, Insurance companies.

2. **Private wealth managers**: manage rich people's assets, so called high net-worth individuals. Private wealth managers will meet with their clients to set out goals on what sort of assets the client is comfortable investing in and the investor's time horizon.

Key concerns of an asset manager: firstly, they do not want to lose any money that has been entrusted with them. After that, they want to earn a decent return on those funds.

Pension Fund Manager versus Insurance Fund Manager

Many companies have a **pension plan** for their employees. Normally, both the company and the employee pay money into the pension plan on a regular basis. All this pension money can either be managed in-house by the company or assigned to a third-party asset manager. In addition to a corporate pension, we all have the choice of saving towards a private pension.

The assets of a pension fund manager belong to a large group of people at different stages in the cycle of life:

- Some are already retired, others are not
- Some will live beyond the average life expectancy, others will not

The money a pension fund manager has to pay out forms her **liabilities**. Her **assets** consist of any un-invested cash, debt instruments, equities and

27

commodities. On an ongoing basis, the asset manager needs to endeavor to have a **present value (PV) of assets** at least equal to the **present value of liabilities**.

If the PV of liabilities exceeds the PV of assets, the pension plan is **underfunded**. This exercise of managing assets so that they are at least equal to liabilities is called **asset-liability management**.

A fund manager whose liabilities are insurance contracts is also tasked with **asset-liability management**; the liabilities, however, are much less predictable. Insurance is paid out when an unexpected, unplanned for event occurs. History can only act as a rough guide because in any given year 'accidents' will be higher or lower than the historical average. If a disaster happens, e.g. a flood, more people will call on their buildings insurance than would be the case in an 'ordinary' year.

The contingent nature of insurance contracts adds an extra dynamic to the asset-liability models of insurance asset managers.

A pension fund manager, on the other hand, has to deal with predicting how long people will live. With improvements in living standards, we are all living a lot longer than pension models assumed and this major change in life expectancy means pension fund managers have more liabilities than they anticipated. Extra assets are needed to match against these liabilities.

Both pension asset managers and insurance asset managers have to make assumptions about the nature of their liabilities and manage their assets to meet those liabilities.

Private Wealth Management (PWM)

Working in PWM you will meet many individuals with a large asset base. They give you their cash and guidelines on how to invest that cash. Level 3 of the Chartered Financial Analyst Program (CFA) goes into a lot of detail on the dynamics and considerations that a private wealth manager needs to think about:

- How risk averse is the client?
- How close to retirement is the client? For instance, a young client probably doesn't need much liquidity in the near term so you can invest in assets that need to be held long-term.
- Is the client averse to any industries or products?

What does a career in asset management mean for you?

On average, your working day will be shorter than it would be in corporate finance, say 8:00 a.m. to 6:00 p.m. and less intense than it would be in the capital markets.

A career in asset management should be more stable relative to both of the above and your earnings trajectory, especially in the first five to seven years, will probably be lower.

2

GETTING INTO AN INVESTMENT BANK

NETWORKING

Above all else, building a cache of contacts helps your career in direct and indirect ways. Ten pointers on networking:

1. Attend networking events and aim to leave with about two business cards. Don't stretch yourself thin by trying to meet with everyone; it's much more useful to have a proper conversation with two people than ten superficial conversations. The two people you connect with are more likely to remember you later on.

2. When talking to people look engaged, maintain eye contact, don't keep on looking away and don't check your phone – not even once.

3. Go to local recruitment events. If you manage to find out the names of any speakers in advance, do some research on them so that you can ask very specific questions, based on the speaker's own experience of the industry.

    *   People tend to prefer questions that can be linked back to their own (awesome) life over technical questions that cannot be correlated with their day-to-day job or previous experiences.

- Do enough research to enable you to ask astute personal questions, e.g. "Ms. X, I understand that you led Project B. Can you tell us a little about what it was like to work on the largest telecom deal of the century and to be featured in Forbes on the back of it?" Notice how the question contains an element of flattery. Ms. X will be thinking, *I like that kid*, and she'll probably remember you if you approach her afterwards.

4. If you don't have business cards, get some made, even if you are still in university; I did this and found them handy in creating an impression. Let's face it, it's very unlikely that the investment bankers that you give your card to will actually call you. However, you will look like a real keeno if you have cards when most of your peers do not. *Vistaprint* produces good quality affordable cards.

5. Join any professional organizations or societies related to investment banking. You will probably find some in your local careers magazines or on careers websites.

   - Personally, I joined Sponsors for Educational Opportunity, SEO, which helps to place people from ethnic minorities in investment banking (and other professional) internships after providing them with intensive training.

   - To be a member of SEO you have to qualify by passing their interview process which is identical to normal investment banking interviews.

   - That said, SEO provides pre-internship training, so if you're very strong in two out of three areas you could still make the cut and you'll receive the necessary coaching.

6. Catch up with your peers, especially any economics students, on how they are going about hunting for a job.

   - In the couple of months before I started applying for internships I was constantly chatting about it to my peers. I knew nothing about banking. I would say these conversations are half of the reason I managed to secure an internship in the first place.

- Discuss different ways of handling technical questions, where people are applying, what recruitment events people are attending, whether they can share contacts with you, what they know about the different banks, which newspapers they are reading, what questions they have been asked at interviews and so on.

- To get ahead it is best to treat your peers as collaborators not as competitors. The more open you are, the more others will share information with you.

7. Always send a follow up email to new contacts: a 'thank you' or 'great to meet you' email always goes down well. In addition, you can elaborate on a discussion you had or perhaps remind them to send you something that they said they would or vice versa.

8. Join LinkedIn. You can use this as a tool to connect with any new contacts you have made.

- Try to get your lecturers, colleagues and your manager at your part-time job to give you a recommendation on LinkedIn. Potential employers may see it.

- Check out your friends' Connections. See how you can use their contacts to progress your own job hunt.

9. Find a mentor or a coach. I myself received some coaching from Harrison Careers. I found their help useful. You can also receive one-on-one coaching from Girl Banker®. See girlbanker.com for details

10. Finally, ask intelligent questions! As part of SEO, I had exposure to many high-ranking bank officials at networking events and I made it a point to ask something smart, so much so that my peers began to recognize me as the girl who likes asking questions. At the end of the experience SEO awarded me recognition as 'The Most Insistent Person.' Don't ask me what that means!

If you find it difficult to approach people that you don't know, here are some useful tips to help you strike up a conversation:

1. Practice, practice, practice

- Practice networking with people that you are already comfortable with such as family, friends, teachers or even colleagues. Practice will make you feel better prepared for any networking events and even interviews.

- Ask the person you are practicing with to give you *honest* pointers on how you can make yourself look like the better candidate.

2. Get introduced

- If someone you know already knows the connection you want to make, they will probably be happy to introduce you.

- This way you don't have to think of an ice breaker. More often than not this sort of introduction builds itself up into a conversation.

3. Fake confidence until you actually feel it

- Hold your head up high and smile. No one else knows that you are nervous; you can successfully portray confidence without in fact feeling it.

- A little test for you: next time you walk into a full room, try to identify the confident from the shy and reserved. It's dead easy to spot, right? Their behavior gives each group away.

- The more you put yourself out of your comfort zone, e.g. by approaching strangers at networking events for a chat when you normally would not feel comfortable doing so, the easier it becomes.

4. Be yourself and stick to subjects you are knowledgeable about

- Don't present yourself as something you are not; a little lie can spiral out of control especially if you tell different people different lies. Being yourself obviously extends beyond telling the truth: it's about behaving naturally.

- For instance, just because the interviewer seems to be blue-blooded when you're not, it doesn't mean you have a lower chance of getting the job. To the contrary, you might be perceived as being more hungry to achieve because you weren't born with a silver spoon in your mouth. Indeed, amongst some circles there's a growing belief that recruits from a less-privileged background crave success a lot more and are therefore more willing to give the job their all.

- One of the quickest ways to make yourself look unprepared and hence not worthy of the job is to take the conversation into unfamiliar territory. I see this quite a bit in interviews.

- Do a lot of research. Then focus on those topics that show how well-prepared and well-read you are.

5. Tackle your fear of rejection

- The people you want to talk to are probably just as nervous as you are, maybe more so.

- What's the worst that could happen: the person hurries off looking uninterested? If so, do you care that much? At least you tried. Think of it as their loss.

6. Get the other person talking to take the pressure off of you

- You should find yourself getting less anxious as the other person talks. Hopefully, you'll come up with questions based on what they say.

7. Google or get a book for more tips on tackling shyness

- If you think you need more than the above there is plenty of material out there.

DECIDING WHERE, WHEN AND HOW TO APPLY

Ultimate question: when banks are looking to hire, what are they looking for?

At junior levels all banks want just one thing: someone with the right attitude. They will train you to ensure you have the basic technical skills but underlying all that they want a go-getter, someone who is hungry to excel. That is the fundamental requirement.

In addition to having the right attitude, they look for:

- Someone who has some **technical knowledge** or appears to have the ability to **learn quickly**
- **Personable** people who will work well with others ('team players')
- **Charismatic** people with a **presence** especially for advisory or sales roles
- **Self-starters** i.e. people with initiative

Investment banks vet their applicants with extreme care. The majority of their hiring needs are satisfied through their annual recruitment of new graduates. The vast majority of new hires are recruited after completing an eight to twelve week internship the year *before* they embark on full time employment. Many universities don't emphasize this point hard enough: **if you want to become an investment banker, do an internship <u>a year before</u> you graduate**. That said, a résumé/CV looks more interesting if you have a variety of different experiences: one solid banking internship plus two or three other out-of-the-box experiences (charity work, other industry or business experience) will do much more for you than three banking internships.

I interned at Goldman Sachs in the summer of 2004. When I joined full-time in 2005, I recognized many of the new recruits from the year before. This in itself highlights the value of securing an internship a year before graduation.

The official internship programs in the UK, the US and Europe are held during the summer (from late June to early September).

In the month following the internship, your bank will call, write or email you to let you know if they will be offering you a full-time position. Some banks will do this on the last day of your internship in an '**exit interview**'.

If you are offered a full-time position, you will be given a week or two to confirm whether or not you will be accepting it. I received a phone call and I said yes on the spot. Feel free to take your time.

To get a summer internship, you need to make your application in the winter before. Deadlines for applications are usually in January to February. If you're late, you are going to find it quite difficult to get in another way. Banks normally look to replace lost staff with experienced hires (not inexperienced graduates) usually with the help of a search firm, the so called '**headhunters**'.

To emphasize the point, you will maximize your chance of securing a full time job in investment banking if you have done a summer internship. You will maximize your chances of getting a summer internship by applying to as many banks as is physically possible in December the year *before*, January at the latest. Check the careers section of the bank's website for their specific deadline: **girlbanker.com/banks** (QR code below) has hyperlinks that will take you directly to the recruitment section of 50 top investment banks.

Some banks will read applications on a rolling basis until the deadline; other banks will look at every single application only after the deadline.

When should I apply and what should I be looking for?

To be specific, if you graduate in June/July 2014 start job hunting in October 2012 if you are in the UK or US system of education.

Table 2.1: The summer internship application timeline

Oct 2012 to Jan 2013	Applications for banking internships are made Most applicants are in their penultimate year of university
Jan to Feb 2013	Banks close their doors to new internship applications
Feb to Mar 2013	Banks start selecting who to invite for interviews
Apr to Jun 2013	Internship offer (and rejection) letters start arriving
Summer 2013	Take part in an 8 to 12 week internship The best interns get offered a full-time job to start in 2014
Summer 2014	The permanent job starts (normally in July). You will recognize many new hires as interns from the summer before

If you want a permanent investment banking job to start in 2014, you will be shooting for a very small pool of vacancies if you start this hunt any time after Feb 2013. By 2014, that boat has all but sailed. Most full-time jobs starting in summer 2014 are G.O.N.E.

Okay, now it's clear that you need to start nice and early, what should you look for?

If you are new to the investment banking industry it can be hard to focus your applications. Where you apply depends on your prime interest.

The biggest and most reputable banks frequently pay slightly less than the market rate because they have no problem attracting quality candidates. However, having a well-known bank on your résumé/CV increases your market value; it may be worth accepting slightly less pay now for more in the future.

If pay is a primary driver for you, then a less-well-known bank may in fact do more for your wallet because they tend to pay a premium to attract talent.

I was fortunate to be reading a degree amongst people very familiar with the banking industry, so I just asked my friends where they were applying (and why) and applied there. If you prefer to take a more scientific approach think about the following:

1. **Deal flow**

   For the best learning experience, choose a firm that does many transactions. Tables 2.2 and 2.3 are a great starting point.

2. **Size of the firm by employees or market cap**

   It may be easier to get things done in a smaller investment bank, although, the infrastructure may not be as comprehensive, e.g. support for completing presentations, collecting market data, printing and binding pitch books; you might also feel more included.

3. **Focus of the firm**

   Some firms are stronger in corporate finance than in market-making, or they may be better at asset management. Many new to banking do not realize that asset management is not corporate finance nor is it markets. Some online research will quickly reveal what the bank focuses on and what its reputation is.

   Focus can shift from year to year. For instance, in 2003-2004 when I was applying for internships, HSBC Bank was viewed as more of a commercial bank than an investment bank, although they did have investment banking capabilities. Over time, however, especially during the credit crunch, it built up a huge amount of credibility as an investment bank; whilst many other banks were struggling or even going bust, HSBC grew from strength to strength.

4. Locations of the firm

If you have an interest in working across countries go for a bank with a global platform so that when you do want to move you do not need to get a new job; you can just get an internal transfer.

5. Diversity of the firm

Even today, some firms are a lot more diverse than others. Personally, I think some banks are serious about diversity and view it as beneficial to productivity, whilst others use it as a marketing gimmick and are, as a result, not very diverse. Even within firms, some managers/teams are more pro-diversity than others. Take a good look at whatever stats are available regarding the firm's employee base as well as their diversity initiatives.

For instance, how many women are there in the bank/team? Do women seem to progress in this bank/team? Are there any bank-wide networking groups for your race, your religion, your sexuality? In interviews, feel free to ask about the firm's diversity track record or profile.

6. The team

Once you start interviewing or interning, analyze the team that wants to hire you very specifically. I cannot emphasize this enough. Even within one firm, the culture from one team to the next can be radically different. After my Goldman Sachs internship, several teams were happy to hire me; after my formal offer, I was asked to go back to meet with the teams before I made my decision. It was difficult because, even after ten weeks, you have only scratched the surface but, ultimately, I believe I chose the best team for me. If you are in the same situation don't be afraid to ask to go in and talk to teams again.

The scope of bank hiring

If you think you are competing only with people in your country, think again. Recruitment is now a very global event, especially at the big US banks. They want the smartest person they can find for the job and they will comb the globe to find her (or him). Over the last decade, banks have been recruiting quite heavily straight out of Asia, especially India which is known for its rigorous MBA program at the Indian Institute of Management (IIM). More recently, banks have been recruiting straight out of Africa. These recruits are hired not only for their local office but also for head offices in New York, London, Paris, Frankfurt and beyond.

League Tables

To provide you with a framework for where to start, have a look at the league tables 2.2 and 2.3. Each table was compiled from Bloomberg, Girl Banker®'s favorite news portal.

How was the data picked?

The data is for the 2011 calendar year. The products and the dates chosen to compile a league table can have a huge impact on the rankings. It all depends on when companies close transactions and submit the information that will be included in league tables to data agencies, such as Bloomberg. I chose to demonstrate league tables for 'Global Equity, Equity Linked & Rights Issues' and 'All Corporate Bonds' because they are both very broad.

With so many league tables, how do analysts select a few to show clients in a presentation?

As an analyst, you will become familiar with the importance of selecting the best data to present your firm. For instance, your company may rank higher if you present the last six months rather than the last one year. You may rank higher under European equities rather than Global equities, under high yield bond issuance rather than investment grade issuance and so forth. The data can be sliced and diced in·many different ways.

As a new analyst you should aim to work where you will get the best exposure. Chase work, rather than money, to increase your market value.

There are so many banks, how can I choose where to apply?

The firms nearer the top of the league table have the most deal flow. Each league table shown here has data from hundreds of banks; if I had included the entire list you would have seen that many near the bottom of the table closed only one or two transactions in the entire 12 month period.

Does that mean you shouldn't apply to smaller firms?

Certainly not, but it does mean you may have to work that much harder to get execution experience in the format that you want. Indeed, a large institution may need you to focus on a very narrow product category (e.g. high yield bond issuance) from the outset because there's enough work to occupy all of your time, whilst in a smaller institution you'll get a broader, more general, experience (e.g. high yield and investment grade corporate bond issuance plus private placement).

Table 2.2: Global Equity, Equity Linked & Rights Issues

- The total amount issued in this period: $560.4bn
- The number of issues in this category: 3,209
- The number of underwriters involved in this product category: 592

Table 2.3: All Corporate Bond Issues

- The total amount issued in this period: $3.2 trillion
- The number of issues in this category: 19,712
- The number of underwriters involved in this product category: 781

Table 2.2: League Table for Global Equity, Equity Linked & Rights Issues, 2011

Rank	Underwriter	Mkt Share (%)	Amount USD (bn)	Number of Issues
1	Goldman Sachs & Co	9.0	50.3	202
2	Morgan Stanley	8.4	47.1	273
3	Bank of America Merrill Lynch	7.5	41.8	235
4	JP Morgan	7.3	41.1	261
5	Credit Suisse	6.5	36.2	188
6	Deutsche Bank AG	6.2	35.0	203
7	Citi	5.8	32.2	210
8	UBS	5.3	29.6	185
9	Barclays Capital	4.1	23.0	155
10	Nomura Holdings Inc	1.8	10.3	58
11	Wells Fargo & Co	1.5	8.5	98
12	HSBC Bank PLC	1.4	8.0	47
13	RBC Capital Markets	1.2	6.5	108
14	China International Capital Corp	1.1	6.2	23
15	BNP Paribas Group	1.1	6.2	34
16	Daiwa Securities Group Inc	1.1	6.1	38
17	TD Securities	0.9	4.8	50
18	Macquarie Group Ltd	0.9	4.8	47
19	Ping An Insurance Group Co	0.8	4.5	33
20	UniCredit	0.7	4.1	24
21	Banco Itau BBA SA	0.7	4.1	27
22	CITIC Securities Co Ltd	0.7	4.0	11
23	Guosen Securities Co Ltd	0.7	4.0	28
24	RBS	0.7	3.8	69
25	Guotai Junan Securities Co Ltd	0.6	3.6	17
26	BMO Capital Markets	0.6	3.5	42
27	Jefferies Group Inc	0.6	3.5	55
28	CIBC	0.6	3.2	36
29	DBS Group Holdings Ltd	0.5	2.8	14
30	Bank of China	0.5	2.8	16
31	China Securities Co Ltd	0.5	2.6	9
32	ING Groep NV	0.5	2.6	14
33	Credit Agricole CIB	0.4	2.5	20
34	Mizuho Financial Group Inc	0.4	2.4	18
35	China Merchants Securities Co Ltd	0.4	2.4	22
36	Scotia Capital Inc	0.4	2.4	33
37	Societe Generale	0.4	2.2	14
38	Banco BTG Pactual SA	0.4	2.2	12
39	Banco Santander SA	0.4	2.1	20
40	Standard Chartered PLC	0.4	2.1	19
41	Commerzbank AG	0.4	2.0	7
42	Raymond James & Associates Inc	0.3	1.9	34
43	Intesa Sanpaolo SpA	0.3	1.9	5
44	CIMB	0.3	1.9	24
45	Essence Securities Co Ltd	0.3	1.8	8
46	Bradesco BBI SA	0.3	1.8	10
47	VTB Capital	0.3	1.7	8
48	Haitong Securities Co Ltd	0.3	1.5	18
49	Sumitomo Mitsui Financial Group Inc	0.3	1.5	16
50	GF Securities	0.3	1.5	13
Source: Bloomberg		86%	483	3,111

Heather Katsonga-Woodward

Table 2.3: League Table for All Corporate Bond Issues, 2011

Rank	Underwriter	Mkt Share (%)	Amount USD (bn)	Number of Issues
1	JP Morgan	6.2	199.5	1,017
2	Deutsche Bank AG	5.3	171.8	1,039
3	Bank of America Merrill Lynch	5.2	167.0	2,638
4	Citi	4.8	155.7	1,094
5	Morgan Stanley	4.5	143.9	2,339
6	Barclays Capital	4.5	143.8	952
7	Goldman Sachs & Co	4.2	134.6	611
8	HSBC Bank PLC	3.7	119.4	839
9	UBS	3.1	100.3	1,146
10	BNP Paribas Group	3.0	95.0	511
11	Credit Suisse	2.9	94.9	542
12	RBS	2.7	87.3	582
13	UniCredit	1.8	58.7	195
14	RBC Capital Markets	1.8	56.4	371
15	Wells Fargo & Co	1.5	49.7	1,727
16	Intesa Sanpaolo SpA	1.4	45.9	136
17	Credit Agricole CIB	1.4	43.8	221
18	Societe Generale	1.2	40.1	188
19	Mizuho Financial Group Inc	1.1	35.0	273
20	WestLB AG	1.0	33.2	280
21	Nomura Holdings Inc	1.0	31.8	290
22	Bank of China	1.0	30.9	124
23	Natixis	0.9	29.3	140
24	Banco Santander SA	0.9	28.2	156
25	Landesbank Baden-Wuerttemberg	0.8	25.6	168
26	TD Securities	0.8	24.9	197
27	Daiwa Securities Group Inc	0.7	24.0	225
28	Sumitomo Mitsui Financial Group Inc	0.7	23.5	171
29	Commerzbank AG	0.7	22.7	161
30	CITIC Securities Co Ltd	0.7	22.2	54
31	DZ Bank AG	0.7	21.6	211
32	Scotia Capital Inc	0.6	19.6	114
33	Standard Chartered PLC	0.6	19.2	349
34	Industrial & Comm Bank of China	0.6	19.2	78
35	China International Capital Corp	0.6	18.8	37
36	Norddeutsche Landesbank GZ	0.5	17.7	91
37	ANZ Banking Group	0.5	17.0	134
38	ING Groep NV	0.5	16.4	122
39	Agricultural Bank of China Ltd	0.5	14.7	56
40	BayernLB	0.5	14.5	95
41	China Construction Bank	0.4	14.2	68
42	National Australia Bank Ltd	0.4	13.8	64
43	Banco Popolare SC	0.4	13.3	46
44	Banco Bilbao Vizcaya Argentaria	0.4	12.8	93
45	Westpac Banking	0.4	12.6	58
46	BMO Capital Markets	0.4	12.6	64
47	CIBC	0.4	12.0	71
48	Commonwealth Bank Australia	0.4	11.9	53
49	Mitsubishi UFJ Financial	0.4	11.3	94
50	Landesbank Hessen-Thuringen Girozer	0.4	11.3	73
Source: Bloomberg		79%	2,543	20,358

43

The tables above are very heavily skewed towards large banks. You should definitely consider looking at the 'boutique' banks below

A key feature of boutique investment banks is that they have no connection to commercial banking, don't take any trading risk and tend to focus on smaller deals. Some specialize exclusively on given sectors, e.g. Arma Partners focuses exclusively on corporate finance advisory services to Technology, Media and Telecoms (TMT) companies. See girlbanker.com/banks for more information.

There are hundreds of boutique investment banks out there; the below list of 50 was compiled by Girl Banker® based on industry knowledge and contacts. In alphabetical order:

Table 2.4: Boutique and other Noteworthy Investment Banks

	Founded		Founded
Allen & Company	1922	Houlihan Lokey	1972
Arma Partners	2003	Lancaster Pollard	1988
Berkery, Noyes & Co.	1983	Lazard	1848
BG Capital (equity & debt brokerage)	2000	Lincoln International	1996
Blackstone	1985	M.M.Warburg & Co.	1798
Brewin Dolphin	1762	Marathon Capital	1999
Business Development Asia	1996	Marlin & Associates	2002
C.W. Downer & Co.	1975	McQueen	1999
Cain Brothers	1982	Miller Buckfire & Co.	2002
Cantor Fitzgerald (bond trading)	1945	Moelis & Company	2007
Capstone Partners	1996	Montgomery & Co.	1986
Centerview Partners	2006	N M Rothschild & Sons	1811
Close Brothers Group	1878	Needham and Company	1985
Collins Stewart Hawkpoint	1991	Newedge (brokerage)	2008
Corporate Finance Associates	1956	Park Lane	2005
CSG Partners	2001	Perella Weinberg Partners	2006
D. A. Davidson & Co. (broker-dealer)	1958	Sagent Advisors	2004
Defoe Fournier & Cie.	1824	Sanford Bernstein (sell-side research)	1967
Duff & Phelps	1932	Sonenshine Partners	2000
Europa Partners	2000	Stephens Inc.	1933
Evercore Partners	1996	Sucsy, Fischer & Company	1972
Financo	1971	Thomas Weisel Partners	1999
Foros Group	2009	Vermilion Partners	2004
Gleacher Shacklock	2003	William Blair and Co.	1935
Greenhill & Co.	1996	WR Hambrecht + Co.	1998

WHAT DEGREE WILL GET YOU IN?

Investment banks want the range of people they hire to reflect the diversity of their client base, so your degree doesn't matter too much. That said, most people who are interested in the field have done economics, business, accounting or some other finance-related degree.

Some of the best investment bankers I know didn't come from a business or banking background and some of the most mediocre ones did; so if you're thinking you don't have a chance because of your degree, don't worry. Those with degrees in economics or business may have the knowledge advantage; however, you can quickly catch up by following Girl Banker®'s tips.

How does it make sense to hire people without financial knowledge?

Every team in a bank focuses its energy on a very narrow field of finance. The required knowledge will be so specific that even 'relevant' degrees will not cover everything you need to know to work with a specific team.

Importantly, a science degree may offer a new hire a deeper understanding of, say, the healthcare industry, making them an invaluable addition to a Healthcare Team in corporate finance.

A lot will have to be learnt on the job, regardless of your subject. A strong go-getting attitude and a real passion for work is more important. Banks find people with the right attitude and train them up. Banks with a very strong culture prefer to nurture bankers from the start of their career to the top.

Where should I start?

The first step for any investment banking hopeful should be to follow the financial press on a daily basis. You don't have to spend a dime; the free sections of Bloomberg.com, reuters.com, ft.com and wsj.com are enough. You can now also follow financial tweets; see Chapter 10/Resources for Girl Banker®'s recommendations.

THE APPLICATION PROCESS

There are two key routes you should look at:

- **Use your university's careers service**. Investment banks may visit your university specifically. If you are at a top-end university they may even have a unique recruitment program that you can use.
- **Apply directly via the bank's website**. Your university careers service won't have knowledge on every single investment bank. It is definitely worth exploring the careers section of banks independently and applying more widely. Use girlbanker.com/banks for quick links.

Whichever method you use, network proactively. Get to know people connected to the industry and learn as much as you can from each.

The following are the key steps in graduate recruitment:

1. An internship application is submitted, usually using a standardized online form (rather than your own stylized résumé/CV).
2. Once your application has been accepted, the interview(s) you are invited to will normally entail all of the following:
   - An aptitude test online or on paper
   - A case study and/or brainteasers
   - A competency based interview
   - A technical interview
3. Accepted to intern in the summer.
4. After the summer internship, you receive a hire letter or a letter stating that you will not be offered a full-time position.

The following will reduce the likelihood of your application being accepted:

- Typos: they suggest you have poor attention to detail and cannot be bothered to check your own work
- Grammatical errors

The proportion of interns offered full-time contracts varies from year to year and from bank to bank; it is never 100%.

If you've interned but have not secured a full-time job, you will have a better chance of securing an alternative entry-level position than if you hadn't interned at all, so do not despair. Some banks may not have filled all of their positions from the internship program and will look to fill in those positions with people like you.

ALTERNATIVES TO THE STANDARD HIRING PROCESS

Sponsors for Educational Opportunity, SEO

- SEO is a not-for-profit organization that places people from ethnic minorities in internships at investment banks (and other professions).
- SEO arose because of the dearth of ethnic minorities in investment banks (seo-usa.org, seo-london.org).
- SEO have partner banks that allocate a portion of their internship pool to SEO. They provide a significant amount of pre-internship training, so your chances of impressing a bank improve with SEO.

Doing a Masters of Business Administration, MBA

- If after three to seven years working in an industry that is completely unrelated to banking you would like to have a career change into banking, doing an MBA is one of the best ways to achieve this.
- Some investment banks have special internship programs for people with a few years of work experience and an MBA.
- MBAs with work experience are normally hired at the Associate level.
- The time limit of three to seven years is my own estimate; generally, the older you are the harder it is to switch into a bank because:
  - If the person hiring is younger than you, they might be concerned about having trouble controlling you.

- o If you have a family there may be doubts over how you might cope with the long hours that banking initially requires.

The Chartered Financial Analyst program, CFA

- The CFA qualification is well regarded because its modules are highly relevant to different areas of banking and because CFA only allow the best 35-45% to pass any sitting.
- Some bankers think the CFA qualification looks a lot better if you did it whilst you were working rather than when you were in university or looking for a job; however, I would argue that it adds a lot of value to your résumé/CV no matter when you do it. It's not easy.
- Case in point: one of my colleagues did his first degree in Lebanon followed by a Master's degree at a good UK university. When it came to looking for a job, he says he didn't get a single response after sending out his résumé/CV so he decided to sign up for CFA Level 1, while he was doing the Master's degree. When he sent his résumé/CV out again he started getting interview invitations. He's one of the best derivative salespeople I know so it just goes to show that banks can have trouble sifting through the many applications.
- I did CFA 1 and 2 whilst I was at Goldman and CFA 3 whilst I was at HSBC – all levels were passed on the first sitting within 18 months (the shortest time possible). I'm not showing off, I promise.
- Why did I do the CFA? I thought there were things that I ought to know that I didn't yet know but I wasn't quite sure what those things were (the unknown unknowns) and reasoned that a course like the CFA would help me to discover them. I'm glad I did it.
- One annoying question you will be asked: "Is the CFA relevant to what you are doing / what you want to do?" My response would be:
  A) It may help you to decide the direction to take your career
  B) You never can tell when something you know will be relevant or even when it might help you take advantage of an opportunity

APPLICATION ENHANCERS

The following may increase the likelihood of your application being accepted.

Participate in a spring internship

- In addition to their summer program, some banks now take in interns over the Easter period for two or three weeks for a more informal introduction to investment banking.
- Such schemes if available are very limited. If you can get onto one this will definitely make you look more passionate about banking.

Be an all-rounder

- If the academics are good and you play a major sport for your university, that shows you must have highly developed time management skills.
- Your academic track record is critical but it is a good idea to have one or two extracurricular activities to talk about.
- If you started or ran a society or a business whilst you were doing your degree, that shows you are a self-starter, have a high degree of initiative and obviously superior time management skills.

Read a couple of books written by insiders

Girl Banker®'s recommended list is in Chapter 10/Resources; I have personally read those books myself. Reading novels written by ex-bankers will help you to get a better feel for the industry, the culture and major points of change in the industry over the years. Specifically:

- When you start making job applications you may be able to reference some of your reading. This will not only show you are keen but that you have done your research.

- Similarly, you may be able to slip in knowledge from your reading into an interview.

- Importantly, when you get to the interview stage or in your first days on the job, your peers will almost certainly be trying to figure you out; they want to know whether you're worthy competition or not. Some won't ever explicitly ask you if you've read 'x book', they'll just start talking about some situation that occurred in a book assuming that 'of course you've read it'. Sometimes the games people play are so subtle that you won't even know they're playing them!

A bachelor's degree from a renowned university

- Investment banks are looking for the best of the best of the best. They depend on the education system to help them filter out candidates and it just happens that top tier universities *tend to* have more stringent entry requirements. Banks therefore expect to find the largest portion of good quality candidates at such institutions. You may not view this as fair but I'm just telling it like it is. Don't shoot the messenger!

- Do not feel discouraged if you're at a second tier university; there are many other things you can do to improve your chances, e.g. getting top grades.

Doing an internship although you have already graduated

- You want a permanent job but you failed to get a summer internship the year before, or indeed you didn't even know that this was a mega necessity. Why not apply for an internship anyway? I have seen many people do this.

- If you really impress, a team might ask you to just stay on with a view to making you permanent immediately or later on.

- Alternatively, you might get a job offer that starts in a year's time. This is no bad thing either: save up your internship money and go travelling, enjoy your life because once that job starts you will be working harder than you have ever worked before.
- On the other hand, you might not get a full-time job out of it. Their loss. You still have the experience and you can leverage that to get other jobs.

Parents, relatives and family friends that know senior bankers

- Close family and friends can help to get your résumé/CV into the right hands.
- If a banker knows your academic record or any other positive things about you, he might be able to put a good word in for you to ensure you get an interview.
- Have a good think about who you might know that could help you get ahead.

Super rich parents that know lots of other rich people

- For those descended from a well connected family, life is a little easier. They will go through the official process for the record but they might get the job regardless. "That's so unfair," I hear you say. It may seem unfair but if you think about it from the bank's perspective, it might not be. See the below example. Again, don't shoot the messenger, I'm just telling you what I've seen happen. I had no connections whatsoever myself when I started out.
- Reminder: banks are businesses and like any business their aim is to turn a profit for their shareholders (in the most ethical way possible).

Hypothetical Scenario: you're a banker. After years of hard graft you've been newly promoted to 'Head of a Team' but three months into the year your team hasn't made any money at all. You need to hire to increase your efforts and are presented with two candidates:

Sofia Katsongas:

- Daughter of a billionaire Greek yacht-maker whose clientele includes large sections of the mega-rich across Europe.
- As a hire, Sofia is pretty average. There is nothing remarkable about her.

Dom Khan

- Middle class. Super bright.
- Extremely motivated, it's clear he'll work his socks off to get results.

You can only hire one of the two. You know that by hiring Sofia you will be able to tap into her father's wealthy network of clients. You'll be able to line up a string of meetings with top-quality clients in pretty short order with her on the team, without having to wait weeks. By the time you and Sofia are arriving at meetings, daddy will have already put in a call to give the client notice - he'll be all keen to hear your spiel.

Who do you hire? It's not so easy to decide, is it? If you're being honest with yourself, you're probably going to say Sofia because if you're not able to produce results, your job could be on the line. As much as you might want to play high and mighty, if you've got a mortgage to maintain and little Johnny's school fees to pay, it's hard to be so sanctimonious. I'm not saying it's right, I'm just saying 'it's complicated'...

Girl Banker®'s experience of the graduate recruitment process:

In December 2003, I made about five to seven internship applications using an über slow dial-up connection in Malawi where I was on Christmas holiday.

I found out about Sponsors for Educational Opportunity, SEO, chatting with a stranger on a coach ride from Heathrow Airport to Cambridge. See how networking and *connecting with people* pushes one ahead in the most unlikely of scenarios? Having already submitted the rest of my applications over the holidays, the SEO one was the final one I made.

In early 2004, I received many rejection letters and a couple of acceptance letters. As confidence-bashing as rejection felt, I chose to think of it as 'their loss'. To make myself feel better I assumed it was because I was a foreign student so they couldn't be bothered to apply for my Work Permit.

The Goldman process is the one that I most remember so I'll take you through that. The University of Cambridge is one of their key hiring venues so for round one, they came to us. They hired out many rooms in a hotel for the day and invited candidates for an aptitude test and an interview. I arrived at the hotel to find a multitude of other equally qualified penguins: I didn't see anything but black suits and white shirts. If this had been Malawi there would have been every color suit you can think of. I was glad I'd sought advice on dress code because my favorite suit at the time was purple. Within fifteen minutes we were chaperoned to the testing room. I recall the test requiring a lot more logic than numeracy skills; some answers were not obvious, and no calculators were allowed.

After thirty or forty-five minutes, however long that test was, we were led to a waiting room and successively called up to interviews. The cornucopia of interviews that day required that some bedrooms be used as offices; I was led into a room where two guys from FICC (Fixed Income Currency and Commodities) interviewed me. I only remember one question from that day, "How would you value this hotel?" I think that was the only technical question.

I answered it well although I was thinking; '*I thought they're not meant to ask technical stuff in this round!*' The rest of the meeting involved competency-based questions. I felt good about the interview; I felt okay about the aptitude test.

A week later, I got an invitation to the second round which was held at Goldman's offices on Fleet Street in London. Goldman Sachs takes diversity very seriously; not just racial diversity, but all forms of diversity. They believe that the more diverse their employees' backgrounds, the more varied the range of ideas they can produce for clients. In addition to inviting me to round two, they advised me that they were signed up to a program that provided free, pre-interview coaching to people of Afro-Caribbean descent. It was up for grabs should I need it. I signed up immediately.

I had two coaching sessions: one group session involving role-play and another one-on-one Q&A meeting in which a recent intern evaluated the strength of my responses. Coaching boosted my confidence immeasurably.

Interview day two involved people from several universities. The shameless Ivy Leaguers were going around trying to out-university the non-Ivy Leaguers. I didn't partake. I had three interviews: the first was with a Chinese man, the second with an Irish lady and the third with two men whose backgrounds elude me.

I blundered on the very first question with the Chinese guy: "Tell me what story has aroused your interest in the press lately?" I repeated the details of some M&A story that had been recurring on the front cover of the FT for the last couple of weeks. He wasn't impressed. He asked me why such a bog standard transaction should amuse anyone. He told me it was too 'vanilla' to be exciting and shared the stories that he thought were far more interesting. It could only go uphill from there and I spent the rest of the interview trying to win him over; by the end of it I felt I had brought him closer to my side. Nonetheless, even recalling that interview, almost exactly six years later to the day, fills me with a degree of trepidation. That said, it does show that one less than perfect interview does not necessarily spoil the lot.

The Irish lady was quite nice but also scary. The way she looked at me said, "I'm sizing up every sentence you emit; I'm not really sure about you." Perhaps the inquiring look was just her character. I don't remember any of her questions but by the end of our chat I had no sense of where she stood.

I thoroughly enjoyed round three; I had a rapport with the two guys from the beginning. Again I remember one question; they drew an economic cycle on the white board and jotted down some industrial sectors, then asked me to explain during which part of the economic cycle each industry would make the most profits. As an economist, this question was right up my street.

I received an internship offer a week or so later. Because Goldman was one of the first to sift through that year's candidate pool, I only had to interview with one other bank but for the life of me I can't remember which one it was.

In addition, I was invited to attend the interview day for Sponsors for Educational Opportunity, SEO. The day involved an aptitude test, a case study presentation which you were given thirty minutes to prepare for and a formal interview. I received an offer a week or so later.

I wanted to be part of SEO because I knew I would definitely benefit from their training program (and the exposure they provide, especially as I came from a very different culture) but I also wanted to work at Goldman because, well, they're Goldman. I explained my dilemma to the two and it was decided I could go to Goldman Sachs as part of the SEO pool.

3

INTERVIEW BASICS

INTERVIEW BEHAVIOR

1. Portray confidence

To get accepted into an MBA program at the age of 40, my mother had to go through a whole day of final round interviews pitched against eight other candidates. Just before she left for the interview, I asked if she was nervous. I was 15 years old at the time. Without a moment's hesitation she said, "Even if they only wanted one person, it would definitely be me." That statement struck a chord with me and I try to carry the same degree of confidence whenever I go to interviews. Indeed, if there is one characteristic common to all bankers, it is a highly inflated sense of confidence and self-worth (sometimes quite frankly misplaced!).

If you believe that you are a worthy candidate, it will show in your interview. Doing your research will help to build your confidence; don't underestimate the competition; there are many high quality candidates out there.

Finally, there is a thin line between confidence and arrogance; don't cross it. A whiff of arrogance and your interviewer will do their damnedest to make it a 'challenging' interview.

2. Smile even as you speak

It makes you seem more likeable and will help to build a rapport with the interviewer. Smile at someone and most of the time they smile back!

3. Give a firm handshake at the start and at the end

A firm handshake is the only physical contact that takes place (or should take place) between interviewer and interviewee and can set the tone for the rest of the interview.

Some research argues that lightly patting the elbow of the person whose hand you're shaking with your free hand is helpful in building a rapport. You might have seen politicians doing this on TV.

Why does the handshake matter? According to Paul G. Mattiuzzi[3], Ph.D.,

- Research has shown that your handshake actually reflects certain personality characteristics and can make a real difference in certain settings, e.g. interviews and business meetings.
- Furthermore, research also suggests handshakes might be a bigger self-promotion engine for women than for men.
- He quotes an article by University of Alabama psychologists, William F. Chaplin et al, published in 2000 in the Journal of Personality and Social Psychology. In this study a panel was trained to recognize and classify: *completeness of grip, temperature, dryness, strength, duration, vigor, texture, and eye contact*. At a high level, there was a close correlation between the handshakes that were classified as creating a 'good impression' versus a 'poor impression'.
  - When matched up against personality, those with a firm handshake were found to be the same people that were *extroverted* and more *open to new experiences*. The rest were more *anxious* and *shy*. The benefit of a firm handshake

---

[3] http://everydaypsychology.com/2006/11/does-handshake-matter.html

was found to be stronger for women because women were less likely to give one so the ones that did stood out more.

- Bad handshakes
    - o   Too wet (uurrgh!).
    - o   Too limp and weak – makes you seem shy and anxious.
    - o   Too firm – don't squeeze too hard, it hurts. Bringing pain to your interviewer can never be a positive start to an interview.
    - o   Barely touching – suggests you want to maintain a distance and perhaps don't want to be touched.
    - o   Hand too straight. In a pleasant handshake, your hands should clasp each other in a sort-of hand embrace; this isn't possible if your hand is proffered rigidly straight.

It doesn't matter who extends their hand first in an interview setting; however, don't forget to shake hands at the end of the interview too. The interviewer might not care about creating a good impression with you so it is very much up to you to ensure that niceties like handshakes happen.

4.   Maintain eye contact AND lean forward

Eye contact and leaning forward portray **confidence** in oneself, **focus** on and **interest** in the discussion. Eye contact especially can help to bring your interesting **personality** across.

When someone fails to maintain eye contact they could just be **shy** (not a good trait in investment banking). On the other hand, it might mean they are **lying** or plain simply **bored** and hence **not that interested** in the job.

5.   Mirror the body language of the interviewer

I recall learning on a sales training course that subtly mimicking the body language of someone you are trying to sell to (and in this case you are trying to sell yourself) can have a positive impact by showing agreement and empathy.

Body language mirroring naturally happens when two people, such as good friends, are in sync and getting along. However, because body language experts have successfully made us aware of this fact, you will put yourself at a disadvantage if you are blatantly following your interviewer's body movements. You have to be subtle.

Importantly, don't create a barrier between you and the interviewer by crossing your arms. Keep your arms on your lap or at your sides.

6. Be careful about cracking jokes

Making your interviewer laugh is a sure fire way of making them like you and will go a long way towards getting you the job or at least into the next round of interviews. Take heed of these two provisos:

- If you tell a joke that is taken as offensive you'll kill your chances.
- Too many jokes and the interviewer might conclude you are all personality and no substance.

7. Don't repeat the question, please

It makes you sound a little stupid.

> "So Ms. Jones, where did you come in from this morning?"
> "This morning, I came in from...."

Umm, I hope that sounded oh-so-kindergarten even to you. It's important to make the interview flow like an ordinary conversation and the chances are you don't repeat the question when you're talking to someone that you're comfortable with.

Sometimes, it is appropriate to repeat part of the questions, for instance, if several questions are asked in one go then repeat each question as you answer it to give your answer more structure.

8. Finally, speak passionately and enthusiastically

INTERVIEW DRESS CODE

Smartness

Smart casual is a no-no for banking interviews; it is okay on the job (if you're not seeing clients on that day) but definitely not for the interview.

Make sure whatever you wear is comfortable and doesn't make you feel self-conscious so that you can focus on the interview.

- Body piercings (apart from earrings for girls) will tend to work against you
- Visible tattoos are associated with a ruffian lifestyle, not with the clean-cut image banks try to reflect to their clients

Before you even emit one word your chosen suit should be saying:

- Smart
- Serious
- Charming (rather than sexy)
- Pays attention to detail
- This boy/girl is going somewhere and I want to be associated with his/her success

Color

Black suit, white shirt for boys; black suit, light colored shirt for girls.

This may sound rigid but interviews are formal events and you want to look 'the business', that is, smart and serious. When you walk into a room full of interviewees you will notice how much you stand out if you're wearing anything slightly different.

Girls have more flexibility on what to wear but this also means it's easier to pick the 'wrong' thing.

To give you an example of how poor dress can detract from a decent interview: I walked out of interviewing a prospective Associate Director / Junior VP thinking he had handled himself well and the first thing my male co-interviewer commented on was the inappropriateness of the brown shoes the guy had worn.

Jewelry and makeup

Guys

- Stick to just a watch. Most people will view earrings on guys negatively. Wristbands are probably acceptable.
- If you have dry skin, moisturize – flaky skin will give you an air of unkemptness.

Girls

- Keep it simple, a watch and a pair of earrings, a bracelet and a necklace.
- Natural tones for make-up are best.
- If you have very bushy eyebrows a tweeze wouldn't hurt either.
- No chipped nail polish, please; and go for a neutral color.

Shoes

Apologies if I'm stating the obvious here, however, closed shoes (in my opinion) are the only correct shoes to wear: there is no room for toes and heels in an interview. I have been to new hire presentations where the same view has been expressed by banking colleagues.

For girls, shoes with a bit of a heel, even a kitten heel help to improve your posture.

Pantyhose / tights / stockings smarten a skirt suit up, definitely wear a pair. Pack a spare set in your bag in case you get a ladder.

Hair

Management tend to favor a more conservative, tidy look. If you have had to rush to an interview and your hair has blown all over the place, it is well worth taking an extra couple of minutes to smarten up.

Unfortunate though it is, some people pick up unintended signals from hairstyles. If you're unlucky, a 'radical' hair-do will form part of the reason you are not hired for the job; if you are lucky you will be advised to tone it down before you start working. I know of only two colleagues who were given hair advice:

A colleague from South-East Africa was told his afro was too large and would need to be trimmed before he started working, which he did although he was hired as a volatility and options trader and would almost never be seeing clients. I didn't think it was that large but his manager thought differently. Within one year he was running a trading book larger than his manager's and within three years he was the top trader on his team.

A chilled out Aussie colleague of Chinese-English origin was told that if he wanted a job on a certain sales team he would need to remove the highlights in his hair.

Beards

Unless it's for religious reasons, you will discover that facial hair is not the done thing.

Natural black (African) hair

If you're a girl with natural African hair, it is okay to keep that but go for more 'unadventurous', protective hairstyles; YouTube has a great selection of videos. I myself watch kimmaytube, Naptural85 and prettydimples01's channels to figure out how to deal with the 'fro.

Most people don't know much about natural African hair. When I went from having chemical straightened hair – the standard for black girls in banking – to having natural textured 'kinky' hair, I got all nature of responses:

- "What happened to your hair?" my manager asked as he waddled into the office on my first day of being 'natural'. Before I had a chance to respond the whole team let out a roar of laughter that they'd obviously been suppressing for the best part of an hour.
- "Did you tease it out?"
- "Why is it so puffy?"
- "Why couldn't you flatten it?"
- "Did you have a perm?"
- "What does it feel like?"
- "I think your hair looks really cool."
- "Should we call her pineapple?" my manager asked on the day I wore it combed out.

Some of the responses hurt but I responded as politely as possible and I even let people feel my hair if they wanted to. Five days later I purchased a £120 Indian Remy lace wig. I put it on for practice on the Sunday night but I hated it and decided to bear with the comments. It took me about two months to learn how best to handle and tame my hair into conservative protective styles and, ultimately, people got used to it. The longer it gets, the easier it is to manage.

The idea of Girl Banker® was born at around this time, hence the logo.

Dreadlocks

Whether it's fair or not, dreadlocks are viewed negatively in banking (yes, I just said that) and if you are applying for a client-facing role they will reduce your chances of getting the job.

I was always cognizant of this view but it was reinforced when I was going to a team drinks event and I asked an MD if a friend of mine could join. He said yes, but when he discovered the friend had dreadlocks (I don't know how this came to light) he vehemently suggested that I shouldn't bring him along because that would reflect badly on me. So of course I didn't take him: I ditched the team and went to meet up with my friend instead because friends are forever; jobs are transitory, especially nowadays.

Of course, not everyone has a negative view on locks but the one or two people that do will act to stop you from getting the job, so if you are very keen on a banking career, cut them off; you can grow them back when you become an MD.

Caucasian hair

For guys, keep it short and neat but not too short. Unless you're balding you shouldn't really go for a skin head.

Straight and wavy haired girls can wear their hair up or down and it will look neat either way.

If you've got curls, however, it's quite easy for your hair to become unruly and do things that you would prefer it did not. For an interview, consider tying your hair back.

Of course, hair will never be the key determinant of whether or not an interview goes well but in the ideal world you don't even want it to be a consideration.

RULES ON ANSWERING INTERVIEW QUESTIONS

GOLDEN RULE: give examples for EVERYTHING you say, everything

- Why? Examples validate claims and statements

Lots of people I have coached assume their résumé/CV has been read by the interviewer and this is generally **not** true. It's best to assume it has not been read in any detail. By answering questions with valid examples, by the end of the interview you should have **run through all the key things that you want the interviewer to know about you** and then some.

- If you say something like "I'm very good at grasping financial concepts" it has less credence than for example, "I'm very good at grasping financial concepts, as you will see on my résumé/CV I took the Advanced Course in Mathematics in High School. I was actually one of only five people out of a class of 40 to do that and only two of us got an A."

SILVER RULE: practice, practice, practice

- If you're strapped for cash get a friend to ask you interview questions and to rate your answers. Feedback is vital.
- Alternatively, record your own responses on camera, either with a friend involved or on your own, and review the footage. Focus on your body language and the quality of your responses.
- Ideally, hire an independent investment banking coach. Friends may find it hard to give negative feedback; a coach will tell you like it is.
  - **Girl Banker® provides free coaching (goodwill coaching) and fee-based coaching. See girlbanker.com for details.**

BRONZE RULE: brevity is paramount

- Don't use two sentences when one will do.
- Bankers have a short attention span. Don't allow boredom to seep in!

4

COMPETENCY-BASED QUESTIONS

Personally, I think it's silly to give people a script for an interview; it makes it a lot harder to act natural. Consequently, in the below I provide only a *framework for thinking* about how to answer questions.

1. **What do investment banks do? How are investment banks different to commercial or retail banks?**

- See Chapter 1

2. **Why do you want to work in corporate finance?**
   Why do you think you would be good at corporate finance?

In addition to having a deep interest in financial concepts, you can discuss one or more of the following.

- Projects in corporate finance tend to be of a long-term nature, so if you like **long-term, project-based work** and like to get involved in the nitty gritty of a project then corporate finance may suit you. When a project is 'live', i.e. when you are preparing a pitch book or about to execute, the transaction will consume 60-100% of your time. You will eat, sleep and drink the project. You are unlikely to be able to deal with more than two or three live projects at any one time. Are you comfortable with the idea of long-term, project-based work?

- Hours tend to be extremely long with weekends thrown into the mix. Does the prospect of such **hard work** excite you or fill you with trepidation?

- For me, I reasoned that **long hours** would suit me just fine, coming out of university as I was young and agile. I thought the harder my working career is to begin with, the easier things will seem to become later on and this turned out to be true. I thought 20 hour days were really cool when I was 21 and intolerable by the time I was 26. Can you cope with working such long hours?

- Even at a very junior level, you will work on projects that may be discussed on the **front page of leading financial newspapers**. Does this excite you?

- Do you like numbers? If you're gunning for a front-office role in corporate finance you are going to have to learn how to **work with Microsoft Excel based financial models**. Entry-level analysts (i.e. new graduates) are not expected to have modeling skills beforehand (the majority don't). Almost all banks provide Excel training for new analysts. Once you have gained sufficient competency in modeling (usually 18 to 24 months into your job as an analyst) you would be expected to work independently and 'run the model' on a project.

  o Most banks have pre-built Excel models ready that need to be modified and adjusted for specific transactions. Despite this, you need to understand modeling fundamentals to work with these models.

  o Although modeling skills are not a prerequisite to get the job you may want to get yourself on a course for two reasons:

    - To see if this is something you would enjoy, especially if you haven't dealt much with numbers in the past

    - To make your résumé/CV stand out a little more

  o That said, I emphasize that most people, even those with an economics or accounting background, will be new to modeling and your bank may in fact prefer to train you because that way you won't have to break or un-learn any old modeling habits.

- When you move from Analyst to Associate you will very quickly be relied upon to **manage projects (not just the financial model) yourself**; you will also be expected to help analysts when they get stuck with their modeling. Does that interest you?

- To last in corporate finance you need a lot of **patience, perseverance and stamina** – does this challenge intrigue you? Would you like to see how far you can push yourself? What life experiences do you have that display these three characteristics? Examples from team sport would come in useful to exemplify this.

- Looking into the future, do you like to spend time **building a relationship over many, many years**? A lot of senior bankers, once they 'graduate' from running models and building pitch books, spend their lives in meeting after meeting preserving the bank's relationship with the senior management of various companies. This could involve **a lot of travelling**, depending on your client-base.

- If you've met **people** who work in corporate finance, you liked them and what they told you about the job, mention it.

3. **Why do you want to work in sales? For instance, selling equities or fixed income products to clients.**
   Why do you think you would be good at sales?

- Although product placement in sales can be part of a larger M&A or leveraged transaction, salespeople are **product and relationship-building specialists** and their contribution to strategy, structure or pricing will mostly relate to the product they specialize in. As such, the contribution of sales on most projects is more sporadic. If you prefer to get more deeply involved in a project, you might dislike this.

- A salesperson needs to be **good at and enjoy dealing with people**.

- Most projects will not consume all of a salesperson's time; and you would likely be **juggling several projects at any one time** and **switching between different customers all day**. Does handling a multitude of different things in one day appeal to you? Does product specialization attract you? If you have a short attention span, a sales or trading role may suit you.
    - o   When I started out in banking I staunchly believed that I was more of a 'project' person but, after CFA Level 1 as a corporate finance analyst at Goldman, I realized I am much more excited by products. So I started looking for jobs in Structured Sales.
- **Structured products tend to be more complex and more time-consuming** to price by nature whilst **flow products are more vanilla and easier to price**. Consequently, structured product salespeople will tend to get more involved on a transaction than 'flow' sales who deal with a lot of volume on smaller transactions. It would probably be relatively uncomplicated to move from structured to flow sales if you change your mind, but a move in the other direction would be more challenging.
    - o   Flow salespeople also handle many more calls in a day than structured sales. Would that suit your personality?
    - o   ' Flow sales are unlikely to be involved in M&A or leveraged acquisitions. Does that bother you?
- Some **modeling skills are needed in the markets** but a product model is very different to a corporate finance model – it is much more specific in nature. Given product models usually involve complex algorithms, e.g. Black-Scholes or Monte-Carlo simulations for risk analysis, banks will usually have proprietary product software designed by quantitative analysts, which make it faster to price products. Although pricing models are available, it is vital for salespeople to comprehend the underlying fundamentals in order to avoid errors.

- o Importantly, it may at times be necessary for salespeople to build a basic model for a customer, e.g. to solve for a swap rate using feeds from Bloomberg or Reuters. Would this sort of quantitative analysis suit your skill set?

- Although the hours in capital markets roles will tend to be shorter, they will also tend to be **a lot more intense**. Corporate finance analysts can normally get away for a sit-down lunch. Salespeople (and traders) have to be constantly near their desk during market hours. Do you think you would enjoy this level of intensity? Do you work well under pressure? Do you have examples that display how well you deal with a high pressure scenario?

- Quite early on in sales you would be expected to manage your own clients, providing them with market color, pricing and product structures with the aim of doing business with the client. Sales people **have to start generating income as early in their career as possible**. A salesperson is very much defined by their ability to generate revenue and come up with product solutions to clients' problems. Once you are given a revenue target, likely from year two or three onwards, if you don't hit the target, you need to justify why. This is unlike corporate finance where revenue goals are ultimately put to the heads of the team. Senior Vice Presidents / Directors and Managing Directors bear the responsibility of hitting corporate finance revenue goals, whereas analysts and junior associates mainly provide superior modeling and presentation skills.

- There is some **pleasure in seeing your customers on TV or in a news article** and telling friends they are your client. Importantly, if you come up with an innovation on a product, it may appear in the financial press. Does that excite you? With the developments in technology, you are more likely to come up with innovative methods in the capital markets than in corporate finance.

  - o Some people think of salespeople as a ditsy bunch with more charisma than brains. This is not generally true (of course, I am biased). One of my colleagues aimed to be what he called a quanto-salesperson, which he defined as a highly technical person with overdeveloped social skills: he ended up structuring a product within two years in sales that was reported in the Financial Times for its innovativeness. Is this one of your ambitions? If so, the capital markets may be for you.

- If you are a salesperson or trader on the public side of the Chinese wall, you will sometimes be asked to **do analysis for M&A transactions without any background information** because any such knowledge may compromise your ability to do the job. Corporate financiers will ask for pricing and ideas based on very generic details. Only when a proposed transaction becomes serious would a salesperson be brought across the Chinese wall from the public markets side to the private side. What do you think of structuring products without knowledge of the wider strategic initiative at play? Does that bore or intrigue you?

- If you've met **people who work in sales**, you liked them and what they told you about the job, mention it.

4. **Why do you want to be a trader?**
   Why do you think you would be a good trader?

- Traders **take on some market risk whenever they trade**. Even if all trades are immediately hedged at the point of trading to minimize risk, the very act of trading is risky in that money can be lost if silly errors are made. Does the thought of taking market positions interest you or fill you with fear?

- Trading jobs **tend to be more technical than sales**; however, this is not necessarily true. Structured sales people are also very technical.

- The key difference between sales and trading is probably that **traders are not client-facing** and for the most part salespeople are. Traders deal via screens and phones; they seldom meet customers.

- Traders tend to have the **shortest attention span** on the trading floor and normally have a temperament to match – volatile, aggressive, edgy. However, it's not usually personal; it's just the nature of the job. If you want to be a trader, you need thick skin; you will find it extremely tough if you are sensitive. Do you have examples that show how hardwearing you are?

- During market hours traders **have to always be on the ball** regarding where the market is; consequently, they tend to have a screen up for every single market or product that they deal with so that they don't waste time flipping between screens. Multiple screens also enable traders to see market movements as they happen.
  - Currently, the average trader has six to eight computer screens, the average salesperson has three to four.
  - One of my friends knows a guy who was in the toilet when Lehman's filing for Chapter 11 bankruptcy was announced. Those three minutes cost him a lot of money and he's got a bit of a phobia about leaving his desk during business hours now. This was obviously an extreme event but it does go to show how present a trader needs to be during market hours.

- Like sales, traders are not usually privy to any M&A or leveraged deals because any such knowledge may have them barred from trading certain names due to a conflict of interest.

- **People with a real passion for trading will tend to continue actively trading throughout their banking career** even as they are promoted to management positions; others will, as they progress in their career, stop trading and take on more of a supervisory role.
  - One of my trader friends (he traded volatility) revealed to me that he hated having to manage people so much that if they expanded his role to include management tasks he would have to quit. He couldn't think of anything worse than having to 'manage' others. His dream was to build enough of a capital base so that he could quit and trade from home. He

had a maths degree and was **extremely passionate about taking calculated positions in the market**. Does this sound like you? You probably don't want to reveal that you hate dealing with people in an interview; I add this little story to provide some idea of the types of character that are attracted to trading.

- If you've **met some traders**, you liked them and what they told you about the job, mention it.

5. Why do you want to work for this bank?

- To answer this question effectively you have to have read the website of your bank, their annual report and searched for any current news on deals that the bank is involved with.
- If you fail to do so, your answer will not be as specific and hence not that good. I really charmed the pants off my interviewers at my first Goldman interviews because I had memorized their 14 business principles and I knew everything that Goldman was doing for the environment and so forth. I came up with this strategy because, as I perused the firm's website, I noticed how frequently they referred to their business principles.
  - Some of my responses went like the following: "According to business principle number 7 which states that ... and I follow exactly the same mantra as exemplified by the time that I did..." – yep, it's official, I'm a suck up and proud of it. A little flattery won't hurt you but don't overdo it.
- If you've met people from the bank and you liked them, mention it.
- Look out for the following as you do your research:

  1) Size of the bank by market cap. If you're looking at a boutique investment bank this is not so relevant. Other metrics, such as the bank's sector focus or client-focus, may be more meaningful to you.

2) Number of countries the bank is located in.

3) Number of employees.

4) Head office of the bank.

5) CEO of the bank.

6) The bank's mission statement and guiding principles.

7) Read the careers section very thoroughly for any hints and tips; you may be surprised by how much info they give away.

8) In the careers section, do they have people profiles? What do they say?

9) Environmental policy of the bank?

10) The bank's pet projects, e.g. are they supporting a big environmental restoration project or something to support a specific group of dispossessed people?

11) Recent news involving the bank: deals they are working on, regulatory rulings affecting them, earnings announcements.

- You can polish up your research by touching base with people that actually work for the bank for any insider tips and advice; go to careers fairs to meet people.

- **Look out for Girl Banker®'s Investment Bank Profiles. These podcasts, blogs and videos will save you lots of time.**

- **To keep updated: 'like' Girl Banker® on Facebook and follow @GirlBanker on Twitter.**

6. **Why should this bank hire you?**
   What do you think distinguishes you from other candidates that have applied for this position?

- Whilst the previous question was trying to elicit what attracted you to the bank in question, in this question the bank would like you to explain why they should be attracted to you.

- This question is not asking for a generic list of attributes that make one a good hire. Rather you need to explain some life experiences that display characteristics that make you a good match for working in *this* investment bank. Is there something about you that makes you **suited to the bank's culture**? You need to understand the bank to talk about the culture and how it complements your own traits.

- Your examples should display three or more of the below:
    - Your **tenacity when operating under pressure.**
    - Your **ability to juggle many things at one time**, e.g. a wide range of extracurricular activities (this does not have to be sports; you can mention all sorts of activities). If all you did in university was your degree it makes you look pretty unidimensional and potentially boring i.e. not fun to work with.
    - **Ability to cope with a job whilst going through university.** A university job probably involves superior time management skills. Many Americans work through university whereas the average UK student does not. Work experience done at the same time as full time studies would definitely enhance the skills you can bring to banking. When I was reading Economics in Cambridge I didn't know a single person that worked during term. Besides the restrictions to working during term time, many just felt they couldn't handle both. More power to you if you can.
    - **Did you start a business in university**? New business ideas really excite interviewers but if you go down this road, be ready to explain your business model, the sort of revenues you pull in or numbers of people that you engaged. If your business is doing so well, you will also need to explain why you aren't pursuing this as your career path. If it's interesting enough, talking about a business you started can take up most of an interview, meaning less time for tough questions!
    - If you did **a course or degree relevant to banking**, mention this but don't make it the highlight of your answer because

75

the majority of applicants will also have this factor on their list.

- The most boring examples, go something like, "I'm doing an economics degree at Oxford University or Harvard so obviously that's a lot of work…" Yawn; every other person that's walked into the room is an Ivy Leaguer so this sort of statement is not compelling at all.

- The more interesting examples use something very unique: something you know no one else will be talking about that day.

- By the time you have finished answering this question you want the interviewer to think: **you work tirelessly, you work long hours, you're a multi-tasker, you work well with other people but can also produce outstanding results when operating independently, you're passionate, ambitious and creative**.

- An effective answer should not just have the interviewer thinking, '*Jane would be good for this bank,*' she should be thinking, '*Jane has to be on my team and I will fight tooth and nail to get her.*'

7. Do you know this bank's key competitors?
What do you know about other investment banks?

- This is a good way of finding out your knowledge of the banking industry. Familiarize yourself with tables 2.2 to 2.4 in Chapter 2.

- Look for Girl Banker®'s investment bank profiles on YouTube, as iTunes podcasts and on the Amazon kindle store to consolidate your knowledge of other banks.

8. Run me through the key aspects of your résumé/CV?

- Frequently, an interviewer will have just dragged their eyes through the first page of your résumé/CV minutes before an interview, picking up just a small percentage of the script. Consequently, it is best for your answers to assume the interviewer knows nothing about you.

- In addition to highlighting your **education, work experience** and **any awards**, give examples that highlight your suitability for the role you're applying for, e.g. your subject choices may suggest you have always been interested in a banking-esque career.

- See the response to question 6: *Why should this bank hire you? What do you think distinguishes you from other candidates that have applied for this position?*

9. Describe yourself

- This can either mean, "Run me through your résumé/CV" or "Why should this bank hire you?" Ask the interviewers to clarify what information they want before you answer.

10. You're currently doing a non-financial course in university. Given this fact, what attracted you to investment banking? With so little financial knowledge, how would you be useful to us?

- Although this sort of question might make you feel uncomfortable, it's a bit of a non-question really because for most roles nearly all applicants will not have covered the specific elements they need to know, in their degree. Even those with maths, business or economics degrees, will have to learn 50-70% of the things they need to operate efficiently, on the job.

- Say that you are **willing and able to rapidly learn the technical things** that are required for the job but even in the absence of that knowledge you are a good hire because:
  - See the response to question 6: *Why should this bank hire you? What do you think distinguishes you from other candidates that have applied for this job?* Note that most of the response to this question focuses on the attributes that make one a good banker as opposed to role-specific knowledge.
  - I once interviewed a man who had done Sports Science for his BA. My eyes immediately gravitated to this point on his

résumé/CV and I thought, *'Why are we even bothering to see this guy?'* (blush blush). He had a few years of banking experience and he completely blew everyone away; you could not at all tell that his background was not in finance and he in fact had better insight than many with a finance-related degree.

- Many **mathematicians** are attracted to banking, especially to trading or structuring roles in the capital markets, because mathematical problem solving skills are very useful in these roles.

- A degree in **languages** may be useful because it may enable one to handle a more diverse client base.

- **Engineering** degrees are viewed as being very technical by nature and signal that you are adept at handling mathematical concepts; many engineers end up forging extremely successful banking careers. Engineers might also understand certain sectors better than non-engineers, depending on the exact nature and focus of the degree.

- If you did a degree in the **sciences** and you end up covering the, say, healthcare sector, you might well understand the fundamentals of this sort of business better than someone who hasn't done much in the way of science.

- If you can coherently articulate your passion for finance and that you are a quick learner, the bank may consider your unusual background a plus point. It may show you are well-rounded in your interests.

- There are those with degrees that don't appear to have any transferrable skills to banking but, ultimately, provided you are passionate about getting into banking, this should not hinder progress; it just means the learning curve will be slightly steeper.

- You can prove your commitment and interest by taking a short banking-related course; this is not necessary but it would help to differentiate you from other applicants.

- Talk about books you've read (including this one), describe products that you find interesting and explain why they fascinate you. The more background research you've done into banking, the more the interviewer will perceive you as a serious candidate.

11. Would you describe yourself as hard-working?

- The answer to this has to be yes. However, you could also say something about **working smart rather than hard**.
- Working smart is about **efficiency and devising solutions** that will save the number of labor hours that you have to commit to any task:
  - For example, if you're an IBD analyst and you've built up a good network of friends within the bank, you might have an idea of who is working on what and that knowledge may help to lighten the load on your own projects;
  - If you know someone that has recently done work relevant to a project that you're assigned to, you can cut your work hours by borrowing slides. This is not cheating: on day one at Goldman we were told that we weren't being paid to reproduce work that had already been done elsewhere in the firm from scratch and that we should always try to leverage from people who had already done something similar. The result was 'blast' emails:
    - That is, analysts and associates regularly sent out emails to everyone in IBD with 'Blast' in the subject, asking for comps, market updates and other such generic slides
- This is one of my favorite answers of all time: when a colleague who had just completed a Masters Degree in London was asked whether he could commit the sort of hours required of an analyst, he said:

"You're asking me if I am willing to work hard? Look at me. I left my country, I left my family, I left my friends and I broke up with my girlfriend of four years because I have one goal and only one goal and that is to work on my career. If my body can deal with it, I will stay without sleeping for the whole week."

The managers interviewing him were wide eyed with glee. "This is exactly the sort of attitude we are looking for; you have the perfect attitude," they told him.

First week on the job, he comes in on Friday rolling his suitcase behind him.

"What's that?" his manager asked.

"Oh, I'm going to see my girlfriend in Paris for the weekend."

"But I thought you don't have a girlfriend?"

"That was in the interview, I told you what you wanted to hear."

His managers burst out laughing at how they'd been duped and ever since then they invite him along to interview candidates because he can smell BS a mile off.

Although I would never advise anyone to lie, most of this guy's answer was true and it did show commitment. He had left his country, friends and family behind for school and a career and, even without the bit about the girlfriend, he would have gotten the job.

12. What are your key strengths?

- Here are some positive characteristics for banking; choose the ones that apply to you and for which you have a good example.
- I would have a minimum of three in any one answer and a maximum of five. Randomly ordered qualities you could discuss:
  - Decisive
  - Hard-working

o Smart-working

o Organized / efficient

o Team worker

o Great at multi-tasking

o Good at accepting a team strategy even where you don't fully agree with it

o Enjoy sharing information with others

o Perform well under pressure, resilient

o Have a strong sense of urgency

o Good at building enduring relationships

o Pro-active

o Driven and ambitious

  ▪ For instance, when I am enjoying a task I can work non-stop for long periods without even realizing how much time has passed; I get lost in the work.

o Good at assessing the risk involved in a situation

o Good listener

o Approachable

o Target driven and always set yourself personal goals

o Good at keeping the future in mind

o Very hard to offend, thick-skinned, not sensitive

o Good at accepting and acting on constructive criticism

o Have great diction and a loud voice (these will be useful on a trading floor)

o Quite competitive but also very patient

o Superior IT skills or financial modeling skills

o Very interested in other cultures and work well with people from different backgrounds

  ▪ Examples of travelling and work experience abroad would be useful here

13. How would someone that knows you well describe you?

- This is another opportunity to explain your strengths but you can also say things that would in another context make you look conceited. Below are examples that I have seen used in the past:
  - o I always give more than 100%
  - o I'm enjoyable to work with
  - o I'm a good mix of funny and serious
  - o I always know what to do when things go wrong
  - o I frequently tackle problems from a completely different angle to what everyone else might come up with; I think very laterally
  - o I never complain; even when a situation looks utterly hopeless I always manage to see the positive side to it; at the same time, I won't flog a dead horse, I know when it's time to move on
  - o I have a strong sense of urgency; I don't sit on work just because it can be done later

    "My professor was very surprised when I turned up to the first term of my final year in September with a first draft of my dissertation; she didn't expect a first draft until January or February of the next year."
  - o I am very responsive

    "Friends always laugh at me because I'll respond to an email just to say I won't be able to read it until later. Far from being over-the-top, I think it's important to set people's expectations. People expect an almost immediate response to email nowadays and if I won't be able to respond that urgently, I let them know or set an out-of-office message."
  - o I flourish when I'm thrown into the unknown; I like to operate outside of my comfort zone and the moment I see myself getting relaxed or complacent I come up with a way of challenging myself

- o I don't see anything as impossible; I see opportunities everywhere
- o I'm a persistent sales person

  You can tell a story about beating a sales target here, e.g. *"My college carried out a phone-athon every year to collect money from alumni. By working two more hours per day than they recommended I called double the number of people I should have over a seven day period and collected 1.5 times more money than the next best person and all it took was committing an extra couple of man hours a day."*
- o Personally, those that know me well would say I am super-efficient. After a day of remarkable efficiency on a personal task a friend said to me, *"Heather, this is what I'm going to insist is written on your tombstone: 'If nothing else, she was efficient.'"* I was too chuffed to ask how she knew I was going to kick the bucket before she did.
- o Another friend said to me, "You are so determined." Without telling her I was writing a book I asked what she meant. She responded with, "You're always doing new things and every time you say you will do something you actually do it. I always tell my mum about you." Chuffed again. She
  ⋅ proceeded to list the things I had said I would do; amongst them were the purchase of my first property, the CFA and several other hobby courses I had done. This is the positive side of impatience; one does not procrastinate.
- Remember to back up everything you say with a good example
- Don't make up examples please!

14. What do you like the most about yourself?

- There's a thin line between confidence and arrogance. You could easily cross that line if you don't structure your answer to this question carefully.

- An answer that portrays a strength that others can benefit from is probably the best one because it makes you look good for the job plus easy or interesting to work with.

Examples:

- I always stay calm under stressful conditions even if I don't feel calm
- I'm good at keeping secrets
- I value producing great work over having lots of money
- I tend to see solutions that no one else can see
- I remain efficient even after very little sleep
- I always ask the difficult questions that everyone else is scared to ask
- People entrust their secrets with me even when I don't expect it. This has led me to believe I am trustworthy and very approachable.
- I always make time to help others even when I don't have much time to spare myself
- Even when I think I have exceeded my own expectations, I always try harder. I think being first is good but staying first is even better and you have to work tirelessly to maintain a top spot.
- I can handle many different projects without getting stressed out. I actually feel energized by a heavy workload. If I feel like I have lots of time to complete a task I just put it off until later so I always take on as much as I can possibly handle.

15. What is your biggest achievement?

This is one of the hardest questions you can be asked. For many people, there won't be one great achievement so impressive that it will enthrall an over-achieving banker with a highly inflated sense of self-worth. If you're interviewing at one of the top banks in the world, what can you possibly tell the guy or gal sitting opposite you that will wow them; they're probably a supersonic performer themselves.

Firstly, don't make it up; tell the truth. Your biggest achievement does not have to involve making lots of money or getting a string of As. Think through the following:

- Have you ever set anything up and succeeded? A campaign? A charity? An appeal for something you believe in?
- Have you ever written a letter to someone very important and received a response back?
- Have you ever saved someone you know from a tragedy? How?
- Have you ever done something that everyone thought you'd fail at, or that was a long shot but which you successfully pulled off anyway?
- Think of the really low points in your life, a time when things were going wrong for you. The chances are, you'll find a big achievement in one of these low points.

What's your employer hoping to see through what you classify as your biggest achievement?

- That you are an over-achiever or at least aim to be
- You are creative
- You're bold; you don't always follow the crowd
- You're a team player and are always looking out for others
- You're an innovative problem solver
- You can spot opportunity even when things are looking bleak
- You're street smart and not just book smart

16. Do you have any weaknesses?

What would you classify as your key weaknesses?

- The funniest answer I ever heard to this question was on a TV show. *'The Fairy Jobmother'* asked a man what he would describe as his key weakness and without a moment's hesitation he said, *"My diabetes."* Even she couldn't stifle her laugh.

- The interviewer is not asking for your health status and generally any health issues should be brought up with the Human Resources department rather than in an interview.

- Also, you should never give a *real* weakness otherwise you will not get the job. Your weaknesses should all be non-events or even strengths if viewed from a different perspective.

- Here are a few examples of weaknesses:
    - I only speak one language and I think that might limit me because I want to work with clients in Europe. I have signed up to a French course so that I can get to a stage where I speak two languages fluently.
    - I am a bit of a stickler for rules and people might find this annoying so I'm trying to be more laid back.
    - I am hyper-organized. As the eldest of three I became accustomed to organizing my younger siblings' lives too and I'm hoping I won't do this with colleagues. This example is borderline good/bad; depending on how you express yourself you could come across as a micromanager or a control freak (both are negative traits).
    - I think more about the future than the present and sometimes I think my life is just wasting away because I am too concerned about the future to enjoy the present. This was a real problem in high school because at times when I had planned a weekend out with my friends I would jump ship if a test came up so that I could prepare for it. However, I

improved in university because I realized it would be better to build a network than just to come out with the top grades.

o I have never used Bloomberg or Reuters before and I believe these are the main portals for information in a bank.

o I haven't done a banking internship before and I wonder if that will hold me at a significant disadvantage.

o I didn't do a finance-based degree and although I think I will have a lot to add, not merely because I think from a different perspective, I wonder if my colleagues will look down at me for not doing economics or something similar.

o When I am enjoying working on something I am at risk of overdoing it because I simply don't know when to stop. I will have to discipline myself to take breaks because I don't want to burn out on the job. I'm thinking of my banking career as more of a marathon than a 100-metre sprint; if I pace myself I'll perform a lot better.

o My personal weakness is that I am not particularly patient (I can be, with much difficulty), however, most of the time when I want something done, I want it done now:

  ▪ This can be a problem at junior levels because you might rush work when you have too much on, thereby making unnecessary errors.

  ▪ It can possibly be a problem as you get more senior and have to manage people, e.g. you ask them to do something but then end up doing the work yourself because you have some extra time thereby a) depriving that person of a learning opportunity or worse b) making them feel insecure about their efficiency.

17. Have you ever failed?

Have your plans ever not worked out?

Tell me about a time when something went wrong. How did you resolve it?

This question is trying to elicit how well you react to negative situations. If you have always been the best in your class: academically, socially and at sports and never failed at anything, you might have some trouble in the 'real' world because you won't win all the time. Things will go wrong, plans will take a direction other than that which is preferred and some things will just outright fail.

- Investment banks ideally want problem-solvers, people that have been tested by going through something difficult but managed to pick themselves up and become a better, more rounded individual for it.
- Lots of people will have examples from university or school; most of them will be dry or downright boring: "I was working on project z and coming up against the deadlines when 'blah' happened...." or "My project partner all of a sudden got ill two days before we were due to hand in our Engineering thesis and I had to complete it all on my own so I went without sleep for 72 hours..." Well, boohoo, poor you. These situations may well be stressful and challenging but, as the majority of candidates will be telling different variations of the same story, it does not set you apart.
- The best examples come from real life; by 'real', I am referring to those experiences that don't come from the controlled environment of a school or university. I coached one of my friends prior to an Asset Management interview and he attributes the job he secured to the answer he gave to this very question: an answer which I told him to use despite him thinking it was silly. He's probably giving me more credit than I deserve but I'll take it:
    - The night before his interview he had three possible answers to this question. The other two involved university

experiences and the third was from work experience: during his gap year he spent a few months looking after a group of children with learning difficulties and once a week he had to take them into town. On one of those jaunts one of the kids disappeared and the process he had to go through to find this child was an interesting adventure. Besides finding the child, he had to ensure the others didn't come out thinking that disappearing would be a fun thing to try in the future.

- o He didn't want to tell the story because he thought the interviewee would find it too weird or random but after I heard it I said he'd be insane not to, so he did.
- o When he told the story, he says the interviewers quite literally sat up in their seats and started listening when they had previously been glancing at their watches every two minutes. The rest of the interview basically focused on the challenges involved in looking after children with learning difficulties: an area that was well within his comfort zone.
- o He left the room feeling confident about his performance and he had an offer a week or so later.

- Have a deep think about what might be interesting to an interviewer. By all means use experiences from university or school but if you have other stories to tell don't neglect them. I would definitely recommend using something rather different to make you more unique and hence more memorable.
- Whatever story you choose to tell, tell it well. Make sure it brings out what you learnt and why you are better for having been through the experience.
- Overall, the interviewer wants to know that you have encountered a failure before, that you kept your cool under the circumstances and that you learnt something valuable from it.
- Hopefully, as a result of facing a challenging situation you did not:
  - o Breakdown completely

- o Alienate a group of people
- o End up losing a whole lot of money and never got it back
- o Start using underhand tactics to bring down the competition
- o Give up
- Ask someone who's quite opinionated what they think of your potential answers.

18. What is the biggest failure you have ever had?

This is a very tough question especially if you're a bit of an optimist.

- Although very similar to the above, this question is looking at the big knock-back of your life, the most devastating failure you have ever had, and the truth is most people in their late teens or early twenties will likely not have experienced a big failure.
- Your example can either be a plan going wrong or something completely unexpected happening.
- Whereas "What's your biggest weakness?" is looking for something that is not really a weakness, this question is asking for a real failure and the positives that (hopefully) came from it.
- In your answer mention:
  - o What the failure was
  - o When and how it occurred – could it have been avoided?
  - o The repercussions – besides you, was anyone else affected? How?
  - o The resolution – if the problem was solved, who solved it and how?
  - o The lessons – what did you learn? Are those lessons valuable to working in an investment bank?

19. The grades on your résumé/CV are not the best I have seen today. Why should I hire you over someone with a better academic profile?

- If you attended the best private schools that money can afford there's generally no excuse for bad grades. By nature, students per teacher numbers are kept low and it's so much easier to get one-on-one attention and all the learning aids available.

- When I was being coached for my Goldman interview, the coach said in one group session, "a B can never be an achievement," so I told my story:

    o My high school, Kamuzu Academy, in Malawi (think the back-of-beyond Africa) thought some of the pupils in my year were good enough to take A-level Further Mathematics: me, my best friend Patience and my good friend Lolo; so they introduced this as a new subject on the curriculum.

    o Problem: we didn't have any text books for Further Maths nor did we have examples of previous Further Maths exams. Nonetheless Lolo, Patience and I took this on as a fourth subject when the rest of our year was taking just three subjects (the norm).

    o This was just prior to the modular AS system in the UK that splits exams into six bite-sized exams. In my day you studied for two years and took all the exams in one go at the end.

    o The school managed to find a very old book that covered some of the material (e.g. complex numbers) and we used this until they got a more recent text book from which photocopies were made for the three of us; our teacher kept the main copy.

    o Two-thirds of the way through the first year, Lolo said it was too tough. He dropped out and maintained his other three subjects.

- o By the beginning of year two the school had sourced about four or five past exam papers. Patience and I were ecstatic.
- o One-third of the way through year two, Patience concluded that she was spreading herself too thin and that to maximize her chances of getting three A grades in her other subjects she needed to drop Further Maths, so she too quit.
- o Did I want to quit? Of course. I didn't want to be the only student in the class for two-thirds of the year but I soldiered on; whenever the going got tough I called my dad for a pep talk and in the end I took the exam and got a B. The paper was split into Pure Maths and a combined paper with Statistics and Mechanics. If my memory serves me right (I don't have the breakdown), I got a good A in Stats and Mechanics and a C in Pure Maths and averaged out a B.
- o You know what? I am more proud of that B than the three As I got in biology, economics and 'standard' maths. Those subjects were all well resourced and a plethora of past papers existed – not to mention the moral support from other students who were taking the exam.

- When I finished my story, the coach immediately said, *"I change my mind. When you put it like that, a B can be classified as an achievement."* Indeed, the story showed that I'm not a quitter, I'm not put off by a lack of resources and I will do the best I can with what I have – all desirable qualities.

- If you don't have a good academic record, think about how best you can explain it away. If you simply didn't work hard, apologize for that and give examples that show you have turned over a new leaf. Give **other examples that demonstrate you are a high achiever**: prizes? Anything you have set up such as a business or a charity?

- If there's time, work harder to improve your grades because everyone loves a C student that converts herself to a star pupil – that would make a great interview story.

20. Which other firms have you applied to?

Which other firms are you interviewing with?

Have you received any internship / job offers yet?

Somehow candidates always look more attractive when someone else wants them. Listing other firms you have applied to relays the following insights:

- Whether or not you are focused just on banking or are looking at other industries. Generally, I would only list other banks you are applying to as it shows commitment to the industry. If you are applying to too many non-financial companies it will look as though you are undecided or indeed indecisive in general.

- This question can bring out how well you know the industry, e.g. if all your banks are of the same caliber, it could show you have done some research. If you have applied to a mixture of boutiques and big banks you might want to explain why this is the case, e.g. you may have interned in both types of firm and know that you would fit well into either, despite having a preference for one or the other.

- If you have already received a job offer, you will immediately put pressure on the interviewer. If you have an *exploding offer*, i.e. if you need to accept the offer within a given amount of time, that will add even more pressure on the interviewer. I know a man who had had over 40 interviews at a Big US Bank and appeared no nearer to securing a job offer but the moment he got an offer from another Big US Bank, he was promptly offered the position!

- Rejection can make you look less appealing. Avoid talking about rejections but if directly asked about it, be honest. If you know why you were rejected, explain. It's better to state that you are still interviewing with several banks and you are confident of receiving a job offer. Explain why you have this confidence, e.g. have your interviews been going very well?

21. Are you only applying for positions in investment banks or are there other sectors you are considering?

Some of my peers applied to banks and academia because they were undecided as to whether to do more study or go into work; others applied to management consultancy and banking; a few applied to industry.

If you have an interesting reason for applying to different sectors, mention it. Personally, I applied only to investment banks and initially, only to corporate finance roles.

Reasons you could give for applying widely:

- "There are some things about an industry that you can only find out by talking to people that work in the industry. My family doesn't have any connections to the banking industry so I decided to apply to banks to meet people that actually work on the front line."

- This is a good reason, however, you could go on to add what your research has shown so far, for instance, have you found that you get along with the bankers you have met so far? If so, why is that? e.g. "So far I have had seven interviews across three firms and I can definitely see that banking would be a perfect match for me because everyone I meet shares a similar passion for hard work and the need to stretch out of their comfort zone."

- You could also say that there are aspects of both investment banking and 'career x' that interest you and are a good match for your skill set. Since you haven't experienced working in either, you were keen to interview for both. Indeed, through the interview process you may discover that you have a definite preference.

- If you just applied to many sectors to maximize your chances of getting a job anywhere, don't give that as a reason. Think of something more solid. This is because such an answer could show you are not confident in your own abilities; banks want people who are confident enough to take bold steps.

22. How did you prepare for this interview?

The interviewer wants to know you have done a lot of research and therefore that you are committed to finding a banking job. To the interviewer, the harder you have worked for the interview, the more worthy a candidate you are. Mention:

- The careers / recruitment fairs you have been to
- Help received from your university's careers service
- Any practice trading or selling you have done
- The practice interviews you have had with friends or professionally
- Banking related newspapers, magazines and journals you have been reading
- The books you have read (see Girl Banker®'s list of recommended books in Chapter 10/Resources)
- Courses you have taken specifically with a view to enhancing your chances as a candidate, e.g. courses in modeling, advanced courses in MS Excel, learning to build macros
- Internships you have taken part in, for instance, this would be a great time to bring up a spring internship
- Any banking related Tweeters you have been following:
  - This will be something rather different to mention in an interview; many in banking, especially at the senior level, have not yet realized the benefits of using Twitter
  - Girl Banker®'s suggested list is in Chapter 10/Resources
- Anything else that you believe to be relevant

23. Are there any questions you would like to ask me?

The answer to this is always yes. Asking questions portrays keenness. Ideally:

- Ask something that is very current and hopefully contentious; asking questions about bog standard market activity will not excite your interviewer in any way.

- Ask things that the interviewer can relate back to his own life. People love talking about themselves and will warm towards a candidate that shows interest in them as a person, e.g. *What three things have you learnt over the course of your career that you wish you had learnt earlier?* If an MD, *I have heard that making the step from Director to MD is very tough, what do you think did it for you? In addition, to being super smart, of course?* **Flattery will get you everywhere!**

- Don't ask compensation-related questions; it's too early. For internships it will be standardized so there is no point; if you are looking for a full-time position get the offer first and only then should you start discussing pay.

Most competency-based questions will be variations on the above. Competency normally forms just a third or a quarter of the assessment so time is too limited to ask much else. Any one interviewer will be exposed to you for only a limited period and each will want to cover the basics, so expect to answer the same question several times at the same bank.

Expect the unexpected. You'll be thrown a curveball every now and again: take it in your stride, just apply logic and common sense.

- If you're unsure about an answer you've given, feel free to ask whether what you said covers what your interviewer was looking for
- If you don't understand a question, ask for clarification

5

BASIC ECONOMICS

Some knowledge of economics will make it a little easier to understand the financial concepts in this book. Economics will help you to understand market movements, industry and deal dynamics. This is not an economics book so I will only touch upon those elements of economics that I feel are vital.

The first time I picked up an economics book seriously I was about twelve years old. My father had been telling me about the subject for a while already so I was very curious about it. On my own, I couldn't get beyond the first couple of chapters because it was so different to anything I had ever studied before. I returned the library book and took it up as a subject in school the first chance I got, when I was thirteen. I love economics; it is extremely intuitive. However, if like me you don't initially get it, don't be deterred; just read on; it will make more sense over time.

Demand

The demand curve is downward sloping. This means that, all things constant, as the price of a good or service falls, the quantity demanded rises.

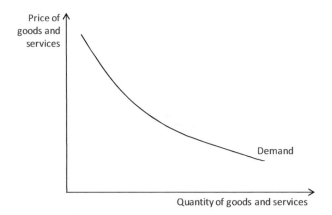

Figure 5.1: Demand curve

Note that this relationship between price and quantity demanded is a general rule, but doesn't always apply. For instance, luxury goods are commonly bought to signal one's wealth or status. For such products, demand rises with price.

Supply

The supply curve is upward sloping. This means that, all things constant, as the price of a good or service rises, the quantity supplied rises.

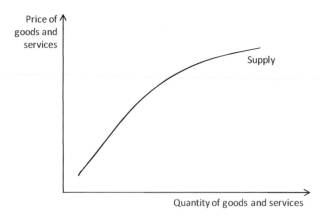

Figure 5.2: Supply curve

For example, if you were a fruit farmer selling bananas and apples and making an identical profit (margin and absolute level profit) from both, what would happen if the market price of bananas doubled but the cost of growing them stayed exactly the same? You would want to sell more bananas than apples. The higher profits from bananas may even encourage you to stop growing apples and focus on bananas.

Equilibrium price

The point at which demand equals supply is called the **equilibrium price** (P_e). At this price there is no tendency for the price to change.

What happens if the price is higher than the equilibrium price (at P_s)?

Suppliers produce quantity B, whilst buyers only purchase amount A, resulting in an excess supply. The only way to clear this excess supply is to reduce the price. As the price falls toward P_e, the amount bought rises whilst that supplied falls until we reach P_e. At P_e, demand equals supply and there's no tendency for the price to change.

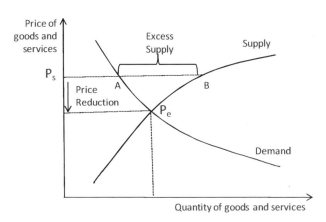

Figure 5.3: Excess supply

What happens if the price is lower than the equilibrium price (at P_d)?

Suppliers produce quantity C, but buyers want to purchase amount D, resulting in an excess demand. It's clear when there is excess demand for a product: the phone doesn't stop ringing (if you can order by phone) and there are endless queues of customers. The seller doesn't have to work very hard at all to get rid of her stock or to fill up her schedule.

The only way to clear this excess demand is to hike the price up. As the price rises towards P_e, supply rises and the quantity demanded falls because a) some people can't afford the product anymore or b) some buyers think it's not worth the higher price. At P_e, demand equals supply and there's no further impetus for the price to change.

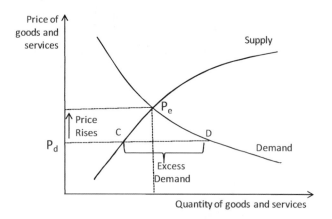

Figure 5.4: Excess demand

These forces of demand and supply may be prevented from working by rules and regulations. For instance, at times governments explicitly set the price for a commodity.

What are some of the adverse consequences of price fixing?

Price setting is relatively common under a communist/socialist regime. The intentions of capping the price of various commodities may be noble, e.g. a government may want all basic commodities to be affordable even to the poorest members of society. However, by keeping the price fixed anywhere other than P_e, incentives are also adjusted. If the price is kept artificially low, some suppliers will opt not to supply the controlled product, e.g. if wheat prices are government-set, a farmer might choose to grow some other crop whose price isn't regulated. The result? Wheat would be in short supply.

Because supply is limited, the Government may try to prevent unequal distribution by rationing, using coupons, so the price is set *and* the amount that can be bought is also set. With a rationing system, another can of worms is opened up:

- How do you account for different family sizes? If the community set-up is such that people live with extended families, setting limits is made even harder.
- How do you stop people lying about the number of dependents they have?
- How do you control the informal/illegal market that will inevitably materialize?

To get more wheat, the rich may offer bribes and thus end up getting more anyway. The Government has to spend money policing people to ensure the rationing rules are being followed. It all gets very costly for the taxpayer.

Overall, the objective of limiting price was to make sure everyone, rich and poor, can afford a basic commodity. The end result is that nobody gets as much as they want; plus you introduce a whole plethora of other problems that are not easy to solve. This is why price controls often break down.

How do governments exert their influence on prices today?

Price fixing still occurs in some countries but in the western world it has mostly been accepted that letting market forces determine price is more effective than price controls.

That said, governments still exert indirect price control using the tax system.

Governments can discourage people from buying certain goods by increasing taxes on them, e.g. higher taxes on cigarettes and alcohol. An increased level of tax shifts the whole supply curve left from Supply$_1$ to Supply$_2$: *for every quantity, the cost of supplying the good goes up.* A new equilibrium at P$_{e2}$ is created.

Improvements in technology reduce production costs and therefore have the opposite effect: the supply curve shifts right/down.

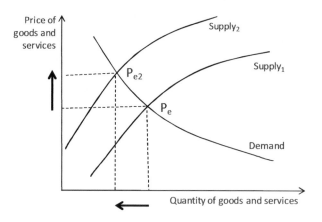

Figure 5.5: Example of a supply curve shift

Alternatively, governments can encourage consumption with subsidies or by removing existing taxes, e.g. books and milk will frequently have no tax applied or a much lower tax.

The concept of demand and supply is wide ranging and can be applied to a varied spectrum of events, e.g. if the demand for loans went up, what would lenders do? Increase interest rates (the price of a loan).

In summary:

- Excess supply is cleared by reducing price
- Excess demand is cleared by increasing price
- Prices can be explicitly fixed by government policy, often with dire consequences
- Prices can be manipulated by changes in taxes and subsidies

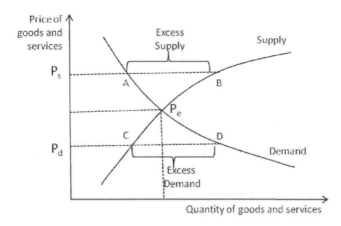

Figure 5.6: Summary of the interaction between demand and supply

Inflation

Inflation refers to a situation in which the average price of goods in the economy is rising and the value of money is decreasing.

Inflation can get out of hand if the Government doesn't step in to control it, resulting in high inflation or even **hyperinflation**. During World War II, hyperinflation meant that German pub-goers bought four beers at a time; by the time they'd finished drinking one, the price would have gone up[4]. By the time they got on to drinking beer number four it was warm but hey, at least it was cheaper.

High levels of inflation mean the same amount of money buys fewer goods, so workers start demanding higher pay to keep up with the increased cost of living. You can see how this can turn into a vicious cycle: companies have to pay workers more, so they have to charge more for their goods to maintain profit margins, so prices go up even further.

Wages form a large component of most companies' costs so even small wage increases can have a huge impact on the cost base. At times **cost-**

---

[4] I read this story when I was in high school. The source is unclear.

push inflation will be limited, for instance, in a recession when many are losing their jobs, many people simply put up with lower wages without complaint; they are just grateful to have a job.

Overall, **monetary policy** is necessary to achieve stable pricing and it also helps to smooth out the economic cycle.

The two types of inflation:

- **Demand-pull inflation** brought on by excess demand
- **Cost-push inflation** is driven by the higher cost of producing goods and services

Low, stable inflation is desired by all governments.

Gross Domestic Product (GDP)

GDP represents the total value of output in an economy and can be summarized in the following way:

$$GDP = C + I + G + (X - M)$$

- C = the value of goods and services bought by household **consumers**
- I = the value of **investment** in the economy
- G = the value of goods and services bought by **government**
- X = the value of **goods exported**
- M = the value of **goods imported**

This formula is the **expenditure method** and is my preferred way of thinking about GDP because it makes it easy to visualize the economic impact of a component's change.

GDP can also be calculated in two other ways:

- **Income method**: the value of *income* generated in the economy from all sources, i.e. the sum total of wages to employees, dividends to shareholders, rents to landlords and interest to lenders.
- **Output method**: sums up the value of goods produced in every economic sector: agriculture, manufacturing and services.

In theory, all three methods should give the same answer but in practice, they don't because it's so hard to sum up everything accurately. For instance, how do you capture the informal market economy where traders deal in cash and therefore aren't in tax records? The income method will fail to capture any informal sector activity, whilst the expenditure method will capture some of it.

The economic cycle

GDP fluctuates over time as shown in the diagram below. The fluctuations are referred to as the economic cycle.

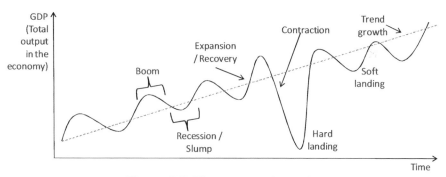

Figure 5.7: The economic cycle

- In an **expansionary** phase when the economy is **recovering** from hard economic times, GDP, employment and income rise; after some period of expanding growth, the economy is said to be in a **boom**.

- In a **contractionary** phase, GDP, employment and income fall; technically, when an economy has had two consecutive quarters of negative GDP growth, it is said to be in a **recession** or a **slump**.

- A very sharp fall in growth before recovery is sometimes called a **hard landing**; governments hate hard landings because they result in very tough times for large swathes of the population, making them politically unattractive.

- A **soft landing**, in which economic growth goes down without sharp declines, is what every economy aspires to achieve.

How does the government influence the direction of the economy?

Governments *attempt* to smooth out the economic cycle through **monetary policy** and **fiscal policy**. Policy designed to promote growth is called **expansionary policy**. Policy designed to stop a boom from creating inflationary pressure is called **contractionary policy**.

FISCAL POLICY

Fiscal policy is government influence achieved through its tax and spending policy. The money governments have available to spend comes from:

- Tax
- Borrowing from companies, financial institutions and individuals
- Profits from state-owned businesses

Tax is used to influence household consumption ('C')

- In a boom, governments increase taxes to reduce household consumption and temper demand-pull inflationary forces. C in {C+I+G+(X-M)} falls or rises more slowly and GDP growth is tempered.
- In a recession, the Government can reduce tax to increase household consumption. C in {C+I+G+(X-M)} rises and GDP growth is stimulated.

By far the majority of tax comes from taxing individuals (income tax), goods and services (sales tax or value-added-tax, VAT) and businesses (corporate tax).

After the 2007-2009 credit crunch, although tax cuts would have helped to stimulate growth, governments were so heavily in debt that this tool was not available to them.

Government spending ('G')

In a boom, governments can spend more by:

- Borrowing more (both locally and from foreigners)
- Taxing more
- Running down its savings (if it has any). However, as most governments in the developed world are running massive **deficits**, they have no **surpluses** to fall back on

Money borrowed from foreigners has a bigger impact on GDP because a portion of funds borrowed from domestic companies and individuals would have been spent in the economy anyway.

Increasing taxes and increasing government spending by the same amount is likely to have a more positive (**multiplied**) impact on GDP than reducing taxes by an equivalent amount. This is illustrated below. The government can decide to spend all tax income. However, if they chose instead to reduce taxes and thus allow households to do the spending, some taxpaying consumers would choose to save rather than spend the tax windfall, thus reducing the impact on GDP.

Figure 5.8: Tax, spending and saving

Some revenue is earned from state-owned businesses, e.g. public transport (if it hasn't been privatized) but this tends to be so small in developed economies that it is not really that effective a tool for driving GDP.

MONETARY POLICY

The amount of money floating about in the economy is controlled by the government to manage the ups and downs of the economic cycle. Any system used to control the stock of money is classified as monetary policy. The main monetary policy tools available are:

1. Interest rates (the main one used nowadays)
2. Buying and selling of government bonds via open market operations – can involve printing money or 'quantitative easing'
3. Exchange rates

Central Bank

Every country has a '**central bank**' tasked with overseeing monetary policy.

- The Federal Reserve (the Fed) in the United States of America
- The Bank of England in the United Kingdom

- The European Central Bank (ECB) for Eurozone countries

The central bank, a government institution, is the '**lender of last resort**'. This means that if a commercial bank or other organization is having severe financial trouble, the central bank of the economy is the only institution that is likely to lend them any money. Failing that, the troubled entity would have to declare bankruptcy or be taken over by a competitor.

In the 2007-2009 credit crunch many banks had to be bailed out by their central banks to avoid going bust. Those that didn't get bailed out were taken over or went bust; Lehman Brothers went bust, Merrill Lynch was taken over by Bank of America and Bear Stearns taken over JP Morgan, for example.

Table 5.1: Some banks rescued by their lender of last resort

Banks bailed out by the Fed	Bailed out by the Bank of England
• Bank of America	• Royal Bank of Scotland
• Citigroup	• Lloyds TSB
• JP Morgan	• HBOS
• Wells Fargo	• Northern Rock

Source: US Treasury website, Bank of England website

1. Monetary policy instrument: interest rates

The base rate (UK) or prime rate (USA)

The base rate is the interest rate that the central bank charges borrowers. Generally, only banks and other specified financial institutions can borrow from the central bank.

The base rate is the primary benchmark for borrowing and lending in an economy. It is also a key tool for controlling inflation in developed economies.

Banks will always charge more than the base rate to lend to their customers, companies and private individuals.

In a boom or recovery when inflationary pressure is high or rising, central banks increase base/prime rates:

- Increasing the base rate curbs spending in the economy. A higher base rate means it costs banks more to borrow from the central bank so they in turn increase their interest rates (on credit cards, loans, mortgages, overdrafts and so on) making it more expensive for customers to borrow money.

- Higher mortgage costs reduce disposable income, that is, the money household consumers have available to spend.

- Furthermore, by spending, consumers now miss out on a good rate of interest on savings, so higher rates encourage increased saving over spending.

- Equally, companies have to pay more interest for their loans, leaving less money available for investment. At the higher rate of interest, some company projects may even become completely unattractive.

- **The result**: a higher base rate, leads to less spending by consumers, less investment by business, more saving by both and it tempers inflationary pressures.

The opposite is true in a recession. The central bank reduces the base rate to encourage spending and investment.

- Mortgage costs fall hence disposable income rises.

- Furthermore, lower interest rates mean consumers choose spending over saving.

- Equally, lower borrowing costs mean there's more money for investment.

- Overall, lower interest rates boost spending and economic growth, helping to push an economy out of recession.

There's one problem. The base rate cannot be reduced below zero. When the base rate is very low it becomes a blunt instrument and the central bank has to use other tools to influence the economy. This problem occurred during the 2007–2009 credit crunch.

2. Monetary policy instrument: buying and selling of government bonds and 'quantitative easing'

A central bank can increase the amount of money in an economy by simply printing more money. Nowadays, this is not the preferred option because it can result in very high levels of inflation.

Assume in the below discussion that the overall amount of money in the economy is fixed.

In a boom

In a boom when the economy is awash with cash, the Government can draw money out of the economy by **issuing bonds** (Bonds are covered in Chapter 8/Technical Questions for DCM or FICC/Bonds and Loans): investors give their money to the Government and in return the Government pays interest.

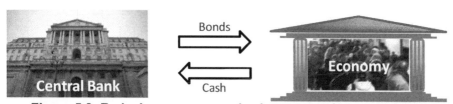

Figure 5.9: Reducing money supply via open market operations

Once the Government receives the money, it can choose not to spend it, thus reducing the amount of money floating about in the economy. Less money means less pent up demand and less inflationary pressure.

In a recession

In a recession, more money is needed to encourage spending and investment. The government can inject money into the economy by buying bonds. If it doesn't have the money to buy the bonds **it can just print more**.

The government can buy back its own bonds or purchase corporate bonds. Buying private bonds is a direct way for the government to lend money to the private sector. The company issuing the bond receives the money it needs for investment; the government earns interest.

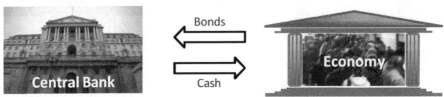

Figure 5.10: Increasing money supply via open market operations

It's not very conventional for a government to buy corporate bonds. Only in dire straits will it resort to this measure. This sort of intervention was required in the 2007-2009 credit crunch: so many banks were in so much trouble that central banks in the west had to set up special programs to stabilize the financial sector.

- The US Fed set up the Troubled Asset Relief Program or TARP[5] in September 2008:
  - $700bn was committed via the TARP; as at Feb 2012 $356bn had been injected into the financial system.
  - Of the invested amount, $118.5bn had been repaid by the end of 2010.
- The Bank of England set up the Asset Purchase Facility[6] in 2009:
  - £325bn had been injected into the UK private sector (including banks) through this program by Feb 2012.

---

[5] http://money.cnn.com/news/storysupplement/economy/bailouttracker/
[6] http://www.bankofengland.co.uk/markets/apf/index.htm

3. Monetary policy instrument: exchange rates

An exchange rate is used to convert one currency to another. Changes in the exchange rate affect the cost of importing and exporting goods, even if the price has remained exactly the same in the local currency.

Assume GBP1 buys USD2. If a US resident is told they need GBP1,000 for a week's holiday in London, that translates to USD2,000.

- If GBP falls in value to 1.5 before the US tourist has had a chance to exchange their USD, then the same GBP1,000 can be purchased with just USD1,500. The holiday is cheaper.
- If GBP rises in value to 2.5 before the US tourist has had a chance to exchange their USD, then the same GBP1,000 now costs USD2,500. The same holiday is now much more expensive and could even be unaffordable.

To any country, receiving tourists is equivalent to exporting goods: X in GDP=C+I+G+(**X**-M). Tourists spend money in the foreign country and stimulate GDP growth.

If a government thinks their local currency is becoming too costly to foreigners, they might take action to create a fall in the value of their local currency. This is achieved by selling the local currency and buying foreign currencies.

- A fall in the value of local currency could be enough to encourage exporters to buy more goods from the economy.
- A fall in the value of local currency could also discourage imports in favor of buying local.
- Either way more exports and fewer imports both have the desirable impact of increasing the economy's income.

Macroeconomics

Investment banks want to attract worldly people who know about and are interested in what's going on all over the world. You will definitely be asked a macro question in either a competency or a technical interview. Here are some guidelines on polishing up your knowledge in this area:

- Follow financial tweets (Girl Banker®'s picks are in Chapter 10).
- Top news on USA, UK and European economies:
  - Growth and GDP
  - Inflation levels
  - Key interest rates, especially the yield on 10-year government bonds in the US, UK and Europe
- Key news concerning the BRICs: Brazil, Russia, India and China. China is key.
- Key central bank announcements from the Fed, the ECB and the Bank of England. Know the chairperson of each entity.
- Changes in key equity indices: at least the S&P500 and FTSE100.
- Movements in gold prices.
- Movements in oil prices.
- Key foreign exchange rates, at least: GBPUSD, EURUSD, USDJPY. If you are in the UK or Europe EURGBP is also key.
- Key rating agency announcements from S&P or Moody's especially news of any downgrades or pending downgrades.

Relate how macro news might impact the sort of transactions banks are doing, e.g. high growth in emerging markets (EM) relative to developed economies will lead to more EM-related transactions.

Rather than trying to gain all this knowledge the night or even week before an interview, follow financial news on a regular basis and you will find yourself effortlessly imbibing macro knowledge.

Economics and macro questions that you could possibly be asked

1. What is the relationship between demand for a good and its price?
2. What is the relationship between supply of a good and its price?
3. Do you know the concept of equilibrium price?
4. What happens when there is excess supply/demand for something?
5. Is the price of a good always determined according to demand and supply? What else can influence price?
6. Give three reasons why price fixing could be harmful.
7. How might a rationing system work?
8. Describe how a 'perfect' government might be organized.
9. How would you describe inflation?
10. Do you know how inflation is calculated?
11. What causes inflation?
12. Do you think zero inflation is a good thing?
13. What is GDP? How is GDP calculated?
14. Give three methods that can be used to stimulate export demand.
15. Here is a list of five companies. At what point in the economic cycle would each company make the most profit and why?
16. Name three sources of government funding.
17. Do you think that privatization is always a good thing?
18. Name any banks that had trouble during the 2007-2009 credit crunch.
19. Do you know what a lender of last resort is? Can you name three?
20. How would you invest USD100,000?
21. List five things that you know about the state of the US/UK/European economy.
22. What's the current GBPUSD exchange rate?
23. What is the current price of oil and how has it moved in recent days?
24. What is the current price of gold? What's the trend been recently?
25. Where is the S&P500 / FTSE100 trading?
26. Talk about something interesting in the world economy right now.
27. What do you know about China?
28. Who's topping the Forbes 500 Rich List right now?
29. What do you think of the {fill in blank} IPO?
30. Do you think we are hitting the top of another technology bubble?

The list is pretty endless. Integrate the economics knowledge provided here with what you are reading in the financial press.

Apply the knowledge; don't memorize it.

6

BASIC TECHNICAL QUESTIONS

What is a basis point or bp?

1bp = 0.01%

100bps = 1.00%

It is often much easier to talk about interest rates in basis points. This is especially true if very small percentages are being discussed.

What is a pip?

For most currencies, 1 pip is the fourth decimal place i.e. 1 pip = 0.0001

- For example, if the exchange rate between GBP and USD is 1.5000 and you're told to add a pip, that would take you to 1.5001.
- If GBP appreciates to 1.5100 we say it has moved by **one big figure** (0.01); you now need more USD to buy the same amount of GBP.

In other currencies, notably JPY, 1 pip is the second decimal place i.e. 1 pip = 0.01

- For example, if the exchange rate between USD and JPY is 110.00 and you're told to add a pip, that would take you to 110.01.
- If USD appreciates to 111.00 from 110.00 we say it has moved by **one big figure**; you now need more JPY to buy the same amount of USD.

Common mistake! Some people discuss a pip as being the 5th significant figure but this is wrong. When JPY appreciated against USD to sub-99, a pip remained the second decimal place. This means that when the exchange rate was 99.50, adding a pip took you to 99.51 not 99.501 which is what it would be if a pip was the 5th significant figure. You've been warned.

What is time value of money? What does the phrase present value refer to?

Whether you're in corporate finance or the financial markets this concept will be very central to your life.

Time value of money refers to the idea that $100 today is worth more than $100 tomorrow. Why is that?

- The main reason is **interest**. If you received $100 today rather than in a year's time, you could place it in a bank account and earn interest on that money. For instance, if the one-year interest rate was 5%, at the end of the year you would get $105 back.
    - It therefore follows that if all other risks are held constant and you were offered $100 today or $105 in a year you should be indifferent.
- **Inflation risk**. This is especially important if you're living somewhere with a high rate of inflation. The value of money is eroded by rising prices; this means that $100 tomorrow will buy fewer goods than $100 today.

- **Credit risk**. The probability that tomorrow you won't get paid. If my cousin TK offered me $100 today vs. $200 tomorrow I'd go for $100 today because tomorrow will come but I know he certainly won't. Credit risk is frequently ignored in discussions on time value of money but it is a real risk.

If $100 tomorrow is worth less than $100 today, then what is tomorrow's $100 worth today? The **present value** of a future cash flow is simply its value today. You can work out the present value of a flow by discounting it using an interest rate.

Table 6.1: Formula for calculating a discount factor

If t < 1 year (if the cash flow occurs within less than 1 year)	$\dfrac{1}{(1+rt)}$
If t > 1 year (if the cash flow occurs after 1 year)	$\dfrac{1}{(1+r)^t}$

Where r = interest rate and t = time

Example:

If the six-month interest rate is 3.50% (annualized) and you are expecting $1,000 in six months, what would be the value of that money today?

Answer: $\$1,000 \times \dfrac{1}{(1+3.50\% \times 0.5\,years)} = \dfrac{\$1,000}{1.0175} = \$982.80$

If the two-year interest rate is 4.75% and you are expecting $7,000 in two years' time, what would be the value of that money today?

Answer: $\$7,000 \times \dfrac{1}{(1+4.75\%)^2} = \dfrac{\$7,000}{1.09725625} = \$6,379.55$

Simple Interest versus Compound Interest

The best way to understand these two concepts is through examples.

Simple Interest

You have 100,000 (it can be USD, GBP, EUR, take your pick).

If you can deposit this into an account for one year earning a simple interest rate of 5.00%, you would get 5,000 in interest at the end of the year (100,000 x 5.00% x 1 year).

Table 6.2: Simple interest over 1 year

Amount	Interest	Period	iAmount
100,000	5.00%	1 year	5,000

iAmount is the amount of interest you receive.

Compound Interest

Compound interest is interest on interest.

If you can deposit your 100,000 into an account for one year earning interest of 5.00% compounded monthly, you would get 5,116 at the end of the year:

- iAmount is the amount of interest attributed to each period
- Each month counts as one period
- This amount would remain in your account only to be paid out at the end of the one year deposit period
- For the first period, you get: 100,000 x 5.00% x 1/12 = 417
- This 417 is added to the 100,000 you initially had, so for the second period, you get: 100,417 x 5.00% x 1/12 = 418
- This 418 is added to the 100,417 you had in period 2, so for the third period, you get: 100,835 x 5.00% x 1/12 = 420
- And so on as demonstrated in the table below

Table 6.3: Compound interest over 1 year

Amount	Interest	Period	iAmount
100,000	5.00%	1/12	417
100,417	5.00%	1/12	418
100,835	5.00%	1/12	420
101,255	5.00%	1/12	422
101,677	5.00%	1/12	424
102,101	5.00%	1/12	425
102,526	5.00%	1/12	427
102,953	5.00%	1/12	429
103,382	5.00%	1/12	431
103,813	5.00%	1/12	433
104,246	5.00%	1/12	434
104,680	5.00%	1/12	436
		Total = 1 year	5,116

What is leverage?

Put basically, leverage is the percentage of debt in a transaction or a business. It can be measured in many different ways. See Table 7.9 in Chapter 7 for example metrics.

For someone new to financial concepts, leverage is probably best understood with reference to the property market.

Leverage in the property market (mortgages)

- Say you want to buy a house that costs $100,000 but you only have $25,000, you could borrow the remaining $75,000 from a commercial (retail) bank.
- The money you invest in the house is the 'equity'.
- The amount borrowed is called a mortgage, so the word 'mortgage' generally just refers to money borrowed for the purpose of buying a piece of real estate.

- The value of the loan compared to the value of the house is called the **LTV** or **Loan-To-Value** Ratio.
- In this instance, the buyer has leverage of 75% as measured by the LTV ratio (a loan of $75,000 divided by the property's value of $100,000 = 75%).
- Before the credit crunch many people in the developed world, especially in the UK and the USA, were able to secure 100% LTV mortgages i.e. they were 100% **levered**.
- The bank lent them all the money needed to buy the house, leaving the buyer to pay just the legal costs, any tax and other transactions costs associated with buying a house.
- Some even managed to secure LTVs in excess of 100%; the bank paid for the house and many associated purchase costs.
- There is nothing inherently wrong with taking on that much leverage provided you can make the interest and capital repayments on time, even as interest rates rise.
- This was one of the key factors that led to the credit crunch: *swathes of people taking on mortgages that they ultimately could not afford.*

What was banks' rationale for lending so much for property purchases?

1. Mortgage banks were *planning to sell the loans on to investment banks anyway* so if things did go wrong and borrowers couldn't pay back their mortgages, at least the troubles would be someone else's. *This assumption turned out to be only partly right.* Many mortgage-lending banks were still sitting on loans that hadn't been shifted yet when the credit crunch hit.
2. The key assumption was that property prices would continue to rise. Lenders believed that even if they gave someone a mortgage that exceeded the current market value of a house, over time a rise in the property's value would effectively lead to a fall in the loan-to-value.

This assumption turned out to be completely wrong. It turns out property prices can fall, massively.

What banks *thought* would happen versus what happened:

Year 1

- Juliet buys a house worth $100,000; her bank gives her a mortgage of $105,000.

Year 5

- Juliet loses her job and starts to default on monthly mortgage payments.
- The bank repossesses the house.
- Its value has gone up to $115,000 so they sell it at that price.
- Juliet still owes the bank about $93,000 after five years of repayment. So they subtract this amount off the sale price plus any transactions costs involved in the repossession process. Juliet receives the balance, if any.

But the credit crunch happened:

- After five years, the property's value had fallen 20% to $80,000.
- Even after the sale, the bank remained short.
- This happened on such a massive scale that some banks had to declare bankruptcy.
- Trust between banks plummeted because they had no idea who was sitting on the 'bad' loans.

This led to further problems...

- Willingness to lend to other banks and to companies almost completely fell away.
- Some banks and companies had been funding their operations by borrowing money for a short-term, e.g. one

year (for example via **interbank lending** or the **commercial paper market**) and investing for a long period of time, e.g. five years. They assumed that when a year was up they would easily be able to extend their loans. As it turned out, they found themselves unable to refinance their loans at the one year point.

- Many such companies also went bust. Northern Rock in the UK is a classic example of one such bank. They issued mortgages of 20 to 30 years but borrowed for much shorter periods.

- When their lenders started refusing to extend their loans they couldn't just go to mortgage holders and ask them to repay because that would have been against the mortgage contract; importantly, the vast number of borrowers would not have had access to that amount of money anyway.

Why might it be cheaper for you to enter into a variable rate mortgage than a fixed rate mortgage?

With a fixed interest rate, the mortgage providing bank takes on the risk of central bank rates (Fed Funds, ECB repo or Bank of England base rate) changing. Think about it this way:

- You enter into a 20-year fixed rate mortgage at a rate of 4.00%.
- Five years in the central bank rate is 5.00% and remains at or above this levels for a prolonged period of time;
- When your mortgage bank borrows money, the minimum they pay is 5.00% but they have lent to you at 4.00% so they are effectively making a loss on what they lent to you.

If you go for a variable rate mortgage, rises and falls in central bank rates are passed on to you so it is a less risky proposition for your mortgage bank. Consequently, the bank is willing to lend more cheaply on a variable loan.

What is LIBOR or Libor?

LIBOR is the London Inter-Bank Offered Rate. It is the rate of interest that banks charge to lend money to each other, i.e. it is an interbank interest rate.

- LIBOR levels are compiled by an organization called the British Bankers' Association.
- LIBOR is compiled on a daily basis (Monday to Friday, except public holidays) and is published at about 11:00 a.m. London time.
- For every maturity, the BBA gets 16 quotes from 16 banks; they discard the lowest four and the highest four; the remaining eight levels are then averaged to come up with that day's LIBOR reference for that maturity.
- LIBOR rates are available for a term of up to one year.
- There is a different LIBOR rate for every currency i.e. we have GBP LIBOR, USD LIBOR, EUR LIBOR and so forth.
- LIBOR used to be viewed as a risk-free interest rate because the big banks that LIBOR is compiled from were seen as being "too big to fail" and therefore riskless. However, this view changed radically during the credit crunch, especially after Lehman Brothers collapsed.
- Nowadays, LIBOR is accepted as just a benchmark or reference level of interest rather than a clear reflection of bank credit risk.

Extra Knowledge for the real keeno – LIBOR is published for the following maturities (or tenors):

Table 6.4: Maturities for which LIBOR levels are published

• Overnight	• 3 Month	• 8 Month
• 1 Week	• 4 Month	• 9 Month
• 2 Week	• 5 Month	• 10 Month
• 1 Month	• 6 Month	• 11 Month
• 2 Month	• 7 Month	• 12 Month

If a LIBOR rate is needed for an intermediate point, simple linear interpolation is normally used.

If LIBOR rates are plotted on a graph with time on the x-axis, the result is a LIBOR curve. The LIBOR curve is a type of yield curve, that is, a curve showing interest rates against time.

Historical LIBOR levels are freely available from the BBA website[7].

What is a forward contract?

A financial agreement to buy or sell a given commodity at a given price on a specific future date.

- The underlying commodity of a forward contract can be:
    - 'Real', e.g. agricultural products, precious stones or metals and so on
    - Financial, e.g. market interest rates, foreign exchange rates, equity prices and other financial instruments
- Forward contracts are traded directly between counterparties rather than on a public exchange. This is called trading **over-the-counter**.
- An over-the-counter transaction can be entered into by phone, email, Bloomberg chat or any other means.

What is a futures contract?

This is just like a forward contract with one crucial difference: futures are standardized contracts that are traded on exchanges. The table below highlights the key differences between the two.

---

[7] http://www.bbalibor.com/rates/historical

Table 6.5: Forward versus Futures contracts

Forward contract	Futures contract
• Traded over-the-counter	• Exchange traded
• Very bespoke contract. Everything can be exactly tailored to the customer's needs: the quantity, payment and maturity dates etc	• Standardized contract, e.g. each future is based on a given quantity of the product in question; payment and maturity dates are also preset
• Collateral does not have to be posted unless it has been agreed in underlying documentation	• **Margin** has to be posted. Margin can be defined as collateral against changes in the futures' value
• Credit risk is generally higher	• Credit risk is lower due to margining

What is the difference between a spot and a forward interest rate?

A **spot rate** is an interest rate that is starting immediately or almost immediately.

Without getting into too much detail, you should know that spot means different things in different currencies.

- Spot when you're talking about GBP interest rates is 't' i.e. today.
- Spot for most other currencies including USD and EUR interest rates is t+2 i.e. in two days' time.

Unless you want to work in the capital markets, this difference won't affect you very much on a day-to-day basis. However, if you see derivatives or FX in your career, you'll need to get real intimate with spot versus forward.

A **forward interest rate** is a rate whose first calculation period is set in the future. The forward rate for any given date is constantly changing (from day to day and even within the same day) until that date arrives. For example, see how market expectations of one-month USD, EUR and GBP LIBOR for 15 Feb 2012 evolved below.

Table 6.6: Expectation of 1-month USD, EUR and GBP LIBOR for 15 Feb 2012 (in %)

LIBOR	30-Dec-11	3-Feb-12	8-Feb-12	15-Feb-12 (Actual)
1-month USD	0.6820	0.3175	0.2764	0.24600
1-month EUR	1.4735	0.8223	0.7395	0.6200
1-month GBP	1.2239	0.8703	0.8289	0.7588

Source: Bloomberg. Collected at some point on the above day, not always at the same time.

It makes sense that the market's best guess of what it'll cost to borrow for a month starting on 15 Feb 2012 will evolve over time as market conditions change. Table 6.6 shows that expectations may bear little resemblance to what actually happens. Provided there are no major catastrophes, the closer we get to 15 Feb 2012, the more accurate the market's expectations will get.

Companies can lock in a future interest rate today using **derivatives**. So, if a company expects to be borrowing in the future and it likes current expectations of future interest rates, it does not have to wait until then to lock in the desired rate; that rate can be secured now. The most basic product available to lock in future interest rates is a Forward Rate Agreement or FRA (covered in Chapter 8/Technical Questions for DCM or FICC/Rates).

What is a swap rate?

Swap rates are interbank interest rates with a maturity greater than 12 months (less than 12 months is LIBOR). Spot and forward LIBORs are used to calculate swap rates.

For example, a conventional 2-year USD swap rate is calculated using:

3-month USD LIBOR in:

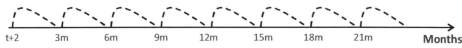

Figure 6.1: LIBOR resets on a 2-year USD interest rate swap

1. Spot 3-month USD LIBOR
2. Expected 3-month USD LIBOR in 3 months
3. Expected 3-month USD LIBOR in 6 months
4. Expected 3-month USD LIBOR in 9 months
5. Expected 3-month USD LIBOR in 12 months

You get the idea

- Once the swap contract is entered into, the interest rate paid by the floating rate payer is **reset** every 3 months.
- Interest rate swaps are explained in Chapter 8/Technical Questions for DCM or FICC/Rates.

What is a yield curve?

A yield curve is a graph that plots interest rates (yields) against time to maturity. Yield curves can be upward sloping ('normal'), downward sloping ('inverted') or flat. To plot a yield curve several data points are needed.

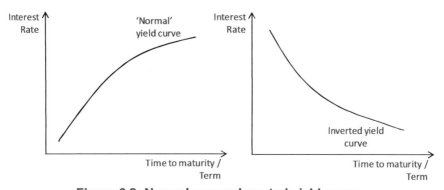

Figure 6.2: Normal versus Inverted yield curve

There are many different types of yield curves. For example:

- You can have a plot of government bond yields.
- Every government has its own yield curve. This makes sense because US Government bond interest rates are different to UK or European Government bonds, for instance.

- A single government can itself have several yield curves.
  - For example, some countries have index-linked bonds (bonds whose yield is linked to the level of inflation in the country) in addition to nominal bonds.
- Some emerging markets have issued bonds in a currency different to the native one, e.g. China has several bonds denominated in USD, EUR and JPY.
- Swap rates (inter-bank interest rates) are available for different maturities, so a swap yield curve can be plotted for many different currencies: GBP, EUR, USD and so on.
  - In some Less Developed Countries a swap market has not been established so a swap yield curve cannot be plotted.
- A yield curve can be plotted for a specific company if it has enough bonds in circulation.

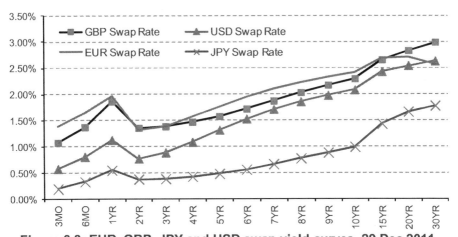

Figure 6.3: EUR, GBP, JPY and USD swap yield curves, 29 Dec 2011

The final maturity of a yield curve will tend to be shorter for emerging markets than it is for developed markets as there will be very limited credit appetite for long maturities in an emerging market. Lending to the U.S. Government for 30 years is less risky than lending to an emerging market (EM) government. Due to limited demand for 30-year EM bonds, such maturities don't get issued, so you would struggle to find a reliable 30 year interest rate quote.

How do companies fund themselves? Where do companies raise money?

The money that is raised to run a business is at a high level classified as either debt (borrowed money) or equity (money put into the business as a token of whole or part ownership).

There are many types of debt and the types available are continually evolving. There are also sub-categories within equity and some funding, hybrid capital, has characteristics of both debt and equity.

Characteristics of Debt

Debt is money that a company has borrowed for either a specific purpose or general corporate use.

Companies borrow from banks, other companies and institutions and high net worth individuals.

Debt capital is borrowed for a fixed period of time and has to be repaid at the end of that term. Typically, at the end of the term companies undertake a 'refinancing' or a recapitalization: they borrow more money to repay the initial borrowings or simply extend the maturity of their borrowed funds. That way, they maintain a constant, desired level of leverage.

Interest is the price of debt. The interest rate paid can either be fixed for the entire term or variable.

Variable interest rates are referred to as being floating, with the rate **reset** periodically (every month, quarterly or semi-annually, for example) based on a reference rate, usually LIBOR but it can also be the country's own central bank base rate or some other reference.

If a company has to be liquidated for any reason, debt-holders are paid back before the equity holders. Debt is therefore said to **rank senior** to equity.

Key Types of Debt

- Bank loans
- Bonds

Bank Loans

Bank loans are almost always LIBOR based.

Why would a company choose bank financing over issuing a bond?

- Diversification of funding
- It may be cheaper at that point in time
- It can be quicker to finalize

Diversification: companies don't like to be dependent on one type of financing so if they've issued a lot of bonds they may choose the bank loan route to spread their risks.

Cost: Whether the bank or the bond market will offer the cheapest funding depends on what's going on the economy; it's cyclical and driven by demand and supply factors.

Speed: for instance, if a company had never issued a bond before and they need funds quickly, a bond will likely take longer to issue because investors have to be educated about the company's profile and their credit history. Their existing bank(s) will already have this knowledge so they should be in a position to make a more rapid decision.

Term Loan versus Revolving Credit Facility (or Revolver)

Revolver

- A revolver is just a corporate-level overdraft facility. Some companies secure a revolver and pay a **commitment fee** for it when they have no intention of using the funds. The money does not have to be drawn down, that is, taken out of the bank account.

- A revolver may be kept as emergency cash or to tide the company over in difficult months. For instance, some companies make most of their revenue in the months leading up to Christmas and will use a revolver to keep going until then.

- Whatever the reason for maintaining a revolver, the money is available whenever a business needs it and once a revolver is agreed there is no need to wait for any further bank approvals in order to access the funding.

- A revolver has a given term (usually three or five years but during the 2007-2009 credit crunch 12-24 month maturities became common). At the end of that term the bank and company will usually renew it.

- At the point of renewal, the revolver's terms may be renegotiated, e.g. the company may ask to change the size, maturity, currency or other detail.

Term loan

- Conversely, term loans are usually drawn facilities with a given repayment schedule. Said differently, in the same way as you think of a revolver as similar to an overdraft on your bank account, a term loan is equivalent to you getting a bank loan.

- With an overdraft you don't have to take the money and if you do, you can pay back whenever you want; on the other hand with a bank loan the money is given to you once the loan is agreed and there are set repayment dates.

- Term loans are usually up to ten years in maturity but they can be much longer, e.g. in Project Finance term loans of 30 years or even longer were very common before the credit crunch.

What sort of information is included in the term sheet for a loan facility?

A term sheet for a loan (a **Facility Agreement**) sets out:

- The exact name of the entity borrowing money
- How much they are borrowing
- What they are borrowing the money for
- When they need to repay the money by
- What the interest rate is
- Any fees the bank will charge for arranging the loan
- Whether or not the borrower is required to hedge the loan using derivatives such as interest swaps or caps
- The penalties that will be imposed if the borrower misses payments
- Specific collateral, if any, that the borrower is required to set aside to secure the loan
- Conditions that must be met before the lender can release the loan
- Conditions that the borrower needs to continually meet throughout the life of the loan, e.g. the lender may specifically request that debt as defined by debt/EBITDA[8] be kept below a given level
- The law that will be applied if either party needs to be taken to court, e.g. New York law or English law etc.

What is the bottom line in a loan transaction?

- The company just wants to borrow a given amount at a reasonable rate and with reasonable conditions.
- The banks want to ensure they get their money back so they look very closely at the cash flow profile of the company, the ingredients

[8] EBITDA is Earnings Before Interest, Tax, Depreciation and Amortization.

that have gone into its revenue projections and any other amounts the company has borrowed. The department responsible for this assessment is the Credit Risk function of the bank.

Bond

A bond is a debt instrument issued by a borrowing company to a group of investors.

The borrowing company receives the money on the 'settlement date' and pays a fixed rate of interest (coupon) to the investors on each 'payment date'. Payments are normally semi-annual on USD and GBP bonds but annual on EUR bonds; the conventions are different for every currency. The money is repaid at 'maturity'.

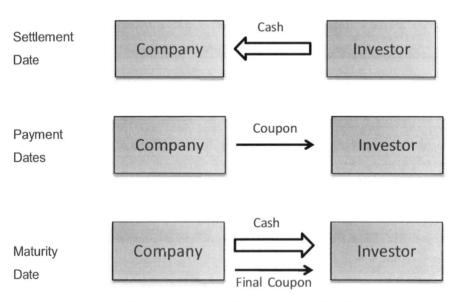

Figure 6.4: Cash flows through the life of a bond

Unrated companies may have limited access to the mainstream bond market and will therefore prefer to seek bank lending instead. This is not necessarily true: there are unrated companies with bonds, e.g. John Lewis in the UK and AP Moller Maersk in Denmark. There's no unrated bond market in the US. However, unrated companies can issue bonds to private investors and institutions through a **private placement**.

Bond ratings help investors to benchmark how they should view or classify one bond relative to another.

If there were no relevant benchmarks, then an issuing company would be unnecessarily punished with an additional credit spread. That is, if investors did not have a standardized rating system to refer to, some companies would end up paying a higher bond coupon than they should and vice versa. It might be worth their while to get a rating in order to avoid such a premium being added on to their bond coupon.

Characteristics of Equity

Equity-holders partake in the ownership of a company.

Equity includes any money that the founders of a company put into the business themselves and any money that they might have received from venture capitalists or other private equity investors. If someone gives you money in return for a share of your company they become an equity-holder or a shareholder.

The money shareholders put into a company does not have to be repaid.

In return for their investment, shareholders receive a share of any profits made. The payments made to shareholders are called **dividends**.

If a company is liquidated shareholders are the last to be repaid. If after the debtholders have been paid there are no assets left to liquidate, then the shareholders get nothing back. Equity is therefore said to be subordinated, or rank junior relative to debt.

Even within debt and within equity there are different subcategories which determine who needs to get paid first if a business goes bust.

Types of Equity

Start-up companies don't have enough of a track record to get a significant bank loan or to raise equity in the capital markets. To fund growth they can obtain equity capital from one of the below. The list is not exhaustive.

Angel investors are businesspeople that invest in high risk start-ups; they typically look to get their money back several times over, five times[9] or more within four to eight years. The decision behind an 'angel' investment usually comes from an individual or family. Some angels group their funds together to enable bigger investments and economies of scale on admin, e.g. project due diligence.

Venture capitalists (VCs) are a special category of private equity investors that invest in early-stage start-ups, typically in technology or some other unproven field. The investment will normally be smaller in size. As VC funds look at higher risk investments than mainstream private equity, they similarly look for higher returns: 10-50 times the initial investment within five years.

Private equity investors (also known as **'Financial Sponsors'**) pool together the funds of various private investors and manage them in a fund. Investors can include high net-worth individuals, companies or even institutions like pension funds and insurance companies. The fund makes investment decisions in a formalized manner as dictated in the **private placement memorandum (PPM)** that is used to set the fund up and attract money from investors. Private equity investors typically look for a return of

---

[9] Source: http://www.businessdictionary.com/article/227/a-beginners-guide-to-angel-investing/

20-30%. To buy an asset, mainstream private equity funds will combine private equity with bank debt

According to PEI 300's 2011 ranking, the ten largest private equity firms in the world are:

1. TPG Capital
2. Goldman Sachs Principal Investment Area
3. The Carlyle Group
4. Kohlberg Kravis Roberts, KKR
5. The Blackstone Group
6. Apollo Global Management
7. Bain Capital
8. CVC Capital Partners
9. First Reserve Corporation
10. Hellman & Friedman

Source: www.peimedia.com/pei300

How do these equity investors get their money back?

*   By selling the asset
*   By listing the asset on a public stock exchange through an Initial Public Offering, IPO
*   Dividends may also be paid by the assets of private equity firms but are not likely in angel or venture capital investments as all funds are typically ploughed back into the business to generate growth

Crowd funding is money sourced from ordinary people normally through some internet based method. Frequently, funds sourced from the crowd don't have to be paid back. For example, every year I try to donate to Wikipedia's fundraising campaign because I like what they do: they democratize access to information. I would encourage anyone to do the same. Every little counts.

A business that raises capital from the crowd receives small amounts of money from many people, most of whom are not professional investors. The contributors will all be people that appreciate the business idea under consideration and possibly see themselves or their friends and family using it.

With the growth of the internet and the ease of making e-payments, crowd funding has grown rapidly in recent years.

Check out milliondollarhomepage.com for the kid who raised over USD1 million in just 128 days to fund his university education through crowd sourcing and he doesn't have to pay it back!

What are shares?

A share is a unit of ownership in a company. Shares and equity are used interchangeably when referring to ownership in a company. Depending on the context, sometimes it makes more sense to use one word rather than the other, e.g. you would normally say, "I want to buy **shares** in Apple Inc."

What is the difference between ordinary shares and preference shares?

Table 6.7: Ordinary versus preference shares

Ordinary Shares (a.k.a. Common Stock)	Preference Shares (a.k.a. Preferred Stock or Preferreds)
• Might receive dividends after Preferreds have been paid	• Get paid a fixed, predetermined dividend
• Have voting rights in proportion to their ownership of the company. Vote on corporate policy and election of the Board of directors amongst many things	• Limited or no voting rights
• If the company is unwound, get paid after Preferreds, i.e. ordinary shares rank junior to Preferreds	• Rank senior to ordinary shares but subordinate (i.e. junior) to bonds and loans
• Much more common than preferreds	• May be convertible to ordinary shares under certain conditions

Overall, preference shares are seen as a hybrid between debt and pure equity. Different types of preference shares exist with different rules, for instance, concerning how and when dividends are paid.

Broadly speaking, debt and equity can be differentiated as follows:

Table 6.8: Notable differences between Debt and Equity

Debt	Equity
• Has to be repaid after a fixed term	• Doesn't have to be repaid
• Doesn't signify any ownership	• Represents an ownership stake
• Paid interest on fixed dates	• Paid dividends, if at all
• Ranks senior to equity	• Ranks junior to debt

What is hybrid capital?

Hybrid financial instruments have features of both debt and equity. Key characteristics:

- They pay a given / predictable return
- They are either convertible to equity at some point or under certain conditions or can immediately be apportioned partly to equity and partly to debt on the balance sheet

In recent times, rating agencies have developed structuring guidelines that allow the same instrument to be simultaneously accounted for partly as debt and partly as equity on a balance sheet, e.g. with certain characteristics an instrument can be categorized as 75% equity and 25% debt or vice versa. Traditionally, 100% of a hybrid instrument would initially be classed as debt.

Two factors that help to get a high equity weighting on a hybrid instrument:

- Very long-dated
- Interest payments that are cancellable or indefinitely deferrable

Preferreds and **convertible debt** are two common hybrid securities.

Why do companies like hybrids?

Because they allow them to raise more debt (i.e. increase leverage) without negatively impacting their credit rating.

Convertible debt

Convertible debt is converted into a given number of shares at or after a given time. Because the debtholder has this additional conversion option embedded into the **security**, they receive a lower rate of interest than would be the case on a 'vanilla' debt instrument.

If on the conversion date the conversion price is lower than the current share price, the convertible debt holder is **in-the-money** and would convert the debt to equity. They immediately lock in a profit by selling at the market price.

Example

Say you bought USD1 million of a convertible loan issued by a book retailer, Blissful Books United, BBU. If the term sheet said you could convert this contract to USD1 million worth of BBU shares in 10 years' time at a price of $25 per share (i.e. 40,000 shares) or receive your $1 million back, what would you do in 10 years' time?

10 years later:

- Market share price = $30.
- So 40,000 shares are worth 40,000 x $30 = $1.2million.
- Your convertible loan contract allows you to buy the same 40,000 shares for $1million, so it is **in-the-money**.
- So you would convert the loan to the 40,000 shares and immediately sell them to lock in a $200,000 profit.

> *Conversion Price < Market Share Price*
> *(in-the-money; convert)*

Alternatively, 10 years later:

- Market share price = $20.
- So 40,000 shares are worth 40,000 x $20 = $800,000.
- Your convertible loan contract allows you to buy the same 40,000 shares for $1million, so it is **out-of-the-money.**
- So you would rather just have your $1 million back than convert your contract. It doesn't make sense to pay $1million for shares that you can easily buy for $800,000 in the equity market.

> *Conversion Price > Market Share Price*
> *(out-of-the-money; do not convert)*

Convertibles can be structured in various ways, e.g. conversion to shares can be mandatory. The above is a simple scenario.

What is market capitalization?

The **market capitalization**, or simply **market cap**, is the total value of a company's equity. It is calculated by multiplying the share price by the total number of shares outstanding in the company.

On 17 June 2011, Apple Inc.'s share price was $320.26; Total Common Shares Outstanding were 924.67 million so the market cap was $296.1 billion (320.26 x 924.67).[10]

Information on the shares of listed companies is very widely available. Besides the company website, Google Finance and Yahoo! Finance will have timely data you can look at.

---

[10] Source: Apple website.

CREDIT RISK

What is credit worthiness?

If a company or a person is **creditworthy**, they are likely to pay back their debts. Such a person or company is said to be a '**good credit**'. Good credits:

- Have **better access to capital**:
    - The likelihood of lenders getting their money back is high so they are more willing to lend.
    - Suppliers are more willing to give the company or person products on credit (i.e. with money to be received later) as they expect to eventually get paid for the goods.
- Have a **lower cost of capital** i.e. borrowing is cheaper for them.
- Have **fewer conditions** attached to the borrowing.
- Have a better overall **reputation** and **access to opportunities**.

A '**bad credit**' would, on the contrary, mean there is a high chance that funds will not get repaid.

It follows that poorly rated entities find it hard and at times impossible to borrow. If lenders do decide to extend credit (i.e. to lend money to a bad credit), the rates tend to be prohibitively expensive with many strings attached.

What is credit risk or credit exposure?

Any entity (bank, investor, supplier etc.) that is owed money is said to have a **credit exposure** as they are 'exposed' to the risk of not being (re)paid.

Within the realm of 'good credit risk' and 'bad credit risk' there are further layers of riskiness. Lenders assess all prospective borrowers using some standardized scale to enable comparison across companies and/or products. The rating given is called a **credit score** (for individuals) or a **credit rating** (for companies).

Any lender, e.g. a bank or a bondholder, is exposed to the risk of not ever seeing their money returned. Companies that sell cars and other big items on credit (i.e. they allow the buyer to pay back over time) will never see some of that money again. Some mortgages will never be fully repaid.

Subprime mortgages are mortgages given to people with a poor credit record. The interest rates are much higher than on a 'normal' mortgage and they would thus only be taken out by people who fail to get a mortgage elsewhere. Subprime mortgages are one class of assets that took a huge hit as a result of the credit crunch and are attributed with helping to create the conditions that led to the credit crunch.

What is a (credit) rating agency?

Investors need a credible and independent organization to rate the credit-worthiness of bond issuers and financial products. Rating agencies perform this function.

The three biggest international credit rating agencies are:

- Standard and Poor's (c.40% market share[11])
- Moody's (c.40% market share)
- Fitch (c.14% market share)

Getting a product rated can help to attract investors for the product because it helps them to validate it and benchmark it against other products that they know.

The rating scales run as in the table below.

---

[11] http://www.washingtonpost.com/wp-dyn/articles/A5573-2004Nov22.html

- S&P and Fitch ascribe a '+' or '-' in front of a rating to indicate if the credit is slightly better or slightly worse than the 'clean' rating.

- Moody's attach a 1, 2 or 3 to a rating where 1 is better than 2 and 2 is better than 3.

- A **downgrade** is a reduction in the credit rating.

Table 6.9: Rating schedule of the main rating agencies

Moody's	S&P	Fitch	Meaning
Aaa	AAA	AAA	Investment grade
Aa	AA	AA	
A	A	A	
Baa	BBB	BBB	
Ba	BB	BB	Sub-investment grade. As you move down the scale, the credit becomes more and more speculative
B	B	B	
Caa	CCC	CCC	
Ca	CC	CC	
C	C	C	
C	D	D	In default

The reputation of rating agencies took a negative hit in the 2007-2009 credit crunch because they had ascribed AAA ratings to many products that were blamed for causing/exacerbating the crunch (e.g. collateralized debt obligations, CDOs).

How is credit risk assessed for a company (or for a person)?

Corporate risk is normally assessed using a top-down approach. That is, the assessor looks at the country of the business, then the current economic environment, then the industry risk and finally the business specific risks.

Table 6.10: Analyzing credit risk

Sovereign	• Some countries are less business friendly than others, e.g. due to onerous regulations or an unstable government

Macro-Economic	• At what point in the business cycle is the economy? • What are inflation and interest levels like?
Industry	• Is the business in a mature, stable industry or not? • Is the industry very competitive?
Business Specific	• Does the business have good management? • Is the business well diversified and operationally efficient? • Does the business have a large market share?

Specifically, in considering whether or not to extend credit or whether or not to sell goods on credit, a lender or creditor considers some or all of the below:

- How will the money be paid back? That is, what is the source of funds that will be used for repayments?
  - **Company**: what's the cash flow profile of the company? How profitable are they?
  - **Individual**: what sort of job does the prospective borrower have? Is it well-paid? Is the job permanent or temporary? How long have they been in that job?
- How stable are the **cash flows**?
  - **Company**: a cyclical business like a media or electronics company is likely to be less creditworthy than a non-cyclical business such as a utility or supermarket (of a similar size); you can postpone the purchase of a new TV, phone or laptop but you can't put off eating for more than just a few hours.
    - That said, different types of supermarket will exhibit different levels of stability: 'value' supermarkets will tend to have a more stable customer base than the posh supermarkets. In tough times, some previously 'posh' shoppers need to take the 'value' route!

- o **Individual**: someone whose employment history contains many gaps will tend to foster less confidence than someone who has never been out of a job.

- What does the **credit history** look like?
  - o Defaults and or late payments will reduce a credit rating.
  - o Longer credit histories are more reliable than shorter ones.
  - o Also, the longer the credit history with a single lender/supplier the better, e.g. a ten year lending relationship with a single bank looks more credit-friendly than a ten year history where one has changed lenders several times. The new lender would have to query why you've had to change bank relationships with such frequency.

- **Liquidity** and **financially flexibility**. How much other **debt** is held?
  - o **Company**: all debt instruments can usually be found in the annual report or other regulatory filing (e.g. 10K and 10Q in the USA), however, debt held off-balance sheet, e.g. in a **special purpose vehicle, SPV** (a company set up to perform specific financial transactions, e.g. a securitization) can be very hard, if not impossible, to isolate. **Leverage ratios** are compared across companies.
  - o **Individual**: all credit and store cards, personal loans including car loans are logged by credit scoring agencies to produce a credit score, e.g. the FICO score in the USA or Experian rating in the UK.

- What is the **risk appetite** of the lender?
  - o For a fairly new business, lenders will look at how realistic projected cash flows are. Banks are typically quite conservative and will take on only those new projects that sound like a done deal.
  - o **Venture capitalists** are more willing to take on a higher level of credit risk in return for a higher expected return.

What is the relationship between risk and return?

Generally, a higher return is expected for taking a higher risk.

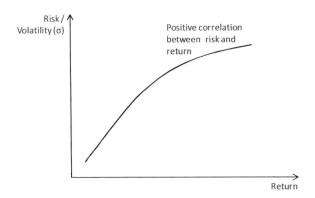

Figure 6.5: Relationship between Risk and Return

The **capital asset pricing model, CAPM**, formalizes this relationship:

$$E(r_a) = r_f + \beta_a(r_m - r_f)$$

- $E(r_a)$ is the expected return from asset or project 'a'
- r_f is the risk free rate
  - Usually assumed to be the return on a government bond with the same maturity as investment 'a'.
  - After the credit crunch, we all know that government risk is most certainly not risk-free but this assumption still holds in 'theory' as governments can print money to avoid default.
- Beta, β_a is a measure of the riskiness of asset 'a'
- $(r_m - r_f)$ is the difference between the expected market return and the risk free rate
  - The expected market return (r_m) is usually assumed to be the average historical return achieved by given market portfolio, e.g. S&P500 for USA, FTSE100 for UK, Nikkei for Japan etc.
  - If available, the return on a portfolio of companies in the same industry as project 'a' can be used.

147

Assume you want to invest in an asset or a project 'a'. The formula above says that the expected return on 'a' is equal to the risk free rate plus a premium. This premium varies with risk factor beta (β_a). The larger β_a is, the higher the expected return.

CAPM is very widely criticized as having unrealistic assumptions. It reflects an ideal world not the real world. That said, it is still widely held as a good approximation of the risk-return relationship. Key assumptions of CAPM[12]:

1. **Perfect markets** i.e. markets where:
- There are a large number of buyers and seller so that no single buyer or seller can influence price with their actions.
- Everyone freely receives exactly the same information at exactly the same time.
- There are no transaction costs, e.g. taxes.
- Investors are rational, utility-maximizing, risk-averse and all have the same expectations.
2. Investors hold a **well diversified portfolio** and as such are only concerned with systematic risk. This is only true for some investors.
- A diverse portfolio does not have unsystematic risk (risk that can be diversified away, e.g. company specific or industry specific risk).
- The risk factor β_a represent only systematic risk (risk that cannot be diversified away and affect all assets, e.g. a global recession).
3. All **assets are held for the same length of time**. Not usually true.
4. Investors **can borrow at the risk free rate**. This is generally not true.

Absolute versus relative risk

Banks and investors have limited funds available for lending. It follows that they cannot lend to everybody that asks and must choose between the different risks, that is, credit risk has to be assessed both:

---

[12] Reference: Hull, J.C., 2012, Options, Futures and Other Derivatives, p73-4

- On an **absolute** basis (how likely is it that company X won't pay?)
- On a **relative** basis (how much more or less likely is it that company X will not pay as compared to company Y)?

Key note on answering questions on credit risk

You will be asked some questions that you have never pondered before. Use common sense. If the interviewer can see that you are successfully making an effort to figure it out, it will score you points.

For example: if asked, "If you saw that a company's interest costs consumed most of its revenues would you still lend to them?" you can say things like:

"High interest payments could be a red flag in a credit risk assessment, however, I would need to find out the reason behind the high interest costs before deciding whether or not to lend. There may be mitigating factors, for instance, the company may have assets far in excess of the money it owes: an oil exploration company, for example, may have just found large oil wells but hasn't exploited them yet. Alternatively, this could be normal for that time of the year or for that point in the economic cycle. The company might also be dealing with a large one-off setback like a fire which might have stopped a factory from operating for a while. Some of these costs may later be covered by insurance and so won't affect long-run profits. Overall, before lending to a company I would need to look at where the company is in the context of the whole economy and with reference to what they are going through now, what happened to them in the past few months or years and what is likely to happen in the future."

This is an example of a common sense answer. I am typing as I think in the same way you would express yourself to the interviewer. There is no banking lingo used above just the expression of a thought process. That's mostly what an interviewer would want to see: how you think.

BRAINTEASERS

Brainteasers are inevitable when applying for investment banking jobs.

Through brainteasers your interviewer:

- Gets an idea of how well you react to questions or situations that you've likely not thought about before. Do the questions appear to excite you or make you unduly nervous?
- He observes the mental process you go through to get to an answer and in so doing can size up your reasoning skills.

The interviewer wants to have as much insight as possible into how your mind works so speak out loud as you work through problems; they will be particularly interested to see if you arrive at an answer in a way that they hadn't considered.

You cannot say 'I don't know' for a brainteaser. You have to give an answer of some form. You can ask for clues and you can check if paper is allowed.

To improve how well, how fast and how broadly you think on your feet I have found the following website: **SharpBrains.com**.

Don't spend too much time on brainteasers if you don't have much time left. Spend more time on preparing your competency and technical questions because they tend to weigh more towards your score.

7

TECHNICAL QUESTIONS FOR

CORPORATE FINANCE &

EQUITY CAPITALS MARKETS (ECM)

Companies frequently require objective advice on **strategy**, **valuation** and **financing**. They hire investment bankers, accountants or management consultants for this advice.

Strategic Advice

Companies may want high level insights on:

- What the key competitors in their industry are doing
- What research analysts are expecting growth to be in the industry or what challenges are expected in the industry
- Companies they could potentially take over and what synergies might be gained by merging with different takeover targets

Valuation Insights

Investment banks need to be able to discuss a business's value in the context of:

- **Market value** as represented by the market share price
- **Relative value** as represented by comparable companies or comparable transactions that have happened in the market
- **Absolute value** as derived from discounted cash flow analysis

Financing Advice

- **Capital raising:** advice on how to issue shares or debt instruments
- **Liability management:** advice on how to protect the financial position of the company given changes in economic factors, e.g. interest rates, currency exchange rates, global economic growth
- **Pension and asset management:** a lot of companies provide pension benefits to their employees. They have the big responsibility of ensuring they can afford to pay a pension to their employees when they retire. There's a lot of regulation covering corporate pension plans and this regulation changes from country to country. Some investment bankers specialize in providing advice on how to manage pension assets.

Corporate financiers, equity sales and trading people need to be able to read financial reports. For interviews, you don't need to get into any detail. However, it will help you to understand:

- The key financial statements
- The key tools used in valuing companies
- The key ratios used to assess a company's financial position including its leverage level

FINANCIAL REPORTING

Registered companies are legally required to file financial reports to the authorities at regular intervals.

The rules on filing are far more stringent for companies publically listed on a stock exchange than for privately held companies.

Key financial industry regulators in the USA and the UK:

- The Securities and Exchange Commission (SEC), USA
- The Financial Services Authority, UK. This is being split into two separate authorities: the Prudential Regulation Authority (PRA) and the Financial Conduct Authority (FCA)

In the US, notable filings submitted to the Securities and Exchange Commission for regulated / listed companies include:

- The annual report or 10K
- The quarterly financial report or 10Q
- 8K - a report detailing a material event that has affected the company
- There are many other filings but for a prospective intern or new hire, knowledge of the above should suffice

Europe, the UK and indeed other regions in the world will have a requirement to file similar information to the regulatory and registry authorities.

What are financial statements?

There are three key statements used to capture a company's financial position:

- **Income Statement** (a.k.a. Profit and Loss Statement or simply P&L in the UK)
  - Shows the revenues and costs or expenses of a company over a period of time, e.g. over a year or a quarter

- **Balance Sheet**
  - ○ Gives a snapshot of a company's assets, liabilities and equities on a given day
  - ○ The asset side of the balance sheet has to equal the sum of liabilities and equity (Assets = Liabilities + Equity)
  - ○ This is the only report that shows the position on one given day rather than over a period of time
- **Cash Flow Statement**
  - ○ Summarizes the cash that has gone into and out of a business over a period of time

The format of financial reports in the developed world is broadly similar. I find the US format of financial reports to be the most intuitive and appealing so I will use that for example purposes. If you can read US reports you can easily read those of other countries, however, the terminology might differ, e.g. Americans say 'inventory', Britons might say 'stock'. With reporting becoming so increasingly unified, anyone familiar with accounting will know what you are talking about regardless of terminology.

All companies that are listed on a stock exchange will have publicly available financial accounts that you can easily get hold of. For instance, Google "Google income statement 2010" and you will be able to view their accounts. You can do the same for any listed company that you want to check out.

I use my fictional company, Blissful Books United (BBU), for many examples. BBU is a large retailer of books with its headquarters in the USA. They own most of their bookshops on a mortgage basis but they also rent some.

What would you expect to see on an income statement?

The income statement below shows revenues and costs over one year but in reality it can be any period of time. Apart from regulators needing to see reports annually or semi-annually, managers will want to see reports more frequently, perhaps even weekly, so that they can dynamically adjust the business strategy.

Table 7.1: Income statement

(in USD '000s)	Year 1	Year 2	Year 3
Revenue or Sales	15,750	16,695	17,530
Cost of Goods Sold (COGS)	(7,560)	(7,680)	(7,713)
Gross profit	**8,190**	**9,015**	**9,817**
Sales, general and admin (SG&A)	(2,363)	(2,504)	(2,629)
EBITDA	**5,828**	**6,511**	**7,187**
Depreciation and amortization	0	(113)	(184)
Operating profit (or EBIT)	**5,828**	**6,398**	**7,003**
Other income	0	0	25
Interest income	102	59	54
Interest expense	(146)	(255)	(238)
Profit before tax (PBT)	**5,784**	**6,202**	**6,844**
Tax	(1,735)	(1,861)	(2,053)
Net income	**4,049**	**4,341**	**4,791**
Weighted average shares outstanding ('000s)	250	250	250
Earnings per share (EPS)	16	17	19

Revenue or Sales

- Revenue reflects the total value of goods (books, in this case) and services sold in the period.
- Provided the good or service has been *delivered,* its value is recorded here whether or not cash has been received by the seller (so any books BBU sells on credit will also be included in this line).
- Some companies receive cash before their product has been delivered, e.g. airlines, property rental companies and online shops. If they haven't yet delivered the good or service, this cash won't count as Sales.

- o It's recorded on the Balance Sheet under Current Assets as 'prepaid items' or 'prepaid accounts'; when the good is delivered, e.g. a flight is taken or the online shop has dispatched the good from their factory or warehouse, it's then taken off the balance sheet and recorded as part of revenue on the income statement.

Cost of Goods Sold (COGS)

- Included in COGS are:
  - o The cost of buying the books sold in the period
  - o The cost of the staff directly involved in selling the books over the same period
- Whether or not the publisher (i.e. BBU's supplier) has been paid for the books sold, the cost of the books has to be reflected in COGS once the book is sold or delivered.
- Depreciation (explained below) is frequently lumped up in COGS.

Gross profit

- Equals {Revenue minus COGS}.

Sales, General and Admin (SG&A)

- Other costs indirectly associated with running a business are classified as SG&A.
- BBU's SG&A would include:
  - o Administrative staff, cleaners
  - o Rent
  - o Stationery
  - o Utilities (water, electricity, phone, internet)
  - o Advertising
- Amortization (explained below) is frequently included in SG&A.

EBITDA

- EBITDA is Earnings Before Interest, Tax, Depreciation and Amortization have been subtracted.
- EBITDA = {Gross profit minus SG&A}.

Depreciation and amortization

- When a company buys a big ticket item, e.g. a machine, land or a building, the cost is not recorded in one go. The number of years over which the items will be used is estimated and the cost split up and recorded over the years of use.
- **Straight-line depreciation** describes the situation in which the cost of the long-term asset is split evenly over the years in which it will be used. This is the simplest form of depreciation but companies do not have to use the methodology and are free to depreciate in some other fashion.
- Amortization is the depreciation of intangible long-term assets, e.g. goodwill. **Goodwill** occurs when a company is bought for more than it is worth. This is best understood with an example.
  Goodwill example:
    o BBU buys a small chain of bookshops for $3.0 million.
    o If BBU sells the tangible parts of the shops, e.g. all the books in stock and the buildings that are owned by the chain, it would only be able to recoup $2.5m.
    o The extra $0.5m that BBU pays above and beyond the tangible value is classified as goodwill.
    o Why would BBU pay more than what the physical assets are worth, I hear you ask? There may be some intangible benefits in buying the chain of bookshops, e.g. a reputable brand name can encourage a buyer to pay extra; good, strategic locations or patents and licenses that are hard to get hold of can also get a seller a premium valuation.

- Here, I have given depreciation and amortization their own line on the income statement, however, a lot of the time:
  - Depreciation is lumped up in COGS
  - Amortization is included in SG&A

Operating profit or EBIT

- EBIT is **E**arnings **B**efore **I**nterest and **T**ax, have been subtracted.
- EBIT equals {EBITDA minus depreciation & amortization}.
- In this example amortization is assumed to be zero.

Other income

- BBU's primary business is selling books but in year three they sell one of the buildings they own and include the profit from that sale under other income so that this one off sale doesn't distort the top line sales figure.
- Other income includes 'other costs' in which case the figure would be negative rather than positive.
- Other income will tend to include **non-recurring,** one-off gains and losses, e.g. the sale or purchase of anything that is not in the ordinary course of business.

Interest income

- Is the interest earned on any interest-bearing **assets**.
- BBU earns interest from cash in their bank account as well as from marketable securities that they are holding.

Interest expense

- Is the interest paid by BBU on any interesting paying **liabilities**, e.g. loans, bonds and mortgages.

Profit Before Tax (PBT)

- PBT equals {EBIT plus 'interest income' and 'other income' minus 'interest expense'}.
- PBT is sometimes called EBT, Earnings Before Tax.

Tax

- Tax equals {'PBT' multiplied by the 'tax rate'}.
- A tax rate of 30% is assumed here.

Net income ('the bottom line')

- Net income equals {'PBT' minus 'tax'}.
- Net income represents the profit made after all costs have been stripped out. It belongs to the shareholders in a company and they can choose whether to reinvest it in the business or pay it out to themselves as '**dividends**'.

Earnings Per Share (EPS)

- Frequently, under the income statement, the number of shares in a company is given and the net income per share provided.
- Net income per share is called **earnings per share (EPS)**.

What would you expect to see on a balance sheet?

Table 7.2: Balance sheet

(in USD '000s)	Year 1	Year 2	Year 3
Current Assets			
Cash and cash equivalents	1,039	2,623	2,556
Prepaid accounts	315	334	351
Accounts receivable	1,323	1,402	1,472
Inventory	709	751	789
Total current assets	**3,386**	**5,110**	**5,168**
Long Term Assets			
Net Property, Plant & Equipment (PP&E)	4,725	4,838	5,022
Goodwill, patents and licenses	0	0	20
TOTAL ASSETS	**8,111**	**9,948**	**10,210**
Current Liabilities			
Accounts payable	1,393	1,152	1,157
Accrued expenses	205	217	228
Deferred income	315	334	351
Taxes payable	434	465	513
Short term debt	0	1,737	1,577
Long Term Liabilities			
Long term debt	2,205	2,337	2,454
TOTAL LIABILITIES	**4,552**	**6,243**	**6,280**
Equity			
Common stock	1,535	1,535	1,535
Retained earnings	2,024	2,171	2,395
Total equity	**3,559**	**3,706**	**3,930**
TOTAL LIABILITIES & EQUITY	**8,111**	**9,948**	**10,210**

TOTAL ASSETS = TOTAL LIABILITIES + EQUITY

If there is a change in assets, there must be an equal and opposite change in the liabilities and equity section.

160

Current Assets are those assets that are expected to be held for LESS THAN one year.

- Assets are listed from most liquid to least liquid on US balance sheets.
- **Liquidity** is the ease with which the asset can be sold for cash.

Cash and cash equivalents

- Includes any cash balances sitting in the company's bank account.
- **Cash equivalents.** Because cash in the bank does not earn much interest, a company may choose to put some cash into *easily saleable* instruments with a higher return, e.g. the bonds of other companies, government bonds or even equity.
- When the company needs the cash, they simply sell the financial instrument for cash.

Prepaid accounts or items (do not confuse with 'deferred income')

- For the shops that it rents, BBU pays rent for the quarter in advance and this payment is recorded as a 'prepaid item'.
  - ○ The rental payment is only transferred to SG&A from 'prepaid items' after the relevant period has passed.
- For shops that it owns, BBU pays for buildings insurance for the whole year at the beginning of the year. This insurance is also accounted for as a 'prepaid item'.
  - ○ Insurance costs are recorded in SG&A after the relevant period that the insurance covers has passed.

Accounts receivable

- Includes goods that have been delivered by the company but for which payment is yet to be received.
- For example, BBU supplies some small independent bookshops with books and invoices them at the point that the books are delivered to

them; before payment is received, the book sales are recorded under 'accounts receivable'.

Inventory

- Includes the stock of goods waiting to be sold.
- Inventories would include books sitting on the shelves of BBU's bookshop and those that are in warehouses or back offices waiting to be displayed.

Long-term Assets are expected to be held for OVER one year.

Net Property, Plant & Equipment (PP&E)

- PP&E includes any factories, buildings and machinery that a company owns.
- Buildings that are being rented but are not owned by the company would not be included under PP&E.
- Over time, depreciation is summed up (**accumulated depreciation**) and subtracted from PP&E to give the current value of the long-term asset. This is Net PP&E.
  - For example, if a machine bought for $1 million is amortized over ten years, it would be amortized by $100,000 every year. In year four, accumulated depreciation would be $400,000 and the machine would now be recorded as worth $600,000 (Net PP&E).

Goodwill, patents and licenses

- Goodwill is the premium paid for a company above and beyond the total value of its assets.
  - See the example under 'Depreciation and Amortization' in the section on Income Statements above.

- Licenses include such things as copyrights, trademarks or any special government licenses needed to operate a given business.
- In year three, BBU registers its trademark. A potential buyer of the trademark offers to purchase it for USD20,000. They refuse to sell but are able to attribute a market value to the trademark for accounting purposes.

Current Liabilities are those liabilities that are expected to be paid off in LESS THAN one year

- Liabilities are listed from the ones with the shortest maturity to the longest maturity item on US balance sheets.

Accounts payable

- Includes goods that have been received from suppliers but have not yet been paid for, e.g. if a publisher has delivered books to BBU in advance of payment, BBU records the invoice value under 'accounts payable'.

Accrued expenses

Are very similar to accounts payable with a subtle difference:

- Accrued expenses includes goods that have been received from suppliers **but for which an invoice has not yet been received**, e.g. BBU may have an arrangement whereby they regularly receive books from a given publisher. However, the publisher might issue an invoice at a date later than delivery of the books.
- The *expected* invoice value is recorded in 'accrued expenses'.
- Once the invoice is received, the invoice value is moved to 'accounts payable' and once it's paid, it is recorded as inventory on the asset side of the balance sheet.

Deferred income (do not confuse with 'prepaid accounts')

- BBU supplies books to some small independent bookshops. Sometimes these shops pay before goods are delivered to them by BBU. This cash is recorded under deferred income on the balance sheet of BBU until the books have been delivered.
- Upon delivery, the value is then recorded as revenue (the top line of the income statement) and removed from deferred income.

Taxes payable

- Includes any taxes that are due to be paid but haven't been settled.

Short term debt

- Includes any debt instruments that will be paid off within the next 12 months, e.g. if BBU took a five year loan four years ago, this loan would now move from the 'Long-term Liabilities' section to 'Current Liabilities'.

Long-term Liabilities have a maturity date in OVER one year.

Long-term debt

- Is borrowed money with a repayment date more than one year in the future.

Common stock

- Is money that has been paid into a business by shareholders.

Retained earnings

- Any net income that is not paid out to shareholders as dividends is recorded as retained earnings.
- In the case of BBU, 50% of net income is paid as dividends and 50% is held as retained earnings.

What would you expect to see on a cash flow statement?

Table 7.3: Cash flow statement

(in USD '000s)	Year 1	Year 2	Year 3
Net income	4,049	4,341	4,791
Depreciation and amortization	0	113	184
Change in operating working capital (OWC)	0	320	44
Proceeds from asset sales	0	0	(25)
Operating cash flows (OCF)	**4,049**	**4,774**	**4,993**
Capital expenditure (Capex)	(4,725)	(113)	(184)
Proceeds from asset sales	0	0	25
Investing cash flows (ICF)	**(4,725)**	**(113)**	**(159)**
Change in long-term debt	2,205	132	117
Dividends paid	(2,024)	(2,171)	(2,395)
Change in common stock	1,535	0	0
Financing cash flows (FCF)	**1,716**	**(2,038)**	**(2,279)**
Net cash flow	**1,039**	**2,623**	**2,556**

The cash flow statement summarizes a company's sources and uses of cash. Cash flows are split according to whether they are from **operating**, **investing** or **financing** activities.

Operating Cash Flow (OCF)

Operating cash flows result from the ordinary course of business.

Net income

- Is included as a positive number because this is the cold hard cash that the company has received after it has paid costs associated with running the business.
- To be clear, **net income is not cash**. It is an accounting figure that has had various cash and non-cash components stripped out of it.

Depreciation and amortization

- Depreciation and amortization costs are stripped out of net income on the income statement.

- Because these do not actually represent an outflow of cash in the business during the time period, they have to be added back.

Change in operating working capital

- Any increase in non-cash current assets (e.g. accounts receivable) is cash positive so it is **added on to OCF**.

- Any increase in non-cash current liabilities (e.g. accounts payable) is **subtracted from OCF** because it represents cash being paid out of the business.

- The table below shows the calculation for operating working capital:

Table 7.4: Operating Working Capital

(in USD '000s)	Year 1	Year 2	Year 3
Accounts receivable	1,323	1,402	1,472
Inventory	709	751	789
Prepaid accounts	315	334	351
Accounts payable	(1,393)	(1,152)	(1,157)
Taxes payable	(434)	(465)	(513)
Accrued expenses	(205)	(217)	(228)
Deferred income	(315)	(334)	(351)
OWC	0	320	363
Change in OWC	0	320	44

Proceeds from asset sales

- Proceeds from asset sales are subtracted from OCF and added to ICF because they are an investing cash flow.

- If 'Proceeds from asset sales' were added to ICF without subtracting from OCF they would be double counted as they are already included as part of Net Income (see the income statement).

Investing Cash Flow (ICF)

Are cash flows that result from buying and selling productive assets. This could be physical assets (property, plant and equipment) or financial investments made by the firm, e.g. if the company buys shares in another company, dividends from that investment would be an investing cash flow.

Capital expenditure (Capex)

- Capex represents an outflow of cash from the business into fixed assets, e.g. new book shelves for BBU stores.

Proceeds from asset sales

- In year three, BBU sold some physical assets for $25,000. This was shown under 'Other income' on the income statement.

Financing Cash Flow (FCF)

Financing cash flow includes any changes in cash due to changes in debt (bonds, loans etc.) or changes in shareholder equity.

Change in long-term debt

- Represents an increase in cash so any additions to debt from one year to the next are added on and any debt repayments are subtracted.
- For simplicity, in BBU's case we assume that all short-term debt is composed only of the current portion of long-term debt. That is,

amounts of previously long-term debt that mature within the next 12 months. As such, there is no increase or decrease in cash arising from the short-term debt line.

Dividends paid

- Are subtracted from FCF because they represent a cash outflow.

Change in common stock

- Any increases in equity capital, e.g. via a rights issue, are added here and any decreases in equity capital, e.g. due to a share buyback, are subtracted.

Notes to the Financial Statements

As the above statements are very brief, a more detailed breakdown is usually given in the '**Notes to the Financial Statements**'. These are normally placed after the statements themselves or in the appendices. If there's further information available in the notes, the line item on the financial statement will have a number by it corresponding to the number of the note.

You should now have a basic idea of the type of information that can be found on the three main financial statements as well as the general format of presentation. If you decide to go into corporate finance you will need to learn how to build up a set of financial statements on your own and project them into the future using realistic assumptions. For equity sales and trading, modeling won't be necessary but a firm understanding of these statements is a must. It will help you comprehend equity research and corporate reports.

To come up with a set of accounts for BBU, I made up all the assumptions on growth, interest and tax rates, the depreciation rate, the proportion of net income paid out in dividends and so on.

Building your own financial statements will require firm knowledge of accounting, including how the different statements relate to each other. You don't need to know accounting to be hired by a bank but it does of course help. Personally, I had very limited accounting knowledge and I was taught everything once I joined Goldman Sachs full-time. I supplemented their teaching with my own reading after work and at weekends.

Table 7.5: Financial statement jargon buster (US versus UK)

United States	United Kingdom
Accounts payable	Creditors
Accounts receivable	Debtors
Check	Cheque
Checking account	Current account
Common stock	Ordinary shares
Income Statement	Profit and Loss Statement
Inventory	Stock
Paid-in surplus	Share premium
Prime Rate	Base Rate
Treasury bonds	Gilts

If you were presented with the financial statement of a company, how would you determine how efficiently the business manages cash?

It is possible to estimate operational efficiency using the below operating ratios:

Inventory days are the average number of days goods are held by a company before they are sold. For BBU, this would be the time frame between receiving books from publishers and selling those books.

$$Inventory\ days = \frac{Inventory}{COGS} \times 365\ days$$

The shorter the inventory days, the more efficient a company is. That said, if stocks are kept too low, a company is at risk of missing sales.

Accounts receivable days are the average numbers of days a company has to wait before it receives cash from its customers. For BBU, books sold for cash have zero receivable days. If books are paid for using credit cards or checks, it may take a few days for the payment to fully clear.

$$Accounts\ receivable\ days = \frac{Accounts\ receivable}{Revenue} \times 365\ days$$

The shorter accounts receivable days, the more cash efficient a company is.

> **Total number of days between receiving a product and receiving the cash from selling that product**
> **= inventory days + accounts receivable days**

Accounts payable days are the average number of days before a company has to pay suppliers. For BBU, this is the number of days between receiving books from publishers and paying for the books.

$$Accounts\ payable\ days = \frac{Accounts\ payable}{COGS} \times 365\ days$$

The longer accounts remain payable, the better for BBU as they can earn interest off any cash sitting in their accounts and it makes cash management easier. Of course, no company wants to get a reputation as a bad creditor so a balance needs to be achieved.

Table 7.6: BBU's operating ratios

(days)	Year 1	Year 2	Year 3
Inventory days	34	36	37
Accounts receivable days	31	31	31
Inventory + accounts receivable days	**65**	**66**	**68**
Accounts payable days	67	55	55

- You can check these operating ratios using the appropriate figures on the income statement and balance sheet above.

- Note how BBU's operational efficiency has deteriorated.
- In year one, BBU paid suppliers after receiving cash from customers.
- In years two and three, cash is only received 11 days and 13 days respectively after suppliers have been paid.
- Management will want to find the underlying cause to tackle this issue.

VALUATION

Market Analysis

Even looking at just the share price of a company can reveal a lot of information about a company's performance over time as well as changes in investor sentiment.

Figure 7.1: Share price of Blissful Books United (BBU), USD

- 52 week high: the highest price reached in the last 52 weeks, $45
- 52 week low: the lowest price reached in the last 52 weeks, $10

Relative Valuation

Relative valuation involves looking at the value of a company from a comparative perspective, that is, in relation to other, similar companies. 'Multiples' are the statistics used to make such an analysis. Popular multiples include:

Table 7.7: Key valuation ratios in corporate finance

Equity Value (Market Cap*)	$number\ of\ shares\ outstanding \times share\ price$
Enterprise Value (EV)	$equity\ value + net\ borrowings$ $net\ borrowings\ = net\ debt + preference\ shares +$ $minority\ interests$
Earnings per share (EPS)	$\dfrac{net\ income}{number\ of\ shares\ outstanding}$
Price-to-Earnings Multiple (P/E ratio)	$\dfrac{share\ price}{earnings\ per\ share\ (EPS)}$
EBITDA multiple	$\dfrac{EV}{EBITDA}$
EBIT multiple	$\dfrac{EV}{EBIT}$
Sales multiple	$\dfrac{EV}{Sales}$

* Cap = capitalization

Multiples are helpful in deciding whether a company is over or undervalued relative to similar companies.

Blissful Books United (BBU), our fictional bookshop chain, is considering acquiring a competitor and it needs help deciding which company to target. They hire an investment bank to advise them on this. As part of the bank's analysis, the following comps are provided (comps is banker lingo for a comparable companies analysis or common stock comparison, CSC).

Comparable Companies Analysis (a.k.a. Common Stock Comparison)

Table 7.8: Comps

Company	52-week High	52-week Low	Current Price	Equity Value ($m)	Enterprise Value ($m)	P/E	EV/EBITDA	EV/EBIT
Arrivederci Books	€ 49.55	€ 38.54	€ 44.30	15,124	18,300	17.0x	8.3x	11.4x
Bonsoir Books	€ 39.75	€ 22.65	€ 31.84	2,598	3,495	15.8x	10.2x	12.4x
Danke Books	€ 36.86	€ 20.25	€ 24.47	4,375	4,884	13.4x	7.7x	11.1x
Konnichiwa Books	JPY1,087	JPY693	JPY795	5,825	6,714	11.3x	11.8x	15.1x
Uptown Books	$52.45	$39.40	$46.78	46,268	57,632	24.4x	12.0x	14.9x
With-it Books	$59.25	$34.23	$52.72	3,285	4,795	13.1x	6.9x	11.4x
Royal Books	£8.15	£4.85	£6.25	9,243	14,232	13.4x	7.7x	13.2x
Berkeley* Books	£4.59	£3.72	£4.50	7,195	11,693	12.4x	8.3x	11.8x

Pronounced 'barclay'

BBU is targeting an acquisition in Europe or the USA but the bankers have thrown in a Japanese company which they think is currently undervalued.

The following *could be* signals that a company is cheap and hence a good buy:

- High earnings per share (EPS)
- Current price is close to 52 week low
- Low price relative to earnings, P/E
- Low value relative to earnings, EV/EBITDA or EV/EBIT
- Low value relative to revenue, EV/Sales

Leverage Ratios

Leverage ratios are useful on an independent basis as well as a tool in relative valuation. They give you an idea of how solvent a company is.

Table 7.9: Key leverage ratios in corporate finance

$$\dfrac{EBITDA \ or \ EBIT}{Interest}$$	• Captures earnings per unit of interest **costs** • If ratio > 1: earnings exceed interest. This is ideal • If ratio < 1: earnings are lower than interest costs • Normally given as a multiple, e.g. 3.4x or 7.5x
$$\dfrac{Debt}{EBITDA}$$	• Captures total debt per unit of earnings • The higher the ratio is above 1, the more debt a company has relative to EBITDA earnings • Normally given as a multiple, e.g. 2.6x or 1.5x
$$\dfrac{Debt}{Market \ Cap}$$	• Captures total debt per unit of equity value • Normally given as percentage, e.g. 44%
$$\dfrac{Debt}{EV}$$	• Captures total debt as a proportion of the entire value of the business both debt and equity (EV) • Will by nature be lower than debt/market cap • Normally given as percentage, e.g. 24%
$$\dfrac{Free \ Cash \ Flow}{Debt}$$	• Captures cash flow per unit of debt • If ratio > 100%: cash flow exceeds debt • If ratio < 100%: cash flow is lower than debt • Normally given as a percentage, e.g. 22% or 7%

Discounted Cash Flow (DCF) Analysis

A DCF analysis is used to discover the standalone current value of a company, irrespective of the valuation of other companies. Using reasonable assumptions, the company's *expected* future stream of cash flows is discounted to work out what the value of the company is today.

Free cash flow represents cash available for distribution to shareholders and debt-holders. It is a very important concept. Whilst earnings can be manipulated using different accounting methods, it's very difficult to fake cash. It is calculated in the following way:

$$Free\ cash\ flow = EBITDA - changes\ in\ working\ capital - capex - tax$$

$$Working\ capital = current\ assets - current\ liabilities$$

The change (Δ) in working capital is simply the working capital in one year (t), less the working capital the year before (t-1). See table 7.4 for BBU's calculation:

$$(\Delta)change\ in\ working\ capital = working\ capital_t - working\ capital_{t-1}$$

Where does one get the discount factor that is used to discount the expected future free cash flows in a DCF analysis?

- The free cash flows are normally discounted using the **weighted average cost of capital, WACC**.
- WACC represents the combined cost of debt and equity:

$$WACC = r_d(1 - company's\ tax\ rate)\left(\frac{Debt}{Debt + Equity}\right) + r_e\left(\frac{Equity}{Debt + Equity}\right)$$

Where r_d is the average cost of debt and r_e is the cost of equity

- BBU has an average of 47% debt and 53% equity over years one to three (check the balance sheet for yourself) so,

$$WACC = r_d(1 - company's\ tax\ rate)(47\%) + r_e(53\%)$$

Cost of debt

- The cost of debt is very easy to calculate if the company has debt liabilities on its balance sheet.
- Because interest is tax deductible (in most countries) this tax benefit has to be subtracted from the cost of debt.

Cost of equity

Coming up with a cost of equity can be more art than science because shareholders do not receive a pre-specified interest rate. The CAPM model discussed earlier shows that the return to equity is a positive function of risk:

$$r_e(BBU) = r_f + \beta_{BBU}(r_m - r_f)$$

- $r_e(BBU)$ is the cost of equity to BBU or said differently, it is the return that shareholders in BBU expect as a result of holding BBU shares.
- r_f is the risk free rate
    - We can use the return on a 10-year US Government bond as a proxy for the risk-free rate, r_f.
    - US Government bond yields are relatively easy to get a hold of online. Some portals will even allow you to download historical data into Excel.
    - The downgrading of the US Government rating from AAA to AA+ by Standard & Poor's rating agency makes the usual text book assumption that the US Government is risk free debatable.
- β_{BBU} is a measure of how volatile BBU's share price is relative to the average of the market as proxied by a domestic stock index, e.g. the S&P500
    - If BBU is less volatile than the market, on average, β_{BBU} will be less than 1.
    - If BBU is more volatile than the market, on average, β_{BBU} will be more than 1.
- $(r_m - r_f)$ is the difference between the expected market return and the risk free rate.

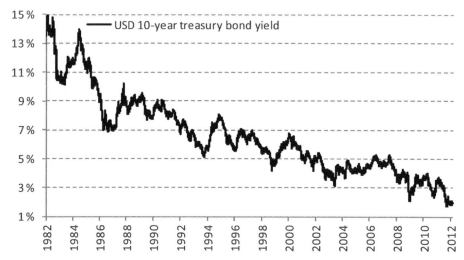

Figure 7.2: USD 10-year Government bond yield Feb 1982 to Feb 2012

Source: Bloomberg

BBU's WACC

- BBU's income statement assumed a cost of debt of 6.60%, 6.25% and 5.90% for years one, two and three respectively, average = 6.25%.
- BBU's tax rate is 30% every year.
- The average 10-year US Government yield from Sep 2001 to Sep 2011 is about 4.00%.
- We will base our risk-free rate, r_f, on this ten year period.
- BBU has a share price less volatile than the average market return as measure by the S&P 500. That is, β_{BBU} is 0.88.
- After analyzing various market equity indices including the S&P500 plus a portfolio of businesses similar to BBU, BBU's Investment Bankers decide on an r_m value of 5.80%.

$$r_e(BBU) = r_f + \beta_{BBU}(r_m - r_f)$$

$$r_e(BBU) = 4.00\% + 0.88(5.80\% - 4.00\%) = 5.58\%$$

$$WACC = r_d(1 - company's\ tax\ rate)\left(\frac{Debt}{Debt + Equity}\right) + r_e\left(\frac{Equity}{Debt + Equity}\right)$$

$$WACC = 6.25\% \times (1 - 30\%) \times 47\% + 5.58\% \times 53\% = 5.02\%$$

The **WACC of 5.02%** will be used in our DCF analysis. Using 'r' to represent the WACC, the discount factor is calculated as:

If t < 1 year (if the cash flows occurs within less than 1 year)	$\dfrac{1}{(1+rt)}$
If t > 1 year (if the cash flows occurs after 1 year)	$\dfrac{1}{(1+r)^t}$

Below is a ten year DCF analysis of Blissful Books United, BBU. The DCF is carried out after BBU has already been operational for three years.

Table 7.10: A basic DCF analysis (all figures in USD)

	Year 1	Year 2	Year 3	Year 4	Year 5	Year 6	Year 7	Year 8	Year 9	Year 10	Year 11	Year 12	Year 13
DCF Year				1	2	3	4	5	6	7	8	9	10
Business Year	Year 1	Year 2	Year 3	Year 4	Year 5	Year 6	Year 7	Year 8	Year 9	Year 10	Year 11	Year 12	Year 13
EBITDA	5,828	6,511	7,187	7,790	8,287	8,651	8,857	9,123	9,396	9,678	9,968	10,267	10,575
Capex	4,725	113	184	193	203	213	223	235	246	259	272	285	299
Δ in working capital	(320)	(44)	(182)	(113)	(147)	(130)	(138)	(134)	(136)	(135)	(136)	(136)	
Tax	(1,735)	(1,861)	(2,053)	(2,225)	(2,368)	(2,471)	(2,530)	(2,606)	(2,684)	(2,765)	(2,848)	(2,933)	(3,021)
Free cash flow (FCF)	8,817	4,444	5,274	5,576	6,010	6,245	6,420	6,613	6,824	7,036	7,257	7,484	7,718
Discount factor				0.95224	0.90676	0.86345	0.82221	0.78294	0.74554	0.70993	1.00000	1.00000	1.00000
Discounted FCF				5,310	5,449	5,392	5,279	5,177	5,088	4,995	7,257	7,484	7,718
Present value of cash flows			59,148										

The DCF only starts in year 4 because BBU is already in year 3 when the analysis is carried out.

Key Assumptions:

Projected EBITDA growth: 8.4%, 6.4%, 4.4% and 2.4% in years 1,2,3 and 4 respectively then 3.0% thereafter

Capex growth: 5.00%

Tax rate: 30%

WACC: 5.02%

To project future cash flows, assumptions were made about EBITDA, capex and tax growth. As a corporate finance analyst you will normally discuss what to assume with the senior bankers on your project. Once you have a feel for how they come to their assumptions, you will be free to make these decisions. You will nonetheless have to justify your assumptions in your pitch books.

Once all the analysis is complete, you could have a summary table showing a company's value range based on different methodologies:

- The current share: the share price's 52 week high and low
- The value of comparable companies or transactions using the ratios in table 7.7
- The leverage compared to other similar businesses using the ratios in table 7.9
- The DCF value

How would you value a company/hotel/this building that you are sitting in (delete as appropriate)?

- This is a common question in corporate finance interviews. The straightforward answer is: by projecting the company's expected future cash flows and discounting them to the present using 'discounted cash flow analysis'. You can then go on to describe the DCF model.

- BUT **what if the company has no revenues whatsoever?** For instance, many internet companies start off as completely free services with a view to 'monetizing' later.
- In this case, you would need to come up with several ways in which a specific company could start making money. Then estimate the proportion of the subscriber base that might be interested in

purchasing the services you come up with and project future revenues on that basis. It makes sense that cash flows based on this methodology will be less accurate than projections which are based on a business with a revenue history.

- It's also possible for a company to develop a free service and a substantial following with the expectation of selling the company on for someone else to grow.

- This is only slightly different to the above example in that the initial creator has no intention of ever charging subscribers.

- The buyer of the business would similarly base the value they pay on subscribers and whatever services they might be able to sell to them.

- In some cases, advertising revenue may be enough to sustain the business.

CASH EQUITIES

What is an Initial Public Offering or IPO?

All businesses are owned by a private individual or group of private individuals when they start out. After a certain point, a company can choose to raise equity capital from the public by **listing** on a stock exchange in an **initial public offering**.

Once shares have been listed on a stock exchange they are available to anyone (even you and me), to buy and sell in the **secondary market**.

Money raised in an IPO goes straight to a company from investors. However, after those shares are listed, they are bought and sold between investors and the company does not benefit from these **secondary market transactions**.

For example, if I bought shares in LinkedIn as a private investor in the IPO when they were listed on the New York Stock Exchange on 19 May 2011, I would have paid USD83 for them. Demand was very hot for these shares; if I had sold them to you the day after the IPO, I could have sold them for as much as USD107 and bagged the difference (USD24, in this case) as profit. The shares were undervalued at the point of listing.

All day long people buy and sell shares: high demand to buy shares pushes the price up; a high supply of shares offered for sale forces the price down.

The IPO process is governed by a lot of documents and conventions. To guide it through the process a company hires specialists; two key specialists are an investment bank and a law firm.

The investment bank knows the process inside and out and it has access to a list of investors that may be interested in buying the listing company's shares. The lawyers understand and draft the transaction documentation. Together they produce an **IPO prospectus**, a legal document filed with regulators detailing any reasonable information a prospective investor needs to make the decision of whether or not to buy the shares being offered.

How does the company choose an investment bank to help it through the IPO process?

It sets up a **beauty parade**. However, rather than show-casing beauty or clothes, investment bankers come to see the company to show off their expertise. They bring along a **pitch book** which illustrates:

- What they think the company is worth based on public information and any other information the company provided prior to the beauty parade
- Details of similar successful IPOs that they have worked on
- Details of any awards they may have won through third party surveys recognizing their expertise in the market

Ultimately, the listing company just wants a bank that will make the process smooth and easy for them and will help to get the best price possible – over or undervaluing the company can both be harmful.

Two key pieces of information that a listing company must decide with their underwriting bank are:

- **Quantity**: how many shares to issue
- **Price**: what price to issue the shares at

An **underwriting contract** states how the shares are to be offered to the public. The four most common type of contract are:

- **Firm commitment**: the underwriter agrees to sell all the shares agreed at a given price. A firm commitment costs the listing company more in bankers' fees because the bank is taking on all the risk.

- **Best efforts:** the underwriter sells as many shares as possible at the agreed price.
- **All or none:** the underwriter either sells all agreed shares at the agreed price or pulls the IPO; that is, the IPO is cancelled or postponed.
- **Bought deal:** before the IPO is marketed to the public, the underwriting banks buy all shares at an agreed, discounted price. They pay the listing company the agreed amount and take on the shares as their own to sell.

What is a greenshoe?

If a company that is listing goes 'live' and there's much more demand for the shares than anticipated, a greenshoe option allows the underwriting bank to issue more shares.

- If the underwriting contract has a **greenshoe option**, up to 15-20% more shares can be issued.

What are the benefits of an IPO to a company?

- It's an exit option for existing equity holders such as private equity investors who wish to recoup their money; an IPO enhances the liquidity of shares significantly.
- The publicity of an IPO is a great marketing tool. For instance, according to Bloomberg's businessweek.com, LinkedIn's May 2011 IPO resulted in a 6.7% increase in subscribers to 33.4 million: that's more than 2 million more users.
- It provides access to a greater pool of equity funding.
- It can be cheaper than incurring more debt.

- Listed companies have access to even more types of funding instruments than private companies.
- An IPO is a prestigious event; it forms a great landmark in the growth of a company.

What are the drawbacks of an IPO to a company?

- Listed companies are under constant public scrutiny and the share price can suffer massively due to unsubstantiated market rumors.
- Listed companies have higher admin costs due to increased legal and accounting requirements.
- The list of disclosures is onerous, taking lots of time and an enormous amount of attention to detail.
- Listed companies have to disclose information that competitors and suppliers can benefit from. This is good for customers, of course.
- Listed companies are much less flexible in acting on new ideas.
  - For instance, in Richard Branson's memoir, *Losing My Virginity,* he reveals that, for him, this was one of the worst things about getting listed as a public company.
  - Before Virgin's first IPO, they would have a good idea and act on it immediately. After the IPO, they had to set up a board meeting and convince the whole board that their idea was good. Mr. Branson hated the whole process. That and having to wear a suit!

After an IPO, a company can raise more equity capital from the public in a Follow-on Public Offering.

What does it mean to underprice an IPO and why does it matter?

Investors buy shares in a company because they believe the business will be successful. You can tell if an IPO has been underpriced if, immediately after the shares are listed, they shoot up in price significantly.

When shares are issued in an IPO, not everyone that wants them will get them. For example, the company may have USD100 million of shares to issue but USD200 million worth of demand.

Those individuals that don't get the full number of shares that they want will try to buy them in the secondary market as soon as the shares are listed. High demand is what drives the share price up.

The **fee that an investment bank earns** for an IPO is normally set as a percentage of the value that they raise for the company.

- So the higher the share price a bank can get, the more money they make. So the bank is incentivized to issue at the highest price possible.
- BUT, if the price is set too high, they would have trouble shifting the shares to investors and may have to hold on to lots of shares that they do not want.
- Importantly, a botched IPO could mean the investment bank will have trouble winning more business.
- Figuring out the issuance price is more art than science and therefore can be difficult to get right at times.

What is a Rights Issue?

A company can raise more equity capital by offering new shares to existing shareholders via a rights issue. Whereas with an IPO the shares are offered to the general public, with a rights issue current shareholders get the right to buy more shares in proportion with their existing shares in the company.

What is a Stock Split?

In a stock split, the company divides *existing* shares into more shares. No new shares are issued.

Example: If BBU has 1 million shares each valued at USD100, then the value of the company is USD100 million (market cap). If they decide to have a 2-for-1 stock split, the 1 million shares become 2 million and their price is halved to USD50 per share. Result? There are more shares but because their price has been proportionately reduced the market cap stays the same.

What's the point of a stock split? A company would undertake a stock split if they believe their share price has become too high (especially relative to competitors) and is therefore unaffordable to small investors. The hope is that once the price is reduced, demand from small investors will rise, and the share price and hence market cap will also rise.

What is a Share Buyback?

A listed company can choose to repurchase its own shares from shareholders. The shares, once bought, can be cancelled or they can be kept by the company as 'treasury stock' and reissued at a later date.

There are several reasons why a company would choose to do this but three important ones are:

1. **Increasing earnings per share and possibly, dividends**
   Earnings per share, EPS, equals net income divided by the number of shares outstanding. Reducing the number of shares outstanding

increases the EPS automatically. By increasing the EPS in this way, it is possible to pay a higher dividend per share without actually increasing the total amount of the dividend; the same dividend spread over fewer shareholders amounts to a higher payout.

2. Belief that the shares are undervalued

A willingness to purchase its own shares signals to the market that a company might be undervalued. If management are confident in the future of a business then they expect the share price to improve. If the shares are truly undervalued, buying back the shares reduces the number of shares in circulation and only those investors that hold on to their shares get the benefits of an improving share price.

In addition, depending on how convincing management are in portraying their belief in the company, the share buyback could in itself improve investors' demand for shares.

3. As a defensive tactic

Having too much cash on the balance sheet makes a company an attractive target for takeover. An acquirer can borrow money, take the cash-rich company over and use the cash on the target's balance sheet to repay its own debtors.

A recent share buyback: Apple announced a share buyback program in March 2012 and also that they would start paying a dividend. In addition to being very cash rich, they may also think they are undervalued. Their official line was that after years of investing all their cash back into the business, they thought they had reached a point where they were producing enough cash to sustain investment *and* dividends.

What is a Block Trade?

If an investor or company wants to buy or sell a large block of shares, it is generally more efficient for them to hire an investment bank to do this for them. This is not an initial public offering because the shares are already in circulation.

Selling a large number of shares could result in the price falling drastically, whilst buying a large number might result in a surge in price. By hiring an investment bank to map out a strategy and handle the process, price volatility is better managed.

A publicly listed company will have a vast amount of information already in circulation so a block trade can be executed much more rapidly. There is no need to produce a fresh prospectus as would have been the case in an IPO. Frequently, the process can be launched and completed all within 24 hours.

Equity teams execute a large number of block trades, especially in years when the flow of IPOs is poor.

What is an equity index?

With an Initial Public Offering, IPO, shares in a company are **listed** on a given stock exchange in a specific country. Once shares are listed, either the prices or the market caps of different shares can be amalgamated to form an index.

An index can be global, national, or representative of a specific sector. For example, the FTSE 100 is an index of the largest 100 listed companies in the UK and the Dow Jones U.S. Technology Index is an index of US tech stocks. There were 139 companies in the index as at 31 Jan 2012 (djindexes.com).

Each company that is included in an index has to be weighted by a given rule:

190

- In a price weighted index, the share price of the company alone determines what proportion of the index the company forms.
- In a market value or capitalization weighted index, the market cap of the company determines what proportion of the index the company forms.

Every index will have a standardized process that determines which stocks are eligible to be included in that index. Eligibility criteria may include:

- The percentage of **free float**: the percentage of shares held by investors that are likely to be willing to sell. This will be subjective. Usually large shareholders are excluded from free float as it is normally safe to assume their hold is strategic. Again, what is considered 'large' will vary from case to case. It's also subjective.
- **Listing**: usually only stocks that are listed on a given exchange may be included, e.g. only US listed companies can go into the S&P500.
- **Liquidity**: many indices will require that to be included; the stock must have a minimum trading volume within any given trading day.

Periodically, some companies will be replaced in an index because they no-longer fit the criteria required to be included.

Although a stock index will have an official inception date, frequently the data is back-tested to provide a longer track record for the index. This is easy to do because the stocks which are included in an index will predate the launch of the index. For example, according to the Dow Jones website (djindexes.com), the Dow Jones U.S. Technology Index was launched on 14 Feb 2000, however, you can find daily data going back to 31 Dec 1991[13].

Below is a list of key indices. Emerging markets are a big market nowadays so it is worth your while to know them in addition to major developed economy indices.

---

[13]http://www.djindexes.com/mdsidx/downloads/fact_info/Dow_Jones_US_Technology_Index_Fact_Sheet.pdf

Table 7.11: Key equity indices

Index	Country	No. of companies	Price/Value weighted	Founded in
AMERICAS				
Bolsa	Mexico	c.50	Value	1978
Bovespa	Brazil	c.50	Value	1968
Dow Jones	**USA**	**30**	**Price**	**1896**
Nasdaq	USA	2,772	Value	1971
Russell 2000	USA	2,000	Value	1984
S&P500	**USA**	**500**	**Value**	**1957**
S&P/TSX	Canada	254	Value	1977
Europe, Middle East and Africa (EMEA)				
CAC40	**France**	**40**	**Value**	**1987**
DAX	**Germany**	**30**	**Value**	**1988**
FTSE 100	**UK**	**100**	**Value**	**1984**
FTSE JSE Top 40	South Africa	40	Value	2002
IBEX 35	Spain	35	Value	1992
MIB, Milano Italia Borsa	Italy	40	Value	1998
PSI 20	Portugal	20	Value	1992
SMI, Swiss Market Index	Switzerland	20	Value	1988
STOXX Europe 50	Europe[14]	50	Value	2004
ASIA				
ASX 200	Australia	200	Value	2000
CSI 300	China	300	Value	2005
Hang Seng	**Hong Kong**	**45**	**Value**	**1969**
Nikkei 225	**Japan**	**225**	**Price**	**1950**
NZX 50	New Zealand	50	Value	2003
Sensex a.k.a. BSE 30	India	30	Value	1986
STI, Straits Times Index	Singapore	30	Value	1966

Source: Index websites (on or around 1 Mar 2012);

Popular indices are in bold.

---

[14] Stocks included in the index come from Austria, Belgium, Denmark, Finland, France, Germany, Greece, Iceland, Ireland, Italy, Luxembourg, the Netherlands, Norway, Portugal, Spain, Sweden, Switzerland and the United Kingdom.

Figure 7.3: S&P500 Index, Feb 1972 to Feb 2012

Source: Bloomberg

What is an exchange-traded fund or ETF?

An ETF is a financial instrument that **tracks a specific underlying basket of assets**. The underlying assets were traditionally equities but now include a wide range of assets including fixed income, currencies or commodities. ETFs can be global, country-specific or sector-specific.

An ETF is not a mutual fund. Mutual funds are not covered in this book.

Why might an investor choose to invest in an ETF?

- They are fairly easy to understand
- They can be bought and sold just like shares
- They offer diversification. Just a few ETFs can include a broad range of assets
- They can be sold short. Selling 'short' is explained later

- They can be bought and sold anywhere (this is different to mutual funds, which generally have to be bought in the country of registration)
- They offer a low fee structure compared to mutual funds

An ETF is developed with objectives defining whether it's targeting capital appreciation (that is, an increase in the value of the ETF) or maximizing current income (such as, high dividend or coupon payments). Therefore, an equity ETF targeting capital appreciation will have more high growth, low dividend stocks; an equity ETF maximizing current income would be balanced more towards high dividend paying stocks. If an investor is following either one of these strategies, ETFs that suit their portfolio can be easily identified.

EQUITY DERIVATIVES

What are options?

Options are financial products that derive their value from a change in the value of another **underlying** product. Options can be bought on many underlying products including but not limited to:

- A share price (i.e. the market value of a company)
- An interest rate
- An exchange rate
- A corporate or government bond
- Real commodities, e.g. oil, gold, wheat, pork bellies

An option is a type of **derivative**. A derivative derives its value from a change in the value of another **underlying** product. All options give the buyer the right but not the obligation to do a given thing at a given time.

Essentially, options can be viewed as insurance contracts. You get paid if a certain undesirable event happens. The price or cost of an option is called the **premium**.

What is the difference between a 'European' and an 'American' option?

A European option can only be exercised on a preset maturity date, whilst an American option can be exercised anytime between two given dates. These distinctions of European and American have nothing to do with the actual regions.

This means that if a European option is bought, it is possible that it can be **in-the-money** to the buyer for a period; but it not be exercised at all because by the time the maturity date is reached, the option will be **out-of-the-money** and hence not worth exercising.

For brownie points: an Asian option

Rather than looking at the underlying's price on one given date to determine the payoff, with an Asian option the '**strike rate**' is compared to the *average price* of the underlying over a given, stated period of time. **The strike rate is the price at which a given derivative can be exercised**.

The volatility of an average price over a given period is generally lower than daily volatility, so Asian options are, all things constant, cheaper than European or American-style options.

What is an equity call option?

An equity call option gives the buyer the right to buy a given number of shares in a given company at a given price on a given date (**European-style option**) or at any point with a given period of time (**American-style option**). Only the option buyer can exercise the option.

To buy a call option is called **going long a call** and selling a call option is **going short a call**.

Example

*Whilst Apple shares are trading at about $80 a share in late 2006 you decide to **buy a call option** that gives you the right to buy 1,000 shares in Apple Inc. at $200 anytime between 1 Jan 2010 and 31 Dec 2010.*

Buying out-of-the-money call options is much cheaper than actually paying the money to buy the shares outright.

The call options are referred to as being out-of-the-money because **the strike price, $200**, is higher than the current share price of $80. If you buy this contract, you would be expressing the view that you believe in the company so much that you expect the share price to more than double over a four year period. This view would be the basis for buying the right to buy the shares at $200 in four years time, though the current value is only $80.

If at any point in 2010 Apple shares exceeded the option strike price of $200, you could exercise your right to buy the shares at $200 and immediately sell them to lock in a profit. Let's say each option cost you $1, this means you would pay a premium of $1,000 for this option contract.

In Dec 2010, the Apple share price went over $320.

- You decide to exercise the option when the market price is at $320.
- You would pay $200,000 to exercise the equity call option contract: $200 strike price multiplied by 1,000 shares.
- You would then immediately sell all those shares at the market price of $320, locking in an immediate profit of $119,000:

    $320,000 current market value of 1,000 shares

    minus $200,000 option contract value received on sale

    minus $1,000 premium paid to enter into option contract

    = $119,000

In summary, buying equity call options implies the buyer believes the share price will go up and they want to profit if this does happen. The higher the share price is above the strike price, the higher the profit as seen below.

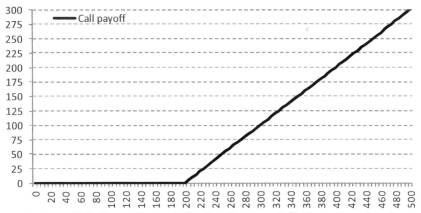

Figure 7.4: Pay-off graph for buying a call (before premium)

What is an equity put option?

An equity put option gives the buyer the right to **sell** a given number of shares in a given company at a given price on a given date (European-style option) or over a given period of time (American-style option). Only the option buyer can exercise the option.

To buy a put option is called **going long a put** and selling a put option is **going short a put**.

Example

Whilst Enron Corp. shares were trading between $80 and $90 a share in July 2000 to August 2000 you could have gone to a bank and bought the right to sell 10,000 shares in Enron at $40 anytime between 1 Nov 2001 and 30 Nov 2001.

> Note: in the world of finance you can sell something you do not currently own. This is called **going short**. You enter into a contract that is equivalent to selling the product. When you short something, if the market price falls below the option contract's strike price, you buy it at the lower market price and then immediately sell it for a profit by exercising your option.
>
> Large corporations can enter into a 'buy' or 'sell' contract with most banks. Banks manage many financial positions and can hedge whatever position a company wants to take.
>
> **This is a basic and important concept for you to understand.**

The **put options are referred to as being out-of-the-money** because the strike price, $40, is lower than the current share price of $85.

To buy this option contract you would basically be expressing the view that you believe the company is overvalued so much that you expect the share price to halve within a year and a half. Option sellers would have been falling over themselves to sell you the contract because in mid 2000 the market had very high hopes for Enron. The company was labeled the "most innovative company in America" for the sixth year in a row by Fortune Magazine in Feb 2001.

If at any point in Nov 2001 the Enron share price sunk below the strike price of $40, you could buy the shares in the market and then exercise your right to sell them at $40, immediately locking in a profit. Let's say each option cost you $1.20, this means you would pay a premium of $12,000 for this option contract: $1.20 premium x 10,000 shares.

In Nov 2001, the Enron share price was on a downward spiral. Share prices fall when there are more sellers than buyers for those shares. Anyone wanting to buy shares when they are plunging in price will find ample sellers.

- On 30 Nov 2001, the last day that your option contract is still valid, Enron Corp. shares are trading at $1 a share
- So you buy 10,000 shares in the market for $10,000
- Then immediately go to your option seller and sell them for $400,000 by exercising the equity put option contract. The option seller has to honor the contract: $40 strike price times 10,000 shares
- In so doing, you would have locked in a profit of $378,000:

    $400,000 option contract value received on sale

    minus $10,000 current market value of 10,000 shares

    minus $12,000 premium paid to enter into option contract

    = $378,000

In summary, buying equity put options implies the buyer believes the share price will go down and they want to profit if this does happen, as illustrated below. The lower the share price is below the strike price, the higher the profit.

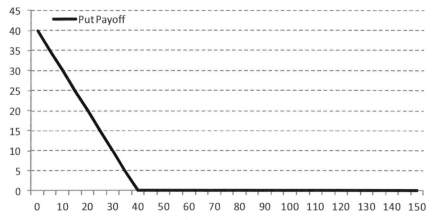

Figure 7.5: Pay-off graph for buying a put (before premium)

An investor believes in Apple. How could it make sense for the same investor to buy call options on Apple and simultaneously sell Apple put options?

This could be done to subsidize the cost of buying the call option.

For instance, in the equity call option example above, whilst Apple shares are trading at $80, an investor could buy a call option with a **strike rate** of $200 for a premium of $1; to subsidize this purchase, they could also **sell** a put option with a strike price that is set so that it also has a premium of $1.

If each contract covers the same number of shares, overall, the investor pays nothing. This is called **a zero-cost collar**. Assume a bank quotes a $1 premium for an Apple put option with a strike of $55.

Given the investor believes the share price will go up, they may well be willing to sell such a put option. They make a profit if the Apple share price rises above $200 BUT they are now taking on the risk that, if the price falls below $55 even temporarily, they may have to pay out.

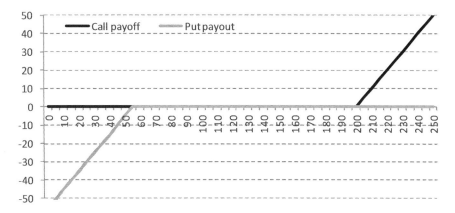

Figure 7.6: Pay-off of buying a call & selling a put (before premium)

The above zero-cost collar is one example of how equity options can be combined to achieve a specific objective, reducing the premium of buying a call in this case. There are many other ways in which options can be combined. Any combination has implicit assumptions and objectives.

For entry level interviews you should not need to have intimate knowledge of how to combine options. From an equity perspective, it should normally be enough to know the difference between going long versus short and a put versus a call option contract. In addition, you should know simple situations of when either could be used.

Black-Scholes and the Greeks

Discussions on options frequently center on the **Black-Scholes** pricing model and **the Greeks**: delta, gamma, vega and theta. You don't need to memorize the formula but should know that the Black-Scholes formula is used to price European-style options.

Table 7.12: The Greeks

Delta, δ	• Measures how much an option's value changes as a result of a unit change in the **price of the underlying**
Gamma, γ	• Measures the rate of change of delta
Vega	• Measures how much the option's value changes as a result of a change in the **volatility (sigma, σ) of the underlying**
Theta, θ	• Measures how much an option's value changes as a result of a change in the **time to expiry**

Understanding the above definitions will be especially important if you are applying for a role in derivatives trading, sales or structuring.

Understanding the 'Greeks' as applied to the equity market

Assume the product is a call option on Apple Shares. That is, Apple shares are the underlying financial instrument.

- The option matures in one month
- The current price of Apple = $80
- The strike price of the option = $120
- The option costs $1 today

So the buyer of this call option has the right to buy Apple shares at $120 in a month.

- If in a month the share price is above $120, say $125, the option buyer will exercise the option: they buy the shares at $120 and sell them at the market price of $125 immediately for a profit.
- If in a month the share price is below $120, say $115, the option expires worthless. Exercising the option contract would require the option buyer to pay $120 for the shares. However, the shares are only $115 on the open market so this would not make sense.

Delta: sensitivity of the premium to the underlying's price

If the price of Apple shares goes up to $90 from $80, would buying a call option cost more or less?

Because the chances of hitting a strike price of $120 are higher when the market price is $90 rather than $80, the option would be more expensive (assuming all other variables are constant).

So call option premia increase with an increase in the price of the underlying.

If the price of Apple shares goes up to $90 from $80, would buying a put option cost more or less?

The opposite would be true for a put option: if someone bought a put option on Apple shares with a strike at $50 and expiry in a month, they would have the right to sell Apple shares at $50.

They would only exercise this option if the share price fell below $50.

An increase in the share price from $80 to $90 moves it further away from falling below the put strike of $50 so the put option premium would fall.

> *So put option premia decrease with an increase in the price of the underlying.*

If the price of Apple shares goes down to $70 from $80, would buying a call option cost more or less?

Because the chances of hitting a strike price of $120 are lower when the market price is $70 rather than $80, the option will be less expensive (assuming all other variables are constant).

> *So call option premia decrease with a decrease in the price of the underlying.*

If the price of Apple shares goes down to $70 from $80, would buying a put option cost more or less?

The opposite would be true for the put option:

A decrease in the share price from $80 to $70 now moves it closer to falling below the put strike of $50 so the put option premium would rise.

> *So put option premia increase with a decrease in the price of the underlying.*

Vega: sensitivity of the premium to the underlying's volatility

If the Apple share price is very volatile, the option will be more expensive. Why does this make sense? Because the chances of hitting the strike price are higher the more volatile the share price is.

Look at the below chart of the Apple share price. If someone in 2001 wanted to buy a call option on Apple shares and they set the option strike price at $50 *above* the market price, that option would probably be cheaper than buying a similar option also at $50 *above* the market price in 2008.

Why? High volatility in 2008 compared to 2001 meant the chances of a $50 price move were higher in 2008 than in 2001.

It makes sense that the same relationship exists between volatility and put option prices. The same logic applies: higher volatility means there is a higher chance of prices falling below the put strike.

So both call and put option premia increase with an increase in volatility.

Figure 7.7: Apple share price, Dec 1991 to Dec 2011

Source: Bloomberg

Theta: sensitivity of the premium to time to expiry

The above option matures in a month; what would you expect to happen to the option price if we moved that expiry date to 1 year?

The chances of the Apple share price moving to $120 from $80 over one year are higher than the chances of experiencing a similar move over one month. This would therefore increase the cost of the option.

So call options are positively correlated with time to expiry.

Similar logic would apply to a put option: the longer the time to expiry, the higher the chance of experiencing any given price fall, the higher the price of a put option contract.

> ***So both call and put option premia are positively correlated with time to expiry.***

Table 7.13: Relationship between option premia and market variables

	Call option premium	Put option premium
Price of underlying rises	increases	decreases
Price of underlying falls	decreases	increases
Volatility of underlying (Vega)	+ve* correlation	+ve correlation
Time to expiry (Theta)	+ve correlation	+ve correlation

* +ve = positive

8

TECHNICAL QUESTIONS FOR

DEBT CAPITAL MARKETS (DCM) or FIXED

INCOME, CURRENCY & COMMODITIES (FICC)

BONDS AND LOANS

Bond Basics

US-based book retailer Blissful Books United, BBU, needs to raise money to fund the purchase of some European bookshops. BBU decides to raise money from investors in the global capital markets via a bond issue.

A bond is a financial contract in which investors called **bondholders** give money to a company (the **issuer** or **borrower**) in return for periodic payments of interest.

The value of a bond has many names which can be used interchangeably:

- Face value
- Par value
- Principal value
- Nominal value
- Maturity value

- Redemption value

BBU decides to issue a two-year bond with a face value of EUR100m.

- Investor appetite sets the bond interest rate at 5.00%. The interest paid to bondholders is called a **coupon**. This is because in the old days bonds came with actual coupons that you tore off and gave to the issuer to claim your interest payment.
- Interest is paid once a year, at the end of the year. Annual interest payments are the convention for EUR bonds. This convention is different in different currencies, e.g. GBP and USD corporate bonds pay interest semi-annually.

The type of coupons paid on bonds

The vast majority of bonds pay a **fixed** coupon.

Floating rate notes (FRNs) pay a variable rate of interest.

- The interest paid is equal to a reference rate plus a spread
- The reference rate would typically be reset every three or six months
- FRNs are a lot less common than pay-fixed bonds

Zero-coupon bonds pay no coupons at all. Zero-coupon bonds are issued at a discount to their par value. For example, a one-year bond with a maturity value of EUR100m can be issued for EUR95.238m.

How does this work? The issuing/borrowing company receives EUR95.238m from bondholders then, at the end of the year, the issuer pays EUR100m back to bondholders.

What is the effective interest rate?

$$\frac{Excess\ paid\ to\ bondholder}{Price\ paid\ to\ issuer} = \frac{100 - 95.238}{95.238} = \frac{4.762}{95.238} = 5\%$$

You can easily work backwards here. If you wanted to work out what the face value would have to be in order to have an effective interest rate of 5%, you would use the below formula:

$$\frac{Notional}{(1+rate)^{years}} = \frac{100}{(1+0.05)^1} = \frac{100}{1.05} = 95.238$$

Zero-coupon bonds can be issued for longer terms. One year was used above to simplify the example but the same logic would apply whatever the maturity.

What would the face value have to be in order to have an effective interest rate of 5%, on a three-year zero-coupon bond?

$$\frac{Notional}{(1+rate)^{years}} = \frac{100}{(1+0.05)^3} = \frac{100}{1.157625} = 86.38376$$

Notice that this formula implicitly assumes compound annual interest.

Bond price

A bond is usually issued at or very close to the par value. The initial bond issuance is called the **primary issuance**. Following issuance, investors can buy and sell corporate bonds to each other in the **secondary market**. Once secondary market trading begins, bonds can trade at a premium or discount to par.

Par is always standardized as 100. A bond trading at a **discount to par** has a value less than 100; a bond trading at a **premium to par** has a value greater than 100. When you hear par, think 100 or 100%.

How is the present value of a bond calculated?

All bond cash flows are discounted at the **yield to maturity**.

$$P = \frac{C}{(1+i)} + \frac{C}{(1+i)^2} + \frac{C}{(1+i)^3} + \cdots + \frac{C}{(1+i)^T} + \frac{M}{(1+i)^T}$$

P = market value of bond

C = coupon payment

i = yield to maturity

T = years to bond Maturity

M = value at maturity, usually equals face value

From the formula you can see that **there is an inverse relationship between bond price and bond yield**. Mathematically, if yield *(i)* rises in the above formula, price (P) will fall and vice versa. This is a crucial relationship which you must be able to repeat in interviews.

Why might a bond sell at a discount to par?

- Emma bought EUR1million worth of the first 5.00%, two-year BBU bond.

- A year later BBU issues another bond at a rate of 8.00%; investors demand a higher coupon because BBU has had a difficult year and they consider giving their money to BBU as a more risky investment than they did previously.

- Emma wants to sell her 5.00% coupon bond. Her bond now has one year left until maturity.

- With the knowledge that BBU bonds with an 8.00% coupon can be bought in the market, no one would be willing to accept a yield of 5.00%.

- To make the effective interest or yield on the 5.00% coupon bond 8.00%, the bond has to be sold at a discount.

- As such, Emma has to sell the bond at EUR972,222 and, at the end of the year when the issuer redeems the first bond, the new buyer receives EUR1million plus the 5.00% coupon: EUR1.05million in total.

- The price of the bond is 97.2222; it's trading at a discount to par:

$$\frac{Payment\ to\ new\ bondholder}{Price\ paid\ by\ secondary\ market\ buyer} = \frac{105 - 97.2222}{97.2222} = \frac{7.7777}{97.2222} = 8.00\%$$

In a similar fashion, if BBU issued new bonds at 3.50%, Emma could sell her bond at a premium to par: EUR1,014,518 in this case or a price of 101.4518:

$$\frac{Payment\ to\ new\ bondholder}{Price\ paid\ by\ secondary\ market\ buyer} = \frac{105 - 101.4518}{101.4518} = \frac{3.5482}{101.4518} = 3.50\%$$

The price of a bond can be quoted in two ways:

- The **clean price**: excludes accrued interest
- The **dirty price**: includes accrued interest

When might this distinction be important?

- Assume you invest in a one-year bond that pays interest at the end of the year.
- However, six months in, you need the money for whatever reason and so decide to sell the bond.
- The issuing company will only pay interest at the end of the year; this interest payment will go to the bondholder that you are selling the bond to.
- As such, you need six months worth of interest in order to be willing to sell the bond. The buyer therefore pays you the dirty price.

In the above two examples where Emma is selling her BBU bond, we assume the transaction happens on the same day as BBU's first coupon so there is no accrued interest to worry about. Emma sells the bond immediately after receiving her first bond coupon.

Where is the secondary bond market?

When an individual or a company wants to buy or sell a bond, they go to a bond broker in a bank or at a specialist bond broking house. Most bond buying and selling takes place in the **over-the-counter** (OTC) market rather than on a public exchange. All trading that is not on an exchange is said to be OTC; this includes trading by phone, email, Bloomberg or Reuters chat.

Bond brokers charge a fee or commission for broking the trade. Brokerage fees have been ignored in all the above examples for simplicity.

Is investing in bonds risk free? No, there are five main risks:

1. **Credit risk**

- The issuing company may for whatever reason (e.g. bankruptcy) default on paying coupons and the bond principal at maturity.
- The bond issuer's rating may be downgraded by ratings agencies; this would immediately reduce the price of the bond in the secondary market.
- Why does a downgrade lead to a fall in bond price?
    - It's simple. Highly rated entities can issue bonds at a lower coupon than entities with a lower rating.
    - Investors are more likely to get their money back from a more highly rated company; consequently, they are willing to invest in them for a lower coupon.
    - To take the risk of investing in a lower rated entity, investors will want to be paid more in the form of a higher coupon.
    - A downgraded company would be expected to issue bonds at a higher coupon than before in order to get investors interested. Therefore, the mechanics explained above in *'Why might a bond sell at a discount to par?'* would occur.

- **High yield bonds** are bonds with a **sub-investment grade** credit rating (see table 6.9 for rating schedules). In days gone by, they were frequently referred to as **junk bonds** but this term fell out of use due to its lack of political correctness. To compensate bondholders for the low credit rating, high yield bonds have higher coupons than **investment grade** bonds. High yield bonds are commonly issued by fast-growing, more risky companies such as media companies.

2. **Liquidity risk**

- There is a chance that an investor might want to sell a bond but there may be no buyers for it.
- Liquidity risk is small when dealing with bonds issued by major governments and big companies. However, the smaller, more niche and specialized the bond issuer, the harder it would likely be to find a buyer for it.

3. **Foreign exchange risk**

- If an individual or a company buys a bond that is denominated in a foreign currency, e.g. a USD investor buys a GBP bond, if the foreign currency falls in value, the investment loses value.
- This is a very real risk even when you are dealing with major currencies.

Example: in Dec 2007 GBPUSD was 2.0000 (i.e. 1 GBP bought 2 USD); by Mar 2009, GBPUSD had fallen in value to 1.4000.

This means a USD investor buying GBP10m worth of a bond would have paid USD20m for it in Dec 2007. Even if they managed to sell the bond at par in Mar 2009, the GBP10m would only have been worth USD14m, that is 30% fall in the value of the initial investment.

Figure 8.1: GBPUSD FX chart (Feb 2006 to Feb 2012)

Source: Bloomberg

Foreign exchange risk can be completely eliminated by entering into a cross-currency swap at the point that the bond is bought. Cross-currency swaps are covered in Chapter 8/Technical Questions for DCM or FICC/Rates.

Important note:

- Foreign currency traders, including electronic systems, e.g. Bloomberg and Reuters, use the notation GBPUSD to mean 1 GBP gives 'x' USD.
- Many text books do not do this, so it was something I had to get used to when I became a banker.
- If you have been writing USD per GBP or USD/GBP, like I used to, start getting used to the conventions ASAP.
- EURUSD is 1 EUR gives 'x' USD, x = 1.3125[15]
- EURGBP is 1 EUR gives 'x' GBP, x = 0.8369[16]
- You get the drift, don't ya?

---

[15] Source: Google Finance, 15 Feb 2012
[16] Source: Google Finance, 15 Feb 2012

4. **Reinvestment risk**

   Reinvestment risk is the risk that the coupons can't be reinvested to achieve a yield equal to or greater than the yield on the bond.

   Zero-coupon bonds don't carry any reinvestment risk because they don't pay any coupons.

5. **Inflation risk**

   This is especially a concern if you buy emerging market (EM) bonds. If you bought a bond in an EM currency, there is a very real risk that inflation will erode the value of the currency.

   The longer the maturity of the EM bond, the higher inflation risk is.

Maturity: are bonds always repaid in one 'bullet' lump sum at maturity?

Not always. This is the conventional format but repayment can be structured in many ways. To mention a few: bonds can be callable, puttable or sinkable.

Callable bonds give the issuer an embedded option to repay the bond fully or in part before the final maturity date.

- Callable bonds can only be called on specified dates, usually set to coincide with coupon payment dates. Alternatively, the call option may be set as compulsory if a pre-specified event occurs, e.g. if the company is taken over by another company.
- The bond prospectus would stipulate the price at which the bond can be called; this would normally be par or higher.

  The issuing company would only call the bond if it is economically beneficial for them to do so, e.g. if interest rates fall they may call the bond and issue a new one at a lower coupon. Because the call option gives the issuer more rights and more flexibility than on a vanilla bond, callable bonds will, all other things constant, have a higher coupon to compensate the bondholder for the optionality that they are giving to the issuer.

Puttable bonds give the bondholder an embedded option to put the bond back to the issuer, fully or in part, before the final maturity date.

- The bond is puttable on specified dates, again usually set to coincide with coupon payment dates.
- The bond prospectus would stipulate the price at which the bond can be called.

A bondholder would only put the bond back to the issuer if it is economically beneficial for them to do so; e.g. if interest rates rise significantly, bondholders may choose to get their money back from the issuing company and invest the proceeds in a newly issued bond with a higher coupon. Because the put option gives the bondholder more rights and more flexibility, puttable bonds will, all other things constant, have a lower coupon to compensate the issuer.

Sinkable bonds are repaid periodically rather than all upon maturity. Spreading out all the payments removes the risk to the issuer of having one large liability all on one date.

Are bonds normally secured against specific assets?

Generally, no. The issuing company is responsible for meeting coupon payments and for repaying the bond at maturity, but overall they do not set aside specific assets to secure the bond.

Covered bonds are a special type of bond with specific security. With a covered bond, a given pool of assets is set aside by the issuer to ensure that bond payments can be met. A typical pool of assets would include public sector assets or mortgages.

Germany is one of the biggest issuers of covered bonds called **Pfandbriefe**.

The biggest difference between covered bonds and other types of secured assets is that the security for covered bonds remains on the balance sheet. Other types of securitized bonds (and loans) are normally ring-fenced in an off-balance-sheet special purpose vehicle, SPV.

What is asset or structured finance?

Structured finance or asset finance or securitization involves pooling similar assets together to create a financial product. For example:

- A credit card company can pool together all the credit card debt of different people and use that as security/collateral to get a loan.
- Car loans can be pooled.
- A mortgage lender can pool together all the mortgages they have to create a **collateralized mortgage obligation (CMO)**.
- Any type of debt instrument (loans, bonds, credit notes etc) can be pooled together to secure borrowing or to create an asset-backed financial security.
- A football club with a good track record of ticket sales can pledge expected future ticket sales to obtain a loan. Arsenal Football Club did this in 2006-2007.

How is a project finance loan different to a regular bank loan?

The type of information that would be expected in a basic loan term sheet is explained in Chapter 6/Basic Technical Questions.

Project financing is a special type of asset/structured financing. It involves getting a loan based on a receivable. However, unlike other asset financing, the receivable does not exist at the time a loan is given.

Traditionally, project finance has been used to build very safe infrastructure-type investments that are not cyclical. Over time, however, it has expanded to include more industries, such as telecom companies which tend to be more cyclical and more risky.

Projects commonly financed in this way include the building of:

- Roads and railways
- Ports and airports
- Mining
- Conventional energy plants
- Renewable energy plants, e.g. wind farms and solar projects
- Hospitals
- Schools
- Telecommunications

Any project built from scratch is called a **greenfield** project, whilst expansions or upgrade projects are called **brownfield** projects.

Characteristics of project finance loans:

- Normally very long-term, 25 years plus; this tenor fell to as short as 15 years in the 2007-2009 credit crunch.
- At the outset, the project has **sponsors** that put in some equity and a **syndicate of lending banks** who inject debt.
- Banks decide whether or not to lend to a project, and how much to lend to the project, based on *expected* cash flows rather than a proper track record as with a regular corporate loan.
- When the project starts, it doesn't have any assets, just cash available to build up an asset that will later produce cash flows.
- Project debt is normally **non-recourse** to the Sponsor Company. This means that, in a default scenario, lenders cannot have any access to the assets of the company that established the project in the first place, only the project's assets and cash flows.

- o If the Sponsor Company is having trouble raising money, they could offer limited recourse or a written guarantee.
- It follows that in deciding whether to lend, the credit rating of the project Sponsors is not considered at all if the debt is non-recourse.
- Many projects are undertaken on behalf of a government rather than a private company.
- If an asset is being built on behalf of a government, lenders usually assume that the government would not allow the project to fail and will hence lend on more favorable terms and will be more willing to take the credit risk. Lenders *implicitly* take the government's low credit risk into consideration.

Like with all lending, lenders set covenants (conditions) to ensure they get their money back. For instance, if leverage exceeds a given threshold, Sponsors may be restricted from paying themselves a dividend until some of the debt is repaid.

The Debt Service Coverage Ratio or DSCR is a key ratio used in project finance. It measures the level of operating cash flow available to pay principle and interest.

	Operating cash flow to service annual debt is:
DSCR < 1	Not enough
DSCR > 1	More than enough

A yield curve can be upward sloping or downward sloping. What do you think drives that?

In economic literature there are three popular theories used to explain the shape of yield curves (**'the term structure of interest rates'**).

Market Expectations Hypothesis

This theory suggests that the yield curve's shape is simply a function of the market's expectations. For instance, if market makers expect interest rates to rise over time, the curve will be upwards sloping and vice versa. Under this theory, investors see different maturities as perfect substitutes and will act to remove any arbitrage opportunities. The theory may be valid for some classes of investor, e.g. pure arbitrageurs, but in general the theory ignores:

- Investors who don't view short and long term rates as perfect substitutes, e.g. Long term investors may not want to take the re-investment risk inherent in short-dated investments.
- Especially nowadays, long-term rates frequently end up being very different to what was expected in earlier periods.
- Interest rate risk. The theory ignores the many risks inherent in being exposed to interest rate changes, particularly **duration** and **convexity**. **Duration** is the sensitivity of a bond or derivative's value to changes in interest rates and **convexity** is the sensitivity of duration.

Liquidity Premium Theory

- This theory suggests that it is more risky to lend for a longer time horizon. Firstly, there's less certainty about distant dates and secondly, the chances of a counterparty having succumbed to an adverse event are higher further in the future. To compensate for the extra risk of lending for a longer term, investors add a **risk premium**.
- Holding constant the extra risk, investors also want to be compensated for tying up their funds for longer so they add a **liquidity premium**.
- This theory is intellectually very appealing because it makes sense that one would charge more to lend for longer. However, under this theory the yield curve would always be upward sloping.

220

Market Segmentation Theory

- This theory suggests that investors who want to invest long-term are entirely different to those who invest for shorter periods of time.
- For example, pension funds and life insurers have long term liabilities so they prefer to invest in long-term assets. Other types of insurers, e.g. employment and vehicle insurers, have shorter term exposures and so will prefer not to lock their money in for very long time periods.
- Under this theory, different parts of the yield curve operate by their own rules; this theory therefore accommodates any shape of yield curve.
- A weakness of the theory is that if the long end is acting of its own accord to the short end, why do rates tend to rise and fall together (yield curve shifts)?
- To accommodate this weakness, there's a milder version of the Market Segmentation Theory called the Preferred Habitat Theory.

Preferred Habitat Theory (of Market Segmentation Theory)

- States that investors do indeed have preferred maturities but can be swayed to invest in different maturities by higher rates.
- This theory would be consistent with any shape of yield curve.

All these theories do hold some truth in them; no one theory is held to be better than the others.

What is hedging?

Although two years into my banking career I chose to join a derivative sales team, before this point I have to admit I had struggled to understand the term 'hedge'. I'm not a gambling woman, hence the first time someone said 'hedge' the image that sprung to mind was green and involved leaves of some form.

To hedge oneself is to protect yourself against an adverse movement in anything. The following pages will help to clarify what hedging means in different financial contexts.

What is a derivative?

A derivative is a financial product whose value depends on a change in the value of some other **underlying** product.

The word derivative tends to scare people (me included when I first encountered it), however, a good proportion of derivatives are quite simple, especially those derivatives that are used for hedging. Below, I present some very basic derivatives. Even if you think you're not going to understand the below, go through it a few times and when it starts to sink in you will agree that this is pretty simple stuff. Importantly, it will help you decide what sort of products you would enjoy covering.

Derivatives are primarily used for:

- **Hedging**: to protect a company against an adverse move in the market price of an input (costs) or an output (prices). The below will focus mainly on hedging.
- **Speculation:** to benefit from an expected change in market prices.
- **Arbitrage:** to take advantage of a perceived mispricing(s) in the market.

By the end of this chapter, you should have a basic concept of how the cash flows work on the below:

Table 8.1: Broad product categories in DCM or FICC

FX	• A spot FX transaction • A forward FX transaction • An FX swap • An FX option
Rates	• Interest rate swaps • A forward rate agreement (FRA) • A cap on interest rates • A floor on interest rates • A cross-currency swap
Credit	• A credit default swap (CDS)
Commodities	• Basic options used by oil producers (e.g. BP or Shell) vs. oil consumers (e.g. airlines) • Basic options used by gold sellers (e.g. miners) vs. gold buyers (jewelry makers)

To give you a feel for when the above products would be needed in real life, by a real company, to solve a real problem, bespoke over-the-counter examples are used below.

If you know the specific desk that you are interviewing with, e.g. rates or FX, you can focus just on those products. That said, hiring into DCM or FICC will frequently be to a general pool for the department and you could find yourself rotating across several product teams.

FOREIGN EXCHANGE (FX)

What is a spot FX transaction?

A spot foreign exchange (FX) transaction involves the exchange of two currencies between two parties.

The standard is for the currency to be delivered two business days after the transaction (t+2). However this varies according to the currencies involved and for some currencies, notably CAD, RUB and TRY, 'spot' means the currencies are exchanged on the next business day (t+1).

The rate at which currency is exchanged is set by demand and supply in the financial markets. This rate fluctuates constantly throughout the day.

Some currencies have their value pegged against another currency, e.g. Hong Kong Dollar (HKD) is pegged to USD; other currencies are pegged to a given basket of currencies, e.g. the Kuwaiti Dinar (KWD) is pegged to an *'undisclosed weighted basket of international currencies of Kuwait's major trade and financial partner countries'*[17]; it used to be pegged just to USD until May 2007. The Central Bank of Kuwait's website has more detail.

Freely Floating versus Managed Currencies

The value of most major currencies fluctuates with changes in demand and supply. High demand pushes a currency's value up (it **appreciates**) and a fall in demand for the currency causes it to fall in value (it **depreciates**). Currencies that can be bought and sold on demand are **freely floating**.

Some governments regularly intervene in currency markets to maintain their currency's value within a certain desirable range. These are **managed currencies**.

---

[17] http://www.cbk.gov.kw/www/exchange_rates.html

Occasionally, a government will intervene to adjust the value of a freely floating currency. For instance, in Sep 2011 the Swiss Government intervened to depreciate the Swiss Franc because they thought its strength was reducing demand for Swiss exports and tourism. One-off interventions don't make it a managed float.

Example of a spot FX transaction:

The exchange rate between GBP and USD is called **cable** in financial markets.

On 20 Jul 2011 the cable rate is 1.6140/**1.6150**. This means you could buy GBP1.0000 with USD1.6150 but if you were selling GBP1.0000 you would only get USD1.6140 for it.

A spot FX transaction in which Blissful Books United (BBU) wants to sell USD and buy GBP (e.g. to takeover a chain of bookshops in the UK) would look as follows:

Figure 8.2: Spot FX transaction: BBU sells USD and buys GBP in order to purchase a chain of bookshops in the UK

Banks embed their profit/risk margin into the exchange rate. This is why the exchange rate for buying a currency is different to the exchange rate for selling it.

Appreciation versus depreciation

If the rate to buy GBP changed from 1.6150 to 1.6200, GBP1.0000 would buy more USD so we would say the pound (GBP) has appreciated or increased in value against the USD.

- In the above example, BBU would now need USD162 million to buy the same GBP100 million i.e. USD500,000 more.

If the rate to buy GBP changed from 1.6150 to 1.6000, GBP1.0000 would buy less USD so we would say the pound (GBP) has depreciated or fallen in value against the USD.

- In the above example, BBU would need just USD160 million to buy the same GBP100m i.e. USD1.5 million less.

What is a forward FX transaction?

A forward foreign exchange (FX) transaction involves the exchange of two currencies between two parties at a given future date at a pre-specified rate of exchange.

This contract to exchange currencies is obligatory once the transaction is entered into. Failure to meet the commitment by either party would be an '**Event of Default**'.

A **forward exchange rate** is calculated by adding or subtracting forward points measured in pips from the spot rate.

Example:

- Assume spot GBPUSD is given as 1.6150
- If the points to buy GBP and sell USD 1-month forward are minus 5
- The all-in exchange rate would be 1.6145

- Forward points can be positive or negative

As with spot FX, forward points fluctuate constantly throughout the day. That said, forward points are less volatile than spot exchange rates.

Why does this matter? As a salesperson or trader, a client will frequently ask you for your points to a given date, rather than for an all-in rate, because it helps them compare across banks. It's very easy to get banks to match on the spot rate because spot levels are very transparent and easily available. On the other hand, forward rates are not as transparent. Banks include their credit, market and liquidity spreads to forward rates so the client can receive vastly different forward points from different banks. Each bank has its own bespoke credit models so there is no reason for credit spreads to match across banks.

Example of a forward FX transaction:

Assume that, on 20 July 2011 the forward rate to buy GBP and sell USD for value 20 August 2011 was 1.6300. This means GBP1.0000 buys USD1.6300 on 20 August 2011.

- BBU decides not to enter into a spot transaction because their acquisition of a UK chain of bookshops is a month away and they don't want to incur the cost involved in holding borrowed money before the sale goes through.
- Instead, BBU enters into a 1-month FX forward transaction to buy GBP and sell USD at a rate of 1.6300. They are not willing to take the risk of GBP appreciating beyond 1.6300 as this would impact the profitability of buying the chain of UK bookshops.

On 20 August 2011, the FX rate turns out to be 1.6233. However, BBU has to exchange at a rate of 1.6300 as they have entered into an FX forward transaction. This could be viewed as a loss but you must keep in mind that it could just as easily have gone the other way.

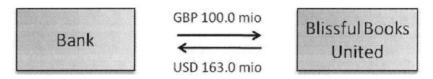

Figure 8.3: BBU sells USD and buys GBP 1-month forward to purchase a chain of bookshops in the UK

What happens if BBU decides they do not need the funds prior to the maturity of the FX forward?

BBU would effectively cancel the FX forward by entering into an equal and opposite transaction.

On 1 August 2011, the takeover of the bookshops unexpectedly falls through. The Competition Commission in the UK decides that the acquisition would be bad for consumers because it seriously reduces competition in the book market.

BBU finds that the forward GBPUSD rate for value 20 August 2011 is now 1.6500, i.e. GBP has appreciated in value against the USD. BBU enters into an FX forward at this rate to **sell** GBP and **buy** USD for value 20 August 2011. As a result of this, BBU makes a gain of USD2 million.

Note that the FX forward was not entered into with a view to making a windfall gain. BBU intended to buy a chain of bookshops and hedged itself at the rate of 1.6300 as it took the view that any further increase in the value of GBP would harm the affordability of making the purchase. However, it has by chance made this gain on FX as result of the takeover's failure. BBU will still have incurred the transaction costs involved in a sale process, e.g. it may still need to pay advisory fees to bankers and lawyers.

Cash Flows on 20 August 2011

Initially, BBU sells USD and buys GBP forward for value 20 Aug 2011 to purchase a chain of bookshops in the UK. Nearly two weeks later, BBU buys USD and sells GBP forward for value 20 Aug 2011 to reverse the FX forward.

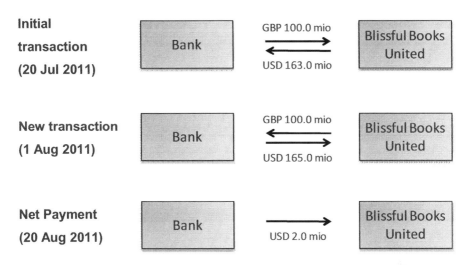

Figure 8.4: Net position of Forward FX deals settling on the same day

What is an FX swap?

An FX swap combines two opposite FX transaction on two different days, e.g. a spot transaction and a forward transaction. The forward transaction reverses the spot transaction.

Normally, the spot and the forward transactions are of the same amount but they do not have to be.

Both the spot and the forward rate of exchange are set on the day of the transaction.

Example of an FX swap transaction:

On 1 September 2011, BBU's headquarters in the US decides to inject EUR10 million into some of its European bookshops in order to buy books from European publishers. The exchange rate is 1.4000 so they pay USD14 million for the Euros.

BBU US needs the money back in six weeks and wants to know the exchange rate they will get at that time, now. In six weeks, EUR10 million could depreciate to less than USD14 million and BBU do not want to take that risk.

On the date of the transaction, the spot rate is 1.4000 and the all-in forward rate is 1.4015.

	BBU buys	**BBU sells**
For value 3-Sep-11	EUR10 million	USD amount based on spot rate, 1.4000
For value 15-Oct-11	USD amount based on forward rate, 1.4015	EUR10 million

Note: the spot transaction is settled at t+2 so a 1 Sep deal settles on 3 Sep.

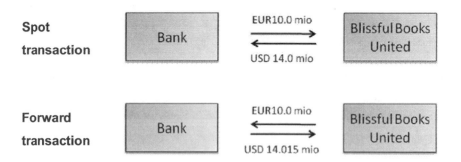

Figure 8.5: Cash flows in an FX swap

What is the cost of entering into the FX swap?

The cost of an FX swap is embedded into the exchange rate by the bank and there are no other upfront payments needed.

BBU could choose not to hedge the forward rate if:

1. They think the cost embedded into the FX rate by the bank is high relative to what they think they should be getting.
2. They may think the EUR will increase massively in value against USD so that EUR10 million would be worth a lot more than USD14 million in six weeks' time.

However, deciding not to hedge is a hedging decision in itself and will affect outcomes. By not hedging, BBU would leave the outcome to chance. By hedging, they know their worst case scenario.

Note that an FX swap is different to a cross-currency swap as explained in Chapter 8/Technical Questions for DCM or FICC/Rates.

How does an FX option work?

In an FX option, one party buys the right but not the obligation to exchange currency at a pre-specified rate on a given date.

Rather than enter into an FX swap as in the previous example, BBU could buy the right to receive USD and pay EUR at a rate of 1.4100 on 15 Oct 2011. The rate of the FX option is called the **strike rate**. The cost of this option is called a **premium**.

The strike rate is normally set at a more disadvantageous rate than would be the case on an FX forward because it's cheaper. Above the '**at-the-money**' (ATM) rate of 1.4015 in this case. The at-the-money rate is the rate that would apply for an outright FX forward to the relevant date. The higher the strike rate is above the ATM rate in this case, the lower the premium.

Table 8.2: EURUSD FX option term sheet

Product	European Option
Type	EUR put / USD call (i.e. sell EUR, buy USD)
Buyer	Blissful Books United, BBU
Trade date	1-Sep-11
Notional	EUR10 million
Maturity date	15-Oct-11
Strike	1.4100
Premium	USD150,000

What happens on the maturity date of the FX option?

If the EURUSD (called 'Eurodollar') FX rate in the market is greater than 1.4100, the option is said to be '**out-of-the-money**' to BBU and they would allow it to expire worthless.

- e.g. if the FX rate is 1.4150 in the currency markets, for EUR10 million, BBU would receive USD14.15 million but, by exercising the option, they would only receive USD14.1 million (USD50,000 less), hence they would rather buy the USD in the currency market.

If the EURUSD FX rate in the market is less than 1.4100, the option is said to be **'in-the-money'** to BBU and they would choose to exercise it.

- e.g. if the FX rate falls to 1.3950 in the currency markets, for EUR10 million, BBU would receive only USD13.95 million but by exercising the option, they would receive USD14.1 million (USD150,000 more) so it is worth it to exercise the option.

Importantly, remember that a premium has been paid for the option so in calculating any 'profit' to BBU, the cost of the premium needs to be taken into account as in the table below. BBU exercises the option if the market FX rate is below 1.4100. However, because the option cost USD150,000, they only start making a 'profit' when the rate is below 1.3950.

Table 8.3: The payoff profile for a EUR put / USD call

Market FX Rate	USD received at market rate	Option payoff (USD)	Option "profit" incl. Premium (USD)	Option exercised?
1.3750	13,750,000	14,100,000	200,000	Yes
1.3800	13,800,000	14,100,000	150,000	Yes
1.3850	13,850,000	14,100,000	100,000	Yes
1.3900	13,900,000	14,100,000	50,000	Yes
1.3950	13,950,000	14,100,000	0	Yes
1.4000	14,000,000	14,100,000	0	Yes
1.4050	14,050,000	14,100,000	0	Yes
1.4100	14,100,000	14,100,000	0	Indifferent
1.4150	14,150,000	14,100,000	0	No
1.4200	14,200,000	14,100,000	0	No
1.4250	14,250,000	14,100,000	0	No
1.4300	14,300,000	14,100,000	0	No
1.4350	14,350,000	14,100,000	0	No

RATES

Do you know how an interest rate swap works?

The interest rate on money borrowed at a variable rate of interest, e.g. LIBOR, rises as the rate rises and falls as the rate falls. If interest rates are expected to rise, it is possible to **hedge** against the rise by entering into an interest rate swap (IRS) so that the floating rate is converted to a fixed rate.

An interest rate swap (IRS) is an agreement between two parties to exchange interest flows.

One party pays a variable rate (normally LIBOR, but it can be another rate, e.g. a government base rate) whilst the other party pays a fixed rate as set on the date that the IRS is executed.

The LIBOR payments are referred to as the 'floating leg'; the fixed rate interest payments are referred to as the 'fixed leg'.

Figure 8.6: Cash flows on an interest rate swap and a loan

Table 8.4: Interest rate swap (IRS) term sheet

Product	Interest rate swap (IRS)
Buyer	The fixed rate payer i.e. BBU
Notional	USD10 million
Trade date	Some date before the 'start date'
Start date	31-Dec-09
Maturity date	31-Dec-11
BBU pays	Fixed rate of 1.500% paid semi-annually

BBU receives	6-month USD LIBOR as set by the BBA
Business days	London, New York (for payments and LIBOR fixings)
LIBOR fixing dates	31-Dec-09, 30-Jun-10, 31-Dec-10, 30-Jun-11
Payment dates	30-Jun-10, 31-Dec-10, 30-Jun-11, 31-Dec-11
Roll convention	Following

What does the above term sheet tell us?

- Blissful Books United has entered into a two-year IRS that starts on 31 Dec 2009 and matures on 31 Dec 2011.

- The amount on which interest is calculated is called the '**notional**' amount because this value isn't paid upfront by either party involved in the swap. What would be the point of the exchanging the same amount of the same currency?

- BBU will pay a fixed rate of 1.500% semi-annually. 1.500% is an annual rate; it needs to be divided by two to make it semi-annual.

- The 6-month USD LIBOR rate paid by the bank on 30 Jun 2010 is set six months before on 31 Dec 2009; we say LIBOR is '**set in advance and paid in arrears**' to describe this phenomenon. It is the market convention.

Table 8.5: LIBOR fixing and payment dates on an IRS

LIBOR paid on:	Is fixed / set on:	Applicable USD LIBOR rate
30-Jun-10	31-Dec-09	0.4343%
31-Dec-10	30-Jun-10	0.9303%
30-Jun-11	31-Dec-10	1.7250%
31-Dec-11	30-Jun-11	2.4400%

- The roll convention of 'following' means that if an interest payment falls on a weekend or a holiday in London or New York, payment is then made on the next good business day.

What cash flows occur on payment dates?

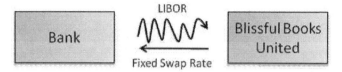

Figure 8.7: Cash flows on an interest rate swap

Table 8.6: Amounts on each interest rate swap payment date

Payment day 1	BBU pays: 1.500% * USD10m * 0.5years = $75,000 Bank pays: USD LIBOR of 0.4343% * USD10m * 0.5years = $21,715
Payment day 2	BBU pays: 1.500% * USD10m * 0.5years = $75,000 Bank pays: USD LIBOR of 0.9303% * USD10m * 0.5years = $46,515
Payment day 3	BBU pays: 1.500% * USD10m * 0.5years = $75,000 Bank pays: USD LIBOR of 1.7250% * USD10m * 0.5years = $86,250
Payment day 4	BBU pays: 1.500% * USD10m * 0.5years = $75,000 Bank pays: USD LIBOR of 2.4400% * USD10m * 0.5years = $122,000

Both payments are in the same currency, so only the net amount is paid.

Table 8.7: Cash flows on each interest rate swap payment date

Payment day 1	BBU pays $53,285 (i.e. 21,715 – 75,000)
Payment day 2	BBU pays $28,485 (i.e. 46,515 – 75,000)
Payment day 3	BBU receives $11,250 (i.e. 86,250 – 75,000)
Payment day 4	BBU receives $47,000 (i.e. 122,000 – 75,000)

How is the fixed swap rate (paid by BBU) arrived at?

Each swap leg has a present value. The present value is the value of each cash flow discounted to the day on which you are calculating it.

Table 8.8: Present value of floating leg cash flows on execution date

Payment Date	Flow	Discount Factor	PV of Flow
30-Jun-10	21,715	0.99835	21,679
31-Dec-10	46,515	0.99363	46,219
30-Jun-11	86,250	0.98507	84,962
31-Dec-11	122,000	0.97300	118,706
		Sum of PVs on floating leg	271,566

Table 8.9: Present value of fixed leg cash flows on execution date

Payment Date	Flow*	Discount Factor	PV of Flow*
30-Jun-10	68,750	0.99835	68,637
31-Dec-10	68,750	0.99363	68,312
30-Jun-11	68,750	0.98507	67,724
31-Dec-11	68,750	0.97300	66,894
		Sum of PVs on fixed leg	271,566

* Based on a rate of 1.375%

On the date of execution, the fixed rate on the swap is set so that the value of each leg is exactly equal before any charges are applied. The swap is said to have a net present value (NPV) of zero; this is the **mid-market rate**. Mid-market is an important concept in the world of derivatives.

At a rate of 1.375%, the present value (PV) of both the fixed and floating leg on the above swap is USD271,566 hence the net PV (NPV) is zero.
1.375% is the mid-market rate of the swap

The discount factors used above are derived via a method called 'bootstrapping' and is beyond the scope of this book. All banks that deal in derivatives will have an automated system for calculating discount factors so don't worry if you look up 'bootstrapping' and find it is rather cumbersome to derive.

- Note that when discounting the future flows on an interest rate swap, a different discount factor is used for every payment date.

- When discounting the future payments on a bond, a single discount factor (the **yield to maturity**) is used for every cash flow. This assumes interest rates remain the same throughout the life of a bond (i.e. a flat yield curve is assumed).

What is the cost of entering into an IRS?

- No upfront cash payment is made.

- In this sort of IRS where the non-bank counterparty pays a fixed rate, the bank charges for the swap by adding a few basis points (1 basis point (1bp) = 0.01%) to the mid rate.

- These basis points reflect the cost of executing the swap (the execution spread), the credit risk to the bank of entering into the swap (the credit spread) and market liquidity (liquidity spread).
  - The higher a trader's execution costs are, the wider or higher the execution spread.
  - The less credit worthy a counterparty is, the higher the credit spread.
  - The more illiquid the market is, the higher the liquidity spread.

- In this particular swap, the mid market rate is 1.375% and the following are added:
  - Execution spread: 0.5 bp

- o Credit spread: 10 bps
- o Liquidity spread: 2 bps
- o Total spread added to mid-market = 12.5bp or 0.125%
- o **All-in rate = 1.375% + 0.125% = 1.500%**

Table 8.10: PV of fixed leg on execution date after charges are added in:

Payment Date	Flow *	Discount Factor	PV of Flow
30-Jun-10	75,000	0.99835	74,876
31-Dec-10	75,000	0.99363	74,522
30-Jun-11	75,000	0.98507	73,880
31-Dec-11	75,000	0.97300	72,975
		Sum of PVs on fixed leg	296,254

*The fixed flow now equals 1.500% x $10million x 0.5years = $75,000 due to spreads.

The end result is that at the point of execution:

- BBU commits to pay a fixed rate of 1.5000%. The fixed payments BBU makes to the bank have a PV of USD296,254.
- The floating payments the bank makes to BBU have a PV of USD271,566.
- The net PV of the swap is USD24,688 (296,254 minus 271,566).
- 12.5bps adds USD24,688 of value to the swap, so every basis point is worth USD1,975 (24,688 ÷ 12.5bps)

How does a Forward Rate Agreement or FRA work?

A FRA is a cash settled contract on a forward interest rate. You can think of it as a single period interest rate swap.

The buyer of a FRA receives a fixed rate of interest and is hence protected from a rise in rates; the FRA seller receives a floating rate and protects themselves against a fall in rates.

FRAs are usually defined by their start and maturity date. For instance:

- A 1 x 4 (1 by 4) FRA is effective 1 month from today and matures in 4 months from today and is based on 3-month LIBOR (4 minus 1).
- A 3 x 9 (3 by 9) FRA is effective 3 months from today and matures in 9 months from today and is based on 6-month LIBOR (9 minus 3).
- A 12 x 13 (12 by 13) FRA is effective 12 months from today and matures 13 months from today and is based on 1-month LIBOR (13 minus 12) and so on.

However, unlike an interest rate swap, settlement happens on the effective/start date of the FRA because, once the LIBOR fixing has happened, the cash flows are known so there's no need to wait until the end of the period for payment. Because of this 'early payment', the amount has to be discounted to the start date.

What is an interest rate cap or simply 'cap'?

An IRS is not the only way that a variable rate payer can hedge against rising interest rates.

Having borrowed money on which the interest rate fluctuates with LIBOR, BBU can protect itself against rising interest rates by buying an interest rate option called a cap.

At the upfront cost of a **premium**, a cap protects the buyer when interest rates rise above a pre-specified strike level. The rate beyond which the buyer is protected is called the **strike rate** of the cap.

Table 8.11: Interest rate cap term sheet

Product	Interest rate cap (or simply, 'cap')
Buyer	Blissful Books United (BBU)
Notional	USD10 million
Trade date	Some date before the 'start date'
Start date	31-Dec-09
Maturity date	31-Dec-11
Strike rate	2.50%
Reference rate	6-month USD LIBOR as set by the BBA
Business days	London, New York (for payments and LIBOR fixings)
LIBOR fixing dates	31-Dec-09, 30-Jun-10, 31-Dec-10, 30-Jun-11
Payment dates	30-Jun-10, 31-Dec-10, 30-Jun-11, 31-Dec-11
Roll convention	Following
Premium	USD195,000

What does the above term sheet tell us?

- Blissful Books United has entered into a two-year interest rate cap that starts on 31 Dec 2009 and matures on 31 Dec 2011.
- The notional amount on which interest is calculated is USD10 million.
- If the LIBOR fixing exceeds 2.50% on any fixing date, on the corresponding payment date BBU will receive an amount equal to:

  Notional * 0.5years * (LIBOR fixing – Strike Rate)

  e.g. if LIBOR fixed at 2.75%, under this cap, on the corresponding payment date (fixing date + 6 months) BBU would receive a payout of USD12,500 i.e. USD10m * 0.5years * (2.75% - 2.50%).
- If the LIBOR fixing was below 2.50% on any fixing date, on the relevant payment date BBU would not receive (or pay) anything under this cap as the option would be out-of-the-money for that date.

How is the strike rate set?

The buyer of the cap decides where to set the strike rate. The further out-of-the-money the strike rate is (or said differently, the higher the cap's strike rate compared to current interest rates), the lower the premium on the cap (i.e. the cheaper the cap).

What does it mean to be out-of-the-money?

If a normal IRS is priced with same details as the cap (dates, roll conventions etc) to achieve the mid-market rate, and this rate is set as the strike rate on the cap, the cap has been priced **'at-the-money'**. From the IRS section, we know that the at-the-money rate is 1.375%.

The cap buyer (BBU) only receives a 'compensatory' payment when LIBOR fixes **above** the strike rate. So the higher the strike rate is set, the less likely it is that LIBOR will fix at that level and hence the lower the premium.

Taken to the extreme, if the strike rate is set at 10.00% when the 'at-the-money' level is 1.375% (as is the case here), the premium would be very low (perhaps close to zero). This is because over a two year period it is highly unlikely that LIBOR will exceed 10.00%; under an option contract with the strike so high the bank probably won't have to pay the cap buyer (BBU) anything over the two year cap term. This low likelihood of hitting the strike makes the premium much cheaper.

What is an interest rate floor?

An entity that receives a variable interest rate (e.g. a bank that lends at LIBOR) may want to hedge against falling interest rates.

The bank can protect itself against falling interest rates by buying an interest rate option called a **floor**.

Extremely low interest rates became a major concern after the 2007-2009 credit crunch because base/prime rates, and hence LIBOR levels, reached unprecedented low levels and banks found themselves receiving rates a lot lower than they had expected when they initially made their loans. As a consequence, some lenders insisted on embedding a floor into some new loans. This meant that a borrower would not benefit if LIBOR fell below the level of the floor.

At the upfront cost of a **premium**, a floor protects the buyer when interest rates fall below a pre-specified level. The rate beyond which the buyer is protected is called the **strike rate** of the floor.

Table 8.12: Interest rate floor term sheet

Product	Interest rate floor (or simply, 'floor')
Buyer	Bank One
Notional	USD10 million
Trade date	Some date before the 'start date'
Start date	31-Dec-09
Maturity date	31-Dec-11
Strike rate	0.75%
Reference rate	6-month USD LIBOR as set by the BBA
Business days	London, New York (for payments and LIBOR fixings)
LIBOR fixing dates	31-Dec-09, 30-Jun-10, 31-Dec-10, 30-Jun-11
Payment dates	30-Jun-10, 31-Dec-10, 30-Jun-11, 31-Dec-11
Roll convention	Following
Premium	USD360,000

What does the above term sheet tell us?

- Bank One has entered into a two-year interest rate floor that starts on 31 Dec 2009 and matures on 31 Dec 2011.
- The notional amount on which interest is calculated is USD10 million.

- If the LIBOR fixing falls below 0.75% on any fixing date, on the corresponding payment date Bank One receives an amount equal to:

  Notional * 0.5years * (Strike Rate – LIBOR fixing)

  e.g. if LIBOR fixed at 0.45% under this floor, on the corresponding payment date (fixing date + 6 months) Bank One would receive a payout of USD15,000 (that is, USD10m * 0.5year * (0.75% - 0.45%).

- If the LIBOR fixing was above 0.75% on any fixing date, on the relevant payment date Bank One would not receive (or pay) anything under this floor.

How is the strike rate set?

The buyer of the floor decides where to set the strike rate. The further out-of-the-money the strike rate is (or said differently, the lower the floor's strike rate compared to current interest rates), the lower the premium on the floor (i.e. the cheaper the floor).

What does it mean to be out-of-the-money?

A floor works in the opposite direction to a cap. Whereas under a cap the higher the rate is from the mid-market price the more out-of-the-money the cap is, under a floor the lower the rate is from the mid-market price the more out-of-the-money the floor is said to be.

If a normal IRS is priced with same details as the floor (dates, roll conventions etc) to achieve the mid-market rate, and this rate is set as the strike rate on the floor, the floor has been priced 'at-the-money'.

The floor buyer (Bank One) only receives a 'compensatory' payment when LIBOR sets **below** the strike rate. The lower the strike is set from the mid-market level, the less likely it is that LIBOR will fix at that level and hence the lower the premium.

LIBOR can never set below 0.00% therefore, when interest rates are already very low, the floor will naturally be quite close to the at-the-money level.

Imagine a world where the 'at-the-money' level is c.7.00%. If the strike rate on a floor is set at 0.75%, the premium would be extremely low because over a two year period it is highly unlikely that LIBOR will fall below 0.75%; in such a world, with a floor at 0.75% BBU (the floor seller) is unlikely to be called upon to pay the cap buyer (Bank One) anything over the two year floor term.

Note that in this example the floor is more expensive than the cap because it is closer to the ATM price:

- (1.375% ATM rate) – (0.75% floor) = 62.5bps
- (2.500% cap) – (1.375% ATM rate) = 112.5bps

Understanding the 'Greeks' as applied to the interest rate market

The Greeks were defined in table 7.12.

In late 2009, Blissful Books United (BBU) had a loan that needed to be repaid in two years. The interest rate on the loan was reset every six months based on LIBOR.

Afraid that interest rates may start to rise, BBU decided to buy an interest rate cap. The cap premium that BBU pays is influenced by the Greeks.

Underlying product: two-year interest rate cap (a call option on interest rates) as demonstrated in the term sheet, table 8.11.

By buying the cap, BBU has the right to be paid a rate of 'LIBOR minus 2.50%' if LIBOR exceeds 2.50%.

- If on a LIBOR reset date LIBOR exceeds 2.50%, BBU (the option buyer) would exercise the option.
- If on a LIBOR reset date LIBOR is less than 2.50%, the caplet expires worthless.
- The current ATM rate is 1.375%

Delta: sensitivity of the premium to underlying interest rates

If interest rates rise such that the two-year ATM swap rate becomes 2.00%, would the cap cost more or less?

Because the chances of hitting a strike price of 2.50% are higher when the two-year swap rate is 2.00% rather than 1.375%, the option would be more expensive (assuming all other variables are constant).

> *So cap premia increase with an increase in*
> *current interest rate swap levels.*

What impact would such a rise in rates have on the cost of a floor?

The opposite would be true for a floor: if a bank bought a two-year floor on interest rates with a strike at 0.75%, they would only exercise this option if interest rates fell below 0.75%.

An increase in swap rates from 1.375% to 2.00% moves rates further away from falling below the floor strike of 0.75% so the floor premium would fall.

> *So floor premia fall with an increase in*
> *current interest rate swap levels.*

If interest rates fall such that the two-year swap rate becomes 1.00%, would the cap cost more or less?

Because the chances of hitting a cap strike rate of 2.50% are lower when the two-year swap rate is 1.00% rather than 1.375%, the option would be less expensive (assuming all other variables are constant).

> *So cap premia fall with a decrease in current interest rate swap levels.*

What impact would such a fall in rates have on the cost of a floor?

The opposite would be true for the put option:

A decrease in swap rates from 1.375% to 1.00% moves rates closer to falling below the floor strike of 0.75% so the floor premium would rise.

> *So floor premia rise with a decrease in current interest rate swap levels.*

Vega: sensitivity of the premium to volatility of underlying interest rates

If interest rates are very volatile, options are more expensive. Why does this make sense? Because the chances of hitting a strike rate are higher when there's a lot more movement in rates than when rates are relatively static.

Look at the below chart of the two-year swap rate. If someone in 1996-1997 wanted to buy a cap and they set the cap strike price at 1.00% *above* the market interest rate at the time, that option would probably be cheaper than buying a similar option also at 1.00% *above* the market price in 2008.

Higher volatility in 2008 compared to 1996-1997 means that the probability of the rate moving by 1.00% was higher in 2008.

It makes sense that the same relationship exists between volatility and interest rate floors. The same logic applies: higher volatility means a higher chance of interest rates falling below the floor's strike rate.

So both cap and floor premia increase with an increase in volatility.

Figure 8.8: 2-year USD swap rate (Feb 1992 to Feb 2012)

Source: Bloomberg

Theta: sensitivity of the premium to time to expiry

The cap discussed has a two year maturity, what would you expect to happen to the option price if BBU were contemplating a five-year cap?

The chances of any cap strike being exceeded over a five year period are higher than the chances of it being exceeded over a two year period. Importantly, a two-year semi-annual cap has four LIBOR reset dates whilst a five-year one has ten LIBOR reset dates. That is, the longer the cap term, the more caplets being priced. This would therefore increase the cost of the cap contract.

So interest rate caps are positively correlated with time to expiry.

Similar logic applies to floor premia: the longer the time to expiry, the higher the premium for a floor contract.

> *So both cap and floor premia increase with*
> *an increase in time to expiry.*

Table 8.13: Relationship of cap and floor premia to market variables:

	Cap premium	Floor premium
Interest rates rise	increases	decreases
Interest rates fall	decreases	increases
Volatility of underlying (Vega)	+ve correlation	+ve correlation
Time to expiry (Theta)	+ve correlation	+ve correlation

+ve = positive

Do you know how a cross-currency swap works?

Please read and fully understand '*Do you know how an interest rate swap works?*' (Under 'Rates' above) before going into cross-currency swaps (CCS). **Only read ahead if you fully understand this section otherwise the below may leave you feeling confused.**

A CCS is simply an IRS in which the two legs are based on different currencies; you can think of it as a more advanced IRS.

Companies do not always borrow money in their operational currency. For instance, BBU a US-headquartered chain of bookshops, may choose to borrow in GBP for its US stores rather than USD because at that point in time UK banks are more willing to lend to it, or perhaps because it's cheaper to borrow from UK banks than US banks (or any other reason). The result is that BBU has an exposure to fluctuations in the value of USD versus GBP on payment dates.

BBU can protect itself from this currency exposure by entering into a CCS. Under the CCS, BBU US would pay USD (the currency in which it earns money) and receive GBP (the currency in which it has borrowed).

In other words, a cross-currency swap (CCS) is an agreement between two parties to exchange interest flows in two different currencies.

The parties can pay each other floating-floating, fixed-floating, floating-fixed or fixed-fixed interest rates as shown in the table below.

Table 8.14: Different structures for a vanilla cross-currency swap

Party 1 (BBU) in a CCS pays:	Party 2 (Bank One) in a CCS pays:
USD LIBOR	GBP LIBOR
USD fixed interest rate	GBP LIBOR
USD LIBOR	GBP fixed interest rate
USD fixed interest rate	GBP fixed interest rate

Assume BBU borrows at GBP LIBOR but wants to convert this to a USD fixed rate exposure. The resulting swap has a GBP LIBOR floating leg and a USD fixed leg.

Figure 8.9: Cash flows on a cross-currency swap and a loan

Table 8.15: Cross-currency swap term sheet

Product	Cross-currency swap (CCS)
USD Notional	USD10 million
GBP Notional	GBP6,191,950 (GBPUSD = 1.6150)
Trade date	Some date before the 'start date'
Start date	31-Dec-09
Maturity date	31-Dec-11
Notional exchange	Initial and final exchange of notionals
BBU pays	USD fixed rate of 2.00% paid semi-annually
BBU receives	6-month GBP LIBOR as set by the BBA
Business days	London, New York (for payments and LIBOR fixings)
LIBOR fixing dates	31-Dec-09, 30-Jun-10, 31-Dec-10, 30-Jun-11
Payment dates	30-Jun-10, 31-Dec-10, 30-Jun-11, 31-Dec-11
Roll convention	Following

What does the above term sheet tell us?

- Blissful Books United has entered into a two-year CCS that starts on 31 Dec 2009 and matures on 31 Dec 2011.
- The amount on which interest is calculated is still called the 'notional' amount because this value does not have to be paid upfront by either party involved in the swap. However, it is customary to have an initial and a final exchange of notional amounts in a CCS.
    - In some CCS there is only an initial exchange of notionals; other CCS have just a final exchange and yet other CCS have no notional exchange at all.
    - A CCS with no initial or final exchange of notionals is referred to as a **coupon cross-currency swap**.
- BBU will pay a fixed USD rate of 2.00% semi-annually; 2.00% is an annual rate and it needs to be divided by two to make it semi-annual.

- The 6-month GBP LIBOR rate paid by the bank on 30 Jun 2010 is set six months in advance on 31 Dec 2009, we say LIBOR is 'set in advance and paid in arrears' to describe this phenomenon. It is the market convention for CCS as for IRS.

Table 8.16: LIBOR fixing and payment dates on a CCS

LIBOR paid on:	Is fixed / set on:	Applicable GBP LIBOR rate
30-Jun-10	31-Dec-09	0.6660%
31-Dec-10	30-Jun-10	1.2150%
30-Jun-11	31-Dec-10	2.0950%
31-Dec-11	30-Jun-11	2.8549%

- Note that GBP LIBOR is different to the USD LIBOR shown for the same dates in the IRS section.
- The roll convention of 'following' means that if an interest payment falls on a weekend or a holiday in London or New York, payment is then made on the next good business day.

How is the fixed swap rate (paid by BBU) arrived at?

The methodology is similar to that used to arrive at a swap rate on an IRS. Each swap leg has a present value. The present value is the value of each cash flow discounted to the day on which you are calculating it.

There is no need to go into detail here but know that, because each leg is in a different currency, the discount factors are also different. This is contrary to an IRS where both legs have the same discount rates because they are both in the same currency.

As with an IRS, on the date of execution, the fixed rate on the swap is set such that the value of each leg when represented in the same currency is exactly equal *before* any charges are applied. The rate at which the net present value (NPV) of the swap is zero is the **mid-market rate**.

What is the cost of entering into a CCS?

- No upfront cash payment is made.
- In this sort of CCS where the non-bank counterparty pays a fixed rate, the bank charges for the swap by adding a few basis points (1 basis point (1bp) = 0.01%) to the mid rate.
- These basis points reflect the cost of executing the swap (the execution spread), the credit risk to the bank of entering into the swap (the credit spread) and market liquidity (liquidity spread).
- In this particular swap, the mid market rate was 1.80% and the following were added:
  - o Execution spread: 2 bp
  - o Credit spread: 15 bps
  - o Liquidity spread: 3 bps
  - o Total spread added to mid-market = 20bps or 0.20%
  - o **All-in rate = 1.80% + 0.20% = 2.00%**
- In a CCS where the non-bank counterparty is paying LIBOR plus a spread (quoted in bps), the charges are simply added to the spread.
- Cross-currency swaps are more credit-intensive than interest rate swaps because of the exchange of notionals at the maturity. This explains the much higher credit charge on the CCS than on the IRS.

What is the difference between an FX swap and a cross-currency swap?

There are two key differences:

- An FX swap does not involve any payment of interest whereas a cross-currency swap does.
- The exchange rate for the initial and final transaction is set at different rates in an FX swap; conversely, in a cross-currency swap both the initial and final exchanges are based on the spot rate set at the outset.

CREDIT

What is a Credit Default Swap (CDS)?

Credit Default Swaps (CDS) provide insurance against default by some known '**reference entity**'. The simplest form of CDS is one where the reference entity is a single company. You can also buy CDS against a portfolio of companies, bonds, loans or even a government (to name a few). As a newbie to banking, it will suffice to have knowledge only of a 'plain vanilla single name CDS' as used in this example.

CDS is traded over-the-counter rather than on an exchange.

Property example: if you buy a house, you can buy a form of insurance called 'buildings insurance'. Armed with this insurance, if something happens to the house, e.g. if it is damaged by fire, a flood or some other natural disaster, you can claim against the buildings insurance to get the house fixed. The costs are covered by the insurance seller.

CDS works in a somewhat similar fashion with one big difference: you don't need to own or have any exposure to the entity that you buy a credit default swap against. This can lead to unintended consequences if that entity defaults, as explained below.

So how does CDS work?

Blissful Books United, BBU, issues a five-year USD bond paying a coupon of 5% per annum.

As a high net worth investor, you buy USD10 million worth of the bond. However, you want insurance that, even if BBU were to go bust, you would get your USD10m back, so you buy a credit default swap (CDS) with a **notional value** of USD10m for the entire term of five years.

For this insurance, you pay a fee every quarter called a **CDS spread**. The more risky the underlying company is, the higher the CDS spread. In this case, you are quoted a spread of 1.20% as a consequence every quarter you would pay USD30,000, i.e. USD10,000,000 × 1.20% spread × 0.25years.

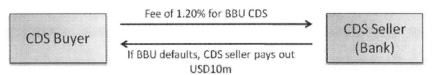

Figure 8.10: Cash flows on a credit default swap

The CDS contract lists the events of default that would lead to a pay out by the CDS seller. Common events of default include:

1. Bankruptcy of the underlying company.
2. A corporate restructuring that impacts the credit rating by a given amount.
3. Failure by the relevant company to pay a financial obligation.

Sometimes it is very easy to classify an event as a default but at other times it is not so straightforward. For example, the CDS contract may classify missed payments by a company as an event of default. What happens if a company misses a payment but somehow manages to pay it some days later? Should the CDS buyer really make a claim? Different people will give you different answers.

In the case of the restructuring of Greek debt in 2011-2012, there was massive debate over whether or not the eventuality was an 'event of default'.

When an event of default occurs, the bond's value does not necessarily plummet to zero. After all's said and done, a market value is attributed to the bond. For instance, if a ratings downgrade is considered an event of default, following a downgrade of BBU, the USD10 million face value bond may be attributed a market value of USD6 million. This is the '**recovery value**'. At the lower rating, the market would not pay the full USD10m that it cost to buy the bond in the first place.

If the entity underlying the CDS does indeed default, the CDS contract is settled in one of two ways: **physically or cash**.

Physical settlement:

1. BBU defaults.
2. The bondholder (you) delivers the bond contract to the CDS seller (the bank).
3. The CDS seller pays you the notional of the CDS: USD10m in this case.

From this point on, you have nothing to do with the bond and whatever payment the CDS seller (the bank) manages to get for the bond is their business.

Cash settlement:

1. BBU defaults.
2. The bondholder (you) holds onto the bond and sells it in the open market for its recovery value: USD6m in this case.
3. The CDS seller pays out the difference between the notional value and the recovery value, that is, USD4 million in this case.

What is the consequence of buying CDS if you don't have an exposure to the entity?

The CDS contract states whether the contract will be settled physical or cash upon an event of default.

Under a cash settled CDS, the CDS seller pays you the notional value less the recovery value. If you don't actually own the reference bond, you have nothing to sell in order to capture the recovery value. So you would have been paying a fee on a value of USD10m but you wouldn't get that same value back from the CDS seller on a cash settled contract. Indeed, if the present value of CDS fees paid is lower than 'notional minus recover' value, you might not care.

You might be wondering: *Well, can't you just go out and buy the reference bond?*

The answer is probably 'no'; the likelihood is that the size of the bond issued is a lot smaller than the total notional value of CDS outstanding. Because a CDS buyer does not have to own the instrument underlying a CDS contract, the notional value of CDS out there could be multiple times higher than reference bond value available (or whatever the underlying is).

If you entered into a physical contract without owning the underlying bond, there is a definite problem. In order to get a payment equivalent to the notional from the CDS seller, you need to present the bond. If you don't already own the bond and can't find one to buy, you're screwed.

When the CDS market first started out, settlement was almost always physical. CDS was bought simply for insurance purposes. Then financial investors and speculators, e.g. hedge funds, realized they could express their market views by buying and selling CDS without the obligation to deliver a bond or loan contract upon the occurrence of a default event. Once CDS began to be used for speculation and not just for protection, growth of the CDS market exploded.

COMMODITIES

What do you know about oil?

This is a very open-ended question for an interviewer to ask. You could talk about the commodity itself, its price over time and how it is used. Alternatively, you could discuss hedging by a producer of crude oil or a consumer that buys a product of crude oil.

Crude oil (a.k.a. petroleum) is the world's most actively traded commodity.

Crude Oil Products

Once crude oil has been dug out of the ground and barreled, it's transported to an oil refinery where it's converted into 'useful' products. In its unrefined state crude oil is pretty useless.

Crude oils dug out of different wells have a different composition. For instance, some crude oil has more sulfur than others – the more sulfur the crude oil contains, the harder it is to refine; among other things, it's heavy and it doesn't flow through pipes as easily.

Government taxes and subsidies on oil products can impact the demand and supply pattern in a country, e.g. In India LPG (liquefied petroleum gas) is subsidized so large sections of the middle class use it as a cooking fuel.

Examples of common products that you get after refining crude oil are:

- **Gasoline** (a.k.a. **petrol**): used to power car engines
- **Diesel fuel**: used to power diesel engines, e.g. for trains
- **Jet fuel**: used to power the engines of certain aircraft
- **Kerosene** (a.k.a. **paraffin**): used to power the engines of certain aircraft & vehicles; in some parts of the world it's used to light lamps and to fire up portable stoves
- **Liquefied petroleum gas, LPG:** used for heating and as a motor and cooking fuel

- **Asphalt**: a sticky, black substance used in road construction and manufacturing roof shingles

Oil Supply

Table 8.17: Countries with the world's largest proven crude oil reserves

Country	Crude oil reserves (million barrels)
Saudi Arabia	264,590
Venezuela	211,173
Islamic Republic of Iran	137,010
Iraq	115,000
Kuwait	101,500

Source: OPEC Annual Statistical Bulletin 2009 (available via the OPEC website)

The dynamic between the countries that consume the most oil versus those that produce the most oil is pretty interesting:

Table 8.18: Top World Producers, Consumers, Importers, Exporters (thousand barrels per day, 2009)

Country	Production	Country	Consumption
1. Russia	9,934	1. United States	18,771
2. Saudi Arabia	9,760	2. China	8,324
3. United States	9,141	3. Japan	4,367
4. Iran	4,177	4. India	3,110
5. China	3,996	5. Russia	2,740
6. Canada	3,315	6. Brazil	2,522
7. Mexico	3,001	7. Germany	2,456
8. UAE	2,795	8. Saudi Arabia	2,438
9. Brazil	2,577	9. Korea, South	2,185
10. Kuwait	2,496	10. Canada	2,147
11. Venezuela	2,471	11. Mexico	2,084
12. Iraq	2,400	12. France	1,828
13. Norway	2,350	13. Iran	1,691
14. Nigeria	2,211	14. United Kingdom	1,667
15. Algeria	2,086	15. Italy	1,528

Country	Imports	Country	Exports
1 United States	9,631	1 Saudi Arabia	7,322
2 China	4,328	2 Russia	7,194
3 Japan	4,235	3 Iran	2,486
4 Germany	2,323	4 UAE	2,303
5 India	2,233	5 Norway	2,132
6 Korea, South	2,139	6 Kuwait	2,124
7 France	1,749	7 Nigeria	1,939
8 United Kingdom	1,588	8 Angola	1,878
9 Spain	1,439	9 Algeria	1,767
10 Italy	1,381	10 Iraq	1,764
11 Netherlands	973	11 Venezuela	1,748
12 Taiwan	944	12 Libya	1,525
13 Singapore	916	13 Kazakhstan	1,299
14 Turkey	650	14 Canada	1,168
15 Belgium	597	15 Qatar	1,066

Source: US Energy Information Administration (data available on their website)

Price of crude oil based on a generic futures contract, USD per barrel

Below is a graph showing one of the most liquid (i.e. most traded) crude oil futures contracts in the financial markets, the WTI light, sweet crude oil futures contract[18]. Light means it has a low density and flows freely at room temperature; sweet means the sulfur content is low.

Light, sweet crude oil is more expensive than heavy, sour crude oil because it is cheaper to refine and produces more high value products, e.g. gasoline, diesel and jet fuel during the refinery process.

This futures contract is very widely used as a pricing benchmark.

---

[18] Data is produced by the New York Mercantile Exchange (NYMEX), a subsidiary of the CME Group.

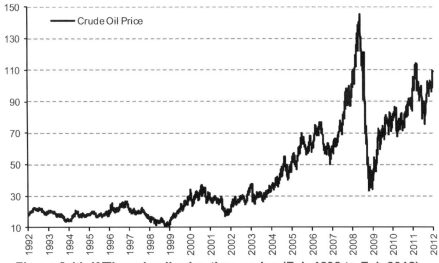

Figure 8.11: WTI crude oil price time series (Feb 1992 to Feb 2012)

Source: Bloomberg

Hedging by a producer of crude oil: put option on crude oil

Gashers Oil Company is an oil producer. Their only source of revenue comes from selling the crude oil they have dug out of their wells to refinery companies.

It costs them about USD45 to produce every barrel of oil. That cost includes interest on their borrowings, the equipment used to dig up the oil and salaries paid to their employees.

Selling their oil for less than USD45 per barrel would result in losses to the company. As such, ensuring their oil is sold for at least this price is a primary concern to them.

To secure the price of oil, they buy a put option with a strike price of USD65. This strike price covers costs as well as a good amount of profit.

The price of crude oil is USD100 when they buy this option, so the option is out-of-the-money.

Table 8.19: Crude oil put option term sheet

Product	Put option on crude oil
Buyer	Gashers Oil Company
Notional	10,000 barrels of oil per day
Trade date	Some date before the 'start date'
Start date	1-Jan-11
Maturity date	31-Dec-11
Strike price	USD65 (average monthly price)
Reference	WTI crude oil price index on Bloomberg
Business days	London, New York
Payment dates	First day of each month for the previous month
Roll convention	Following
Settlement	Notional Quantity * (Strike Price - Average Price)
Premium	USD1 per barrel

To buy this put option Gashers Oil Company pays USD3.65 million for the 365 days in 2011:

10,000 barrel per day x 365 days x USD1 premium = USD3.65 million

What does this put option achieve for Gashers Oil Company?

It gives them the right to sell 10,000 barrels of oil per day for USD65.

- Gashers Oil Co. would only exercise this option if it is in-the-money to them, that is, if the average price of oil falls below USD65 in any given month.
- If any payments are due to Gashers for any given month, they are paid on the first day of the month. For instance, any March payments would be settled on 1 Apr 2011.
- If the payment date is a weekend or holiday, the payment is **rolled** to the **following** good business day.

For every month in 2011 where the average crude oil price falls **beneath** USD65, Gashers Oil Co. would exercise the option because by doing so they secure a better price than what the market is offering.

- e.g. in one month the average price of crude oil is USD50.
- Gashers exercises the option because it is in-the-money.
- In so doing they receive USD150,000 for each day in that month: **10,000 barrels * (USD65 strike price - USD50 average price)**

For every month in 2011 where the average crude oil price is **above** USD65, Gashers Oil Co. would **not** exercise the option because they would achieve a better price by selling in the open market.

- e.g. in one month the average price of crude oil is USD70.
- Gashers would not exercise the option because the strike price of USD65 on the option is worse than selling at the market price.

Above, I have shown a simple outright put option on crude oil. Gashers could subsidize this put option by selling another option or combination of options.

Hedging by a consumer of a crude oil product: call option on jet fuel

Supersonic Jets Inc. is an airline company. To power their fleet, Supersonic Jets buys jet fuel regularly. Jet fuel is their main cost.

They currently buy jet fuel for USD980 per metric ton (MT). In recent days the price of jet fuel has been trending up. A price above USD1,100/MT would make running the airline difficult so they decide to hedge themselves by buying an out-of-the-money call option on jet fuel.

Table 8.20: Jet fuel call option term sheet

Product	Call option on jet fuel
Buyer	Supersonic Jets Inc.
Notional	10,000 metric tons per month
Trade date	Some date before the 'start date'
Start date	1-Jan-11
Maturity date	31-Dec-11
Strike rate	USD1,100 per MT (average monthly price)
Reference	Jet fuel price index on Bloomberg
Business days	London, New York
Payment dates	End of month
Roll convention	Following
Settlement	Notional Quantity * (Average Price - Strike Price)
Premium	USD4 per MT

To buy this call option Supersonic Jets pays USD480,000:

10,000 MT/month x 12 months x USD4 premium = USD480,000

What does this call option achieve for Supersonic Jets?

It gives them the right to buy jet fuel for USD1,100 per metric ton.

- Supersonic Jets would only exercise this option if it is in-the-money to them, that is, if the average market price of jet fuel rises above USD1,100/MT in any given month.

For every month in 2011 where the average jet fuel price fixes **above** USD1,100/MT, Supersonic Jets would exercise the option because in doing so they secure a better price than what the market is offering.

- e.g. in one month the average price of jet fuel is USD1,165.
- Supersonic Jets exercises the option because it is in-the-money.

- In so doing they receive USD650,000:

  10,000MT * (USD1,165/MT average price – USD1,100/MT strike)

For every month in 2011 where the average price of jet fuel is **below** USD1,100/MT, Supersonic Jets does **not** exercise the option because they can achieve a better price by buying in the open market.

- e.g. in one month the average price of jet fuel is USD935.
- Supersonic Jets lets the option expire worthless because it is cheaper to buy jet fuel at the lower market price of USD935/MT rather than exercise the option to buy at USD1,100/MT.

Above, I have shown a simple outright call option on jet fuel. Supersonic Jets could subsidize this option by selling another option or a combination of options.

What do you know about Gold?

Table 8.21: Top world producers[19] of gold (2009)

Country	Production (kg)	Production (troy ounces)*	% of Total World
World Total	2,460,000	79,090,837	100%
1 China	320,000	10,288,239	13%
2 United States	223,323	7,180,001	9%
3 Australia	222,000	7,137,466	9%
4 Russia	205,236	6,598,491	8%
5 South Africa	197,628	6,353,888	8%
6 Peru	182,390	5,863,975	7%
7 Indonesia	127,716	4,106,165	5%
8 Canada	97,367	3,130,422	4%
9 Ghana	97,197	3,124,956	4%
10 Uzbekistan	73,000	2,347,005	3%
Total for Top 10	1,745,857	56,130,606	71%

World Mineral Statistics contributed by permission of the British Geological Survey. IPR/145-07C

Conversion from kg to troy ounce by Girl Banker®: 1 kilogram = 32.1507466 troy ounces

Price of Gold, USD per troy ounce

Figure 8.12: Time series of the price of gold (Feb 1992 to Feb 2012)

Source: Bloomberg

---

[19] World Mineral Production 2005 to 2009 publication available at:
http://www.bgs.ac.uk/mineralsuk/statistics/worldArchive.html

Gold is seen as a safe haven by investors. When risk aversion in the capital markets increases, demand for gold and other financial assets (e.g. USD), which are seen as safe havens, goes up as does their price. You can see the evidence of risk aversion and the subsequent 'flight' to gold in figure 8.12.

Hedging by a gold miner: put option on gold

De Boomers owns gold mines. Gold sales are their only source of revenue.

It costs them about USD250 to produce an ounce of gold. That cost captures interest on their borrowings, the equipment used for mining gold as well as salaries paid to employees.

Selling their gold for less than USD250 per ounce would result in losses for De Boomers. As such, ensuring their gold is sold for at least this price is a primary concern.

To secure the price of gold, they buy a put option on gold with a strike price of USD1,000. This is well in excess of their cost of production because gold prices are hitting all time highs of USD1,800 per ounce when they buy this out-of-the-money option. Even at this strike, the premium is cheap relative to the budget they have set aside for hedging.

Table 8.22: Gold put option term sheet

Product	Put option on gold
Buyer	De Boomers
Notional	100,000 ounces per month
Trade date	Some date before the 'start date'
Start date	1-Jan-11
Maturity date	31-Dec-11
Strike rate	USD1,000 (average monthly price)
Reference	Gold price index on Bloomberg

Business days	London, New York
Payment dates	End of month
Settlement	Notional Quantity * (Strike Price - Average Price)
Roll convention	Following
Premium	USD0.50 per troy ounce

To buy this option De Boomers pays USD600,000:

100,000 ounces x 12 months x USD0.50 premium = USD600,000

What does this put option achieve for De Boomers?

It gives them the right to sell 100,000 ounces of gold every month for USD1,000 per ounce.

- De Boomers would only exercise this option if it is in-the-money to them, that is, if the price of gold is below USD1,000.

If the average price of gold falls **beneath** USD1,000 per ounce in any given month in 2011, De Boomers would exercise the option because in doing so they secure a better price than what the market is offering.

- e.g. in a month when the 'average price' of gold is USD900, De Boomers would receive USD10 million:
  100,000 ounces * (USD1,000 strike – USD900 average price)

If the average price of gold is **above** USD1,000 per ounce in any given month in 2011, De Boomers would **not** exercise the option as they could obtain a better price by selling gold at the current market price.

- e.g. in a month when the 'average price' of gold is USD1,100, De Boomers would not exercise the option because the market price is USD100 better than the price that the option contract secures for them.

Above, I have shown a simple outright put option on gold. De Boomers could subsidize this put option by selling another option or combination of options.

Hedging by a consumer of gold: call option on gold

Rings and Tings is a chain of jewelry shops. They make only gold jewelry: rings, necklaces, bracelets and so on.

Rings and Tings used to buy gold for USD1,000 per ounce but prices have been rising and the wholesale purchase cost is now USD1,200.

Their business is beginning to struggle because they cannot pass the full impact of higher input costs on to their customers without suffering a massive fall in demand. They have already taken a reduction in their profit margin and want to protect themselves against further increases in gold prices. They decide to buy an out-of-the-money call option with a strike rate of USD1,500 per ounce.

Table 8.23: Gold call option term sheet

Product	Call option on gold
Buyer	Rings and Tings
Notional	100,000 ounces per month
Trade date	Some date before the 'start date'
Start date	1-Jan-11
Maturity date	31-Dec-11
Strike date	USD1,500 (average monthly price)
Reference	Gold price index on Bloomberg
Business days	London, New York
Payment dates	End of month
Settlement	Notional Quantity * (Average Price - Strike Price)
Roll convention	Following
Premium	USD1.00 per troy ounce

To buy this option Rings and Tings pays USD1.2 million:

100,000 ounces x 12 months x USD1.00 premium = USD1.2 million

What does this call option achieve for Rings and Tings?

It gives them the right to buy an ounce of gold for USD1,500.

- Rings and Tings would only exercise this option if it is in-the-money to them, that is, if the price of gold is above USD1,500.

If the average price of gold rises **above** USD1,500 per ounce in any given month in 2011, Rings and Tings would exercise the option because in doing so they would buy gold for USD1,500 per ounce when the market price is higher than this.

- e.g. in a month when the 'average price' of gold is USD1,800 per ounce, Rings and Tings would receive USD30 million: 100,000 ounces * (USD1,800 average price – USD1,500 strike price).

If the average price of gold is **below** USD1,500 per ounce in any given month in 2011, Rings and Tings would **not** exercise the option for that month as they could obtain a better price by buying gold at the current market price.

- e.g. in a month when the 'average price' of gold is USD1,300 per ounce, Rings and Tings would let the option expire worthless because it would be cheaper to buy at the lower market price of USD1,300 per ounce rather than exercising the option to buy at USD1,500 per ounce.

Rings and Tings could subsidize the cost of the above vanilla outright call option on gold by selling another option or a combination of options.

Conclusion

Hedging is about protecting the downside. It is good business sense to suss out adverse scenarios that a company might face and take cautionary steps, thus ensuring survival in a tough market environment. **A decision not to hedge is a hedging decision in itself**. To summarize, you have seen derivatives as used by:

- BBU, a chain of bookshops with FX and interest rate exposures
- You, as a bond investor
- Gashers, a producer of crude oil
- Supersonic Jets, an airline and consumer of jet fuel
- De Boomers, a miner of gold
- Rings & Tings, a jewelry maker and buyer of gold

You can apply the same logic used here to other producers and consumers e.g. of coal, agricultural products (wheat, pork bellies etc), other precious metals (platinum, silver etc) or precious stones (diamonds, rubies etc).

Gold and oil prices are well worth following; they are more likely to come up in interviews than any other commodities. However, if you have the time, you should try to look at a few more commodities, e.g. silver has also enjoyed interesting price movements in recent times.

9

ON THE JOB

If someone asked me to describe a good analyst, I would say they were keen, conscientious, thorough, responsible, thoughtful, hardworking, problem-solving, well-informed, positive and admirable.

TIPS THAT WILL HELP YOU TO HIT THE GROUND RUNNING

Whether you're interning or have found a permanent job, you will definitely find the below useful. I didn't come up with all of them myself; in fact, a lot of these gems came from people who had made it quite far up the chain. When I was an intern, I often asked, "*What is the most valuable advice you could give to someone wanting to survive in investment banking?*" Much of the below was collected from responses to my question. Before that, however, here are my top three rules for high performance:

GOLDEN RULE: check your work thoroughly

SILVER RULE: improve your time management skills

BRONZE RULE: be keen and interested

It's very easy to project disinterest, especially when you're tired, and it's even easier to scope out those who don't really have their heart in it. A key aspect of seeming keen is maintaining a positive attitude. Some of the below will help with signaling your keenness. Very simple changes can help you to create the enthusiastic impression you want: ask questions, smile, do more than is required, and answer questions if you know the answer – you don't need me to tell you what keen and interested behavior looks like. You know.

Treat everyone with respect

Desk assistants, cleaners and café attendants all matter. You have NO idea who can be useful to your career. People are remarkably perceptive of those who think they are better than them because of job function. If you're dismissive towards people who you think will have no impact on your career, you could end up limiting your own chances because, whether you like it or not, you really don't have a clue who those people are. You'll be surprised at the number of times you have a casual chat with someone who you later find out runs a business in your firm.

I know one managing director who keeps all his cards close to his chest but he has a lot of respect for his personal assistant (PA); so much so that before he hires someone he asks the PA what she thinks of the person. She bases her opinion on conversations she's had when leading candidates to meeting rooms, or phone conversations held in setting up interviews. Invariably, those who are chatty and friendly towards her get a better rating. Obviously, negative comments from the PA don't necessarily mean the person won't be hired but, if the manager has some standing reservations and she confirms them, that candidate's chances slip even further.

If you want to advance in banking, decide now that you don't care about rank; treat all people like they matter whether you actually believe it or not.

Be efficient

You're going to have a lot on your plate. To improve your efficiency:

- Create a 'spam' folder and redirect any emails that aren't generally useful to there, e.g. research, news that isn't critical, generic announcements. Poor email management will slow you down and will likely lead to you missing the important messages.
- Preferably, get friends to email you on your personal email rather than via work email. We all have a couple of friends who consistently forward weird and interesting clips. It is fun but it's also distracting.
- Create sub-folders by client or project in your inbox and place emails in the appropriate folder once they have been dealt with. It will make finding things a lot easier later on.
- Create appropriately named folders wherever you keep transaction documents; this will probably be a common team server.
- If you receive attachments by email, immediately save them in the relevant project or transaction folder so the docs are available to the entire deal team. This double-saving will also make documents easier to find when someone needs them again.

Maintain a positive and upbeat attitude

You will meet a lot of aggressive characters in the world of investment banking. Some colleagues will inevitably irk you but it's best to portray a positive, unaffected attitude, even if you feel you've been disrespected.

- Someone bumps into you carelessly?
  - Don't give them the look; smile and say it's okay or apologize if you feel you were in the wrong.
- New person on your aisle?

- o Say hello – I found it shocking how new people were simply ignored by the majority.
- Collecting a job from the print room or your bank's presentation center?
  - o Say hi, and have a brief chat. You will be surprised how helpful people will be towards you and what impressions you are creating.
  - o When I left Goldman, I sent a firm-wide goodbye email out, as that was the culture, and was surprised by some of the responses I got from people I had never worked with but had simply been nice to. I still have those emails.
- Dealing with back office inefficiencies?
  - o Some people treat back office staff with disdain; don't be one of them. Sometimes you will want to scream; suppress it.
  - o I was taking a member of the confirmations team through some errors he'd made and out of nowhere he asked,
    "Heather, how come you never shout at me?"
    "What do you mean?" I asked.
    "Well, whenever someone from front office calls me they always yell at me."
    I was touched; I gave some excuse for my colleagues and carried on.
  - o Trust me, I'm no Mother Teresa, far from it.
- Really annoyed by someone's behavior?
  - o Sleep on it and if you still feel upset about it the next day, seek an audience and tell them why they were out of order.
  - o If you're an intern, let it slide; you don't want to risk not getting that job.
- You find your colleagues talking about another colleague behind her back?
  - o Don't join in, period.

- My last point is really quite revolutionary: *say hello to people*, even if they are senior to you!
  - As a summer intern at Goldman in 2004, I met Peter Weinberg, the CEO of Goldman Sachs International at the time, in the corridor and I greeted him. I had met him at an SEO event previously. He started off by actually *thanking* me for simply saying hi because most people ran in the opposite direction when they saw him.
  - At HSBC, the head of my team mentioned how pleasing it was that I always say good morning when I come in and good night when I leave. Until that point, I didn't even know that I did it.
    - If you're wondering why he bothered to make the point, it's because many people come and go without a word.

If you think most of the above is obvious and is natural to your character, great, you're well ahead of many other people.

Remember names!

People love it when you remember their names; it makes them feel special and important. If you're not naturally good at remembering names, you'll have to use a few tricks:

- Keep a detailed spreadsheet of what everyone you meet looks like and does, both front office and back office staff.
- Make memory-prompting notes on the back of business cards.
- Keep notes on what people tell you about other colleagues. Below are examples from my 2004 notebook:
  - John LG – 'make sure work you do for him is pristine'.

- o Ben H - 'approachable', 'do work for him because he'll influence hire decision'.
- o Ronan – 'will make time for interns'.

For instance, because I was very friendly with people in the Presentations Group (they help you produce good-looking presentations) and I always made the effort to remember their names, I found myself being pushed up the queue when I was in a bind and needed a job rushed through.

Similarly, the guy in the Production Room (they print out client presentations) never forgot the bottle of wine I gave him one Christmas and, if I had a massively urgent job, he would always try his best to meet my deadline. I actually gave him the wine because I had a massive supply from a client and there was no way I could get through it myself, not so I could get favors. Be genuine; people can tell the difference; they don't want to be bought.

Fellow colleagues actually noticed my favored status and tried to take advantage of it, "Heather, you know the guy in Production, right? Could you please put in a word for me?" I don't know why a lot of people can't be bothered to form relationships with back-office staff themselves; leave a positive impression on everyone that comes into contact with you, even if they're not that nice!

I cottoned onto the benefit of remembering names in boarding school in Malawi. I realized that when I called the waiters by name I almost always got more food, whereas I didn't if I called the guy anything else. People always asked me how I managed to have a favored position in the kitchens – I selfishly never told them!

If there is something distinctive about you (e.g. I was usually one of very few black girls) people will remember your name and it will look especially bad if you do not remember theirs.

"Coattails"

It was summer 2005. We were at *B.E.D.* in New York City, enjoying team drinks organized for new hires, when a Goldman VP answered "coattails" to my customary question. I was none the wiser; I had to ask for clarification but you don't have to:

Identify someone on your team that you like working for and who likes you and make sure you do an awesome job for them. As they move up the ranks, they carry you up along with them. Attaching yourself to them will be akin to grabbing onto their coattails and holding tight so that they drag you along wherever they go.

Network, network, network

Cliché: it's not what you know, it's who you know; yeah, yeah, we all know that's important. However, just as important: "**It's not who *you* know, it is *who knows you.***" Impress a few people and they will be raving left, right and center about you. People you don't know will think highly of you before they even meet you. Of course, once you meet such people, they will have high expectations that you need to fulfill but still, a good reputation will help to push you along. I have seen this in action myself.

Impress your managers and they will bring you up in management meetings, compliment you publicly and market you with no extra effort on your part.

Have another read through the tips on 'Networking' in Chapter 2. Most of that advice can be put to work after you secure the job. In addition:

- Find out who does what within your division or across other divisions and ask people out to coffee, lunch or dinner so you can learn more about what they do.

Inviting people to dinner might sound awkward and *it is* unless you're applying to Classic IBD (corporate finance) at a bank that has a canteen. In this case, when you're working late, you can casually ask someone along to the canteen so you can have a chat about what they do.

More often than not, they will be more than happy to; people love to talk about themselves.

- Continue to actively build your cache of contacts. People that know (and like) you will put a good word in for you if someone asks them about you; importantly, even if you don't actively need them, you will be able to reach out to your contacts even after you have left the bank.

Before I started out on my 2004 internship, I obtained contact details for some of the previous year's interns and asked them out to coffee so I could gain an understanding of what I was getting myself into and how I could best place myself to secure a job. I recommend you do the same; people who have just been through an internship still have fresh memories of the key lessons learnt and they can tell you many things a seasoned investment banker has long forgotten.

Avoid being too social or too political

This might sound contradictory to the point on networking but it isn't. You'll notice the social butterflies; every so often they'll be organizing a team night out or team drinks; they never seem to be at their desk, always by someone else's having a chat.

How do others perceive this behavior? That you're compensating for lack of competence. If you are constantly spending time with senior people you'll come off looking like you're too political. Too much schmoozing and people won't like you. More so if you make it blatant.

Sit with the team you're working for

A VP on the trading floor gave me this pointer at the start of my internship at Goldman Sachs and I kept it at the back of mind from the start.

As an intern you'll find that at times there isn't a space for you in the aisle of the team you're doing a project for. This is bad for building relationships. If this is the case, make sure you keep an eye on people going on holiday or business trips so that you can take their seat for the duration they are away. ASK someone on the team before you perch yourself in someone else's space; they'll tell you things you need to know, e.g. don't adjust the height of his chair, he hates it when people do that etc.

This tip is a lot more effective than you might believe. I found myself without a seat near the team I was doing a large project for during my internship. The moment I saw an empty seat, I recalled this piece of advice and seized the opportunity to take the empty desk. By virtue of just sitting in the same row I found I was party to all the jokes, I was invited to lunch when they were going and we all got to know (and like) each other very well. Once you start having laughs and cracking jokes with potential managers, you're half way to a full time offer. Indeed, I ended up choosing to work for this team as a full time hire.

Bond with your team

If your team is going out to a club, a pub or for a team dinner, go for a while even if you don't feel like it.

Girls, if you're on a team with very few other women, you may find that the conversation soon culminates in topics that you either have little knowledge of or simply aren't interested in: sport, women (how hot they are, or not, as the case may be) and perhaps strip clubs. Some people argue that you should read up on these subjects so that you can take part; others suggest you stick to what you like and participate where you can.

As an intern, you might want to read up a little on the apparent interests of your team; whatever the case, be yourself.

Have a couple of drinks and a few laughs, then say your goodbyes whilst everyone is still enjoying your company. This is the strategy I tend to use.

Drink sensibly

You may prefer to get smashed before you consider a night out on the town a good one but your colleagues are still your colleagues and, at least initially, you want to establish a reputation for hard work and focus, not for being a party animal.

Regardless of how late you stay out, go into work at the correct time the following day because everyone will know why you are late if you are. Even if you are really ill, everyone will consider it to be an alcohol-induced illness and not something genuine.

Once you have established your reputation as a smart, hard-working individual, most people won't care too much if you have the odd drunken night out; they may even find it amusing, especially if you've just closed or helped to close a big deal.

Do every job well, no matter how trivial

Small things matter. Your reputation for first-rate work will initially be built on your ability to **do simple tasks well**. No one will trust you with the big and interesting deals if you haven't got the basics down to a T. For instance, as an intern, Equity Syndicate asked me to update an investor list using a variety of databases and to write a brief on how it was done when I was finished. Future interns could use the brief to do the same task without further explanation from anyone else. It was a mundane and boring task but, rather than rushing, I did it well and polished the job off with an over-the-top PowerPoint presentation which very comprehensively but briefly explained the process. I sent it off at an ungodly hour and it so impressed the Head of Syndicate that our relationship was pretty much a signed deal after that and she turned out to be a very helpful informal mentor to me. Ultimately, I ended up choosing to work for another team but, based on outperformance on such a simple task, this became one of my options.

Three years later when I left GS, the same Head of Equity Syndicate left to head up a similar team at another firm and she asked me if I'd be interested in moving there. I had only been at HSBC for a month so I said no because I didn't want to tarnish my loyalty card but it goes to show that small and seemingly inconsequential tasks can set forth a trajectory of career-enhancing goodwill. You get only one chance to make a first impression; make sure it's a good one.

Another story comes to mind. As an intern at Goldman, I was given a research project to find out whatever I could about infrastructure funds. This was my big project for the summer. I got the feeling that my VP didn't think I was taking it seriously because, every time he asked me how it was going, I said it was okay but that I hadn't finished it because I was working on something that was 'urgent'. I asked a few questions about what was expected in the presentation at the outset then, over weekends, fleshed out a hefty presentation on every infrastructure fund that I could dig up, no matter how obscure.

A few weeks later, I walked up to the VP and handed him my PowerPoint book. It was detailed and neatly presented. He flipped through this monstrosity, mouth quite literally agape, and told me to take it straight up to the head of the team because it was excellent work. I ended up as a full time hire on this team. When I joined a year later, they were still using a good portion of my slides in management presentations.

Lesson: if you're not able to consistently work on a project, give the team regular updates on progress anyway. I was very lucky to have produced a good job in this case, but if it had been rubbish, it would simply have confirmed the VP's initial thoughts that I wasn't taking it seriously.

Ask for more work (but not too much!)

Say what? To create a reputation for yourself as someone who never shies away from work, always work at your capacity or just beyond. If you feel that you can handle more work, you should definitely go to whoever's responsible for your workload (the 'staffer' if you're in corporate finance, your manager if you're in the capital markets) and ask for more.

Asking for extra work a) makes you look keen, b) makes you look hard-working and c) ensures you are constantly exposed to new people who you can learn something new from. If your staffer says he doesn't have any new projects for you, you can go home earlier than usual without feeling guilty.

I used this strategy myself as a young intern and, based on how available I made myself for more work, by the end of the internship I was pretty sure that Dirk (my staffer) would try his best to ensure I had a job.

Obviously, working beyond your capacity isn't sustainable for the long haul but, once your rep has been cemented, you can ease back a little to working at your capacity. Importantly, if you take on too many projects you'll find yourself doing less than a sterling job on all of them. Don't spread yourself too thin.

Potential Problem: each time you ask how you can help, everyone on your team says there's nothing outstanding or they always give you the *menial* tasks: digging up annual reports, research reports and random data. At times, people can't be bothered to explain something to a junior or an intern; explaining the work and waiting for it to get done may take longer than just doing it themselves. If you get this sort of response, ask people to take you through what they are working on instead.

Example approaches: Fabiana is an Associate. She's highly rated by the managers and you want to work with her so that she can give you a rave review at the end of your internship.

- "Fabiana, could you spend some time explaining the product you're pricing up? I really want to understand derivatives a little better."
- "Fabiana, although you don't need any help at the moment, do you mind if I sit next to you and watch what you're doing to see what I can pick up?"

  It's very hard to have someone sitting right next to you and not explain what you're doing so, although you'll have requested to just sit there and watch, you'll find Fabiana explaining what she's doing as she goes along.

Be the first in and the last out

I love my sleep but when it comes to investment banking, trust me, until you've built up some sort of a rep, face-time matters. Even if you can do the same amount of work within ten hours, it's better to stretch it to twelve (or more). Keeping long hours gives the impression that you're keen, hard-working and tenacious.

You know you're working enough hours when people start cracking jokes about you crawling under your desk for the night.

Be a team player

People can very quickly smell out those who are only out for themselves. If you want to survive at the likes of Goldman Sachs you need to be really hungry to succeed, but also keen to take the team along with you.

Someone who interned the year before I did told me this tasty little tip: the group emails that are set up by HR so that interns can blast out email messages to one another often also have HR officials as part of the group. Therefore, if you find a useful presentation or gain some other knowledge that could help others, by emailing this out to the intern group, you are unknowingly informing HR that you are a team player and you are out to help others. Don't overdo it though; there is a thin line between being a helpful informant and being a spammer; you don't want to cross it.

Needless to say, as an intern I made it a point to share all things useful with my fellow interns; I am the collaborative sort anyway so I would always have done so. However, had I not known that the preset group emails contained HR contact, I might have chosen to share info via a less career-enhancing format, e.g. printing slides out for people or verbal communication.

Work weekends even if you don't have to

Lots of bankers in corporate finance choose to work a little on weekends so this is a great time to signal your enthusiasm.

You don't have to say anything to highlight your presence; just go to the office and do a couple of hours of work, ensuring you walk up and down the office floor so that anyone who's in catches a glimpse of you. This isn't sneaky at all; to get ahead in banking you so definitely need to big yourself up in subtle and not so subtle ways. Shrinking violets find it tough to progress in front office roles because the real keen beans are so aggressively marketing their efforts.

If you don't have any actual project work, review all the concepts that you didn't fully understand in the week. This can be done at home but it is more career-enhancing if done in the office. Your colleagues can't see you working from home.

The more relaxed tone of the weekend also makes this an opportune time to network with people who would otherwise be too busy in the week. Keep in mind this is their free time though; you don't want to be annoying.

Toot your own horn

Exceptional work and results have a nasty habit of not speaking for themselves. If you don't let your managers know what an awesome job you are doing, they might not notice. Men tend to be very good at this but many an article has highlighted that women tend to be awful at 'bigging' themselves up. If you don't take credit for your work, someone else will, trust me.

If you close a transaction or a trade, make sure you are the first to tell your manager; send him an email if he isn't immediately available. Tell him how the bank has benefitted and how long you were working on that transaction for. You don't want your managers forgetting how hard you are working.

Picture this scenario: you transact a piece of business that earns your team a good amount of money, then your team-mate, let's call him Ned, meets your manager and says, "We just traded an interest rate swap with Blissful Books

United. That's a buck for the team's P and L." What does your manager think? That Ned just earned the team a million dollars (that's a buck in banker lingo) and that Ned is a real team player because rather than saying 'I', he used the more magnanimous 'we'. By the time you get to tell your manager about the transaction, his excitement has already waned. Ned has taken the feel-good factor that **you** should have given your manager and used it to promote himself. You see where I'm going with this?

You need to constantly tell your manager(s) what you have done, otherwise they might never know! This is even more important if you are trying your best but your till just isn't ringing.

Make a point of asking intelligent questions...even if you know the answer!

People like to say that there is no such thing as a dumb question but trust me, there is – you should do enough reading and research on banking to be able to differentiate smart questions from the dumb ones.

With Google out to help you, there really is no excuse for asking basic questions. Before you ask anything decide whether it's something that would best be Googled, otherwise you might be exposing yourself as an ignoramus.

Asking no questions at all makes you look uninterested. It's probably worse than asking trivial questions because you might go unnoticed.

At the end of an internship period or an interview day, a panel sits down to debate all the candidates. Asking sharp questions will help people to remember you.

As a full-time employee, you have about six months during which people will give you the benefit of the doubt for asking basic questions. Ask as much as possible at the start otherwise you will make avoidable errors.

Take notes

Most people find it annoying to be asked the same question twice by the same person. In your first few days on the job, you will be inundated with new information. Even if you are well-prepared with technical knowledge, every bank has its own systems, compliance procedures, firm-specific macros and formatting styles for presentation-making and building models. You're bound to forget stuff. The only way to avoid looking the fool by asking for second explanations is to take comprehensive notes.

You may find that you barely have time to look over the notes again, however the very act of writing reinforces the information.

Take a notebook with you to every meeting, even if it's in a café. That said, make sure you are also contributing to the discussion where you can; don't *just* write the whole time.

Keep a list of all the areas you want to understand better and work on them during evenings and weekends.

Take your calculator with you everywhere

Every now and again you'll be in a meeting and a VP or an MD needs to make a calculation. It will look good if you have a calculator, so make a habit of taking one everywhere, along with your notebook and pen.

Get to grips with all the technical skills ASAP

Are you one of those people that types into the Google search engine field then grabs your mouse to hit the search button? Then I'm probably talking to you. Hardcore bankers look down upon those who are not up-to-date with short cuts in spreadsheets and the word processing tools.

You will achieve things faster if you use keyboard short cuts. My IBD training emphasized this point. Ever since then, I've always been conscious of the fact that it looks bad to be using the mouse for everything and indeed, every good analyst I know (myself included) is an Excel shortcut whizz. It really does save a lot of time.

In addition to the basic tools, every team has team-specific software, e.g. for pricing products, calculating risk and so on. Work on mastering the systems from day one and figure them out quickly.

Managers will be more comfortable to have you on their projects if they think you have achieved a good degree of competence with the core tools that your team uses.

Two things you will want to add to your cache of habits:

- Hit the 'save' function as frequently as you blink.
- Never **ever** 'replace all', it can only lead to regret. Rather, find all the words you want to replace one by one.

Don't do 'cliques'

Throw a bunch of prospective interns together and in no time people drift towards people like themselves. I found that these divides were usually according to country of origin or university. The French hang out with the French, the Italians with the Italians, the Nigerians with the Nigerians, the non-Nigerian Africans with the Nigerians (because they were probably the only representative of their country) the Harvard grads with fellow Harvardians and so forth.

It obviously makes sense that people prefer to stick to their comfort zone but you are only going to open doors for your career by making connections with people from a diverse range of backgrounds.

By establishing yourself as part of a clique, you may be making it difficult for other people to approach you.

Achieve go-to status for something

"There are two interns on my team but everyone keeps on giving me all the work," a girl I was mentoring complained.

"That's a good thing," I told her. People only give work to those interns who can handle it. Less work does not mean you're liked more; if anything the opposite is true. If you work well, expect to get plenty more.

Develop your skills by asking people who know more than you lots of questions. For example, people on the Presentation Team know a lot about PowerPoint or Word Processing, whatever program your firm uses, so tap into their expertise. People will notice what you're good at and will start coming to you for help.

If you're facing a problem with an application, e.g. the page numbering has gone all funny or due to section breaks your formats are incongruous or whatever, you can either send your work off to your Presentation Team (if your bank has one) or you can call them up and have someone guide you through the solution. You'll learn a lot more with the latter method.

Find your niche, whatever it is. Just ensure that you are extremely good at something.

Don't bring any negative attention to yourself

Don't gossip or spread rumors; people will stop trusting you. If you've been included on an email you would rather not be part of, ignore it, or reply (don't 'reply all') to the sender and ask to be removed from the list.

Don't originate emails that you wouldn't want to see on the front page of a newspaper: funny or humiliating emails go viral; interns have gone from obscurity to household name in hours. Do something silly and you could find yourself having to change your name to progress beyond the incident!

Case in point: in 2007, an intern at a big bank sent her friends an invitation to her party at the Ritz, dogmatically dictating everything from what they should wear to how they should respond when greeted at the door. She was not only the laughing the stock of The City; t-shirts and mugs with her quotes were on the market a mere two to three days later. Four years on, I still remember her name like it all happened yesterday, but I'll keep it to myself. Her wealthy family must have paid a fortune to have the incident removed from the internet because I can't find a single reference; unfortunately, they can't erase memories.

Under-promise and over-deliver on all work you do

It creates the impression that you are over-achieving and all managers love over-achieving employees. You can over deliver on the quality of your work as well as expected timing.

Know all the latest news

I might come off sounding high and mighty in some of the above but I actually had to learn some of these lessons the hard way.

- As a fresh intern at Goldman, I was seeking out mentors and happened upon Dambisa Moyo. She was from Malawi's neighbor, Zambia, and was therefore immediately attractive for me to talk to. We were the only ones from our region of Africa.

- I went to her desk on the trading floor and after a few moments of small talk she took me straight to the deep end and started asking me questions on the price of oil and the trend in the price over the last week.

- I hadn't looked at oil in at least a week so I gave a very approximate answer. She could clearly see I wasn't very comfortable so she told me to make sure every hour or so I typed 'TOP' into Bloomberg to catch up on the latest news. She said my peers were earning lots of "free brownie points" just by keeping up-to-date with news and I shouldn't lose out.

- I nodded and thought, *Damn, I know who I'm not visiting again*, at which point she said if I didn't come back she would come to find me!

Never act the junior

One of the most enjoyable aspects of banking is the amount of responsibility that will be handed to you very early on; it's also one of the scariest.

As a debut analyst, I was fortunate enough to be with a team that was happy to give me all manner of exposure, but at times I thought I was 'too junior' for the tasks and I would say so. One day, my VP took me aside and said, "Enough of this *I think I'm too junior* rubbish, I only give you tasks I think you are capable of and, even if you think you might be too junior, you have to step up to the plate. You're not going to develop if you keep on doing the same things." Gulp. Until he brought it up, I hadn't even realized I had in fact said this a number of times but from that moment on, I never said it again.

No matter how confident and go-getting you are, you will find yourself given tasks which challenge you and stretch you out of your comfort zone. No doubt you'll feel nervous about doing very new or complicated jobs, taking on risk on behalf of your bank; it's natural; it means you care about getting it right. You'll get less anxious the more you get used to it. The best response is to say you can do it and do the best you can. It goes without saying that if you need help, ask for it!

If your manager jokingly tries to 'scare' you with presenting at a meeting, call his bluff and say, "Yes, I am more than happy to present."

If you're going to a meeting with someone senior and you expect them to be presenting, prepare yourself anyway because they could surprise you and ask you to do the presenting at the last minute, e.g. when you're outside the client's office about to go in.

Auto-send emails out later than you've worked

Now, I think this is mischievous, and I have never actually done this myself, but as I'm telling it like it is I will tell it to you anyway. Some emailing software allows you to set the time at which an email should be sent.

I know some people who left work at 10:00 p.m. but set their emails to go to the sender in the early hours of the morning.

If you're persistently 'working late' but the volume of work you produce is small in comparison, you're just going to look inefficient so if you are going to do this at all, don't do it too often. Obviously, if the email you are sending is going to a client, they won't know anything about your workload so, contrary to looking inefficient, you'll just look very busy.

What I think is much better and more honest is to hold off sending emails until just before you leave. An additional benefit of drafting all your emails for the evening and sending them out in one go is that you might buy yourself a few more hours of sleep. If you send an email out at 8:00 p.m., there is every likelihood that your manager will read it before you've left for the day and ask you to do more work. That possibility falls with every passing hour.

Facebook and other social networks!

How do you use your Facebook? Most people use it as a casual social network; you may be tagged in embarrassing photos, you may put up status updates that you wouldn't care to share with work colleagues, so perhaps it is better not to 'Friend' work colleagues. You need to maintain their respect.

Now that Facebook allows varying levels of 'friendship', if you do accept colleagues limit their access to your profile and your posts. That said, my personal recommendation is to keep colleagues off Facebook. Rather get LinkedIn with them. It's a more formal environment and is less likely to lead to a career-limiting move.

And Twitter? Every tweet is public. Just before you tweet, think about whether you'd be proud to see your tweet on the front cover of the WSJ or the FT. Angry? Don't send that tweet. You'll only regret it later.

Fact: many employers now Google the name of prospective employees before hiring them. Will they like what they find out about you?

Figure out your bank and your team's culture on all things and conform

People have an affinity for people who are like them, so the more your team views your character as 'one of them' the easier it is to get along with them and progress. Figure out how your character can best complement your setting.

One of my favorite quotes: "The reward for conformity is that everyone likes you except yourself" ~ Rita Mae Brown. I'm not recommending a 360 degree character change here, more a realignment.

A final note

Complying with investment banking's conservative code of conduct does not mean you're not being true to yourself. Many people take a more professional attitude on all issues at work, but may hold a completely different stance in their home environment. One day as a bushy-tailed analyst, my mouth dropped when a highly respected and quite serious MD with four kids pranced into the office wearing distressed jeans, a crazy shirt and with his hair gelled up all crazy-like; he was off to a family holiday and had left their tickets at work. It was kind of a pivotal moment for me because it confirmed that your home life and your work life don't have to bear any resemblance to each other: keep that in mind.

Bankers dress smartly because they are providing financial **advice or suggestions** to clients. I don't know about you, but if my banker (or my surgeon) walked into the room in sandals, adorned with a nose ring and tattoos, I'd have second thoughts about the quality of advice I was getting.

PERSONAL HABITS TO WATCH OUT FOR

Much of the below may seem obvious but I'll tell it to you anyway as it might not be obvious to everyone.

- Basic hygiene is important:
  - Shower every morning.
  - Brush your teeth every morning (at least!). I had a colleague who had a bad case of halitosis and nobody told him, yet people continually discussed the issue behind his back.
  - Wear a fresh shirt daily even if yesterday's one looks and smells clean.
  - If you have to do an all-nighter, go to the gym (if your firm has one) and ask to use the showers.
- Don't eat, drink or chew gum when you talk on the phone.
- Try not to get into people's personal space, e.g. standing too close; it makes them feel uncomfortable.
- Don't slurp your tea or your soup; it sounds horrible. I sat next to a serial 'slurper' for a couple of years and I was never able to bring myself to tell him; I just tolerated it.
- Give yourself a limit on personal internet surfing. As a guideline, a total of 15 to 30 minutes in a day should be more than enough.
- Remember your bank records ALL the websites you visit.
- Use the chat rooms sensibly. Reuters and Bloomberg chat, and perhaps firm-specific messaging software, should be available in almost every bank especially on the trading floors. These are designed for business purposes.
  - Someone I know was called up to Human Resources when a random search of the firms' chat rooms picked up negative material from his conversations.
  - When he walked into the office, two HR officials were sitting there with a three-inch thick pile of all his chats. Everything inappropriate had already been highlighted yellow.

- o He realized how much doo-doo he'd landed himself in when a few of his writings were read back to him: cuss words, derogatory comments about women and the like. All he could say was, "If I resign will all this go away?"
- o HR said yes so he resigned on the spot.
- o In terms of intelligence, respect and ability to work hard, the guy was probably in the top 1% at the firm so he went on to do well. However, this is a good example of how careless chatter could damage a good career in a specific firm.
- o If, in ten or twenty years time he decides to go for a more public career, e.g. in politics, this is the sort of stuff journalists will be looking to find out.
- Act out the level you want to reach, e.g. if you want to make it to Managing Director, behave a little like one from the start (but don't forget where you lie in the food chain).

Dress Sense

- If you'll be meeting clients that day, Chapter 3/Interview Dress Code applies even if you have met that particular client before.
- On an on-going basis, office dress sense has become more smart-casual rather than business; as a new hire it might be wise to err on the side of caution and dress as well as you can. If you observe that it is acceptable to dress down a little then you can tone it down.
- Boys, people will notice if you always wear a tie because nowadays most people wear them exclusively when they have a client appointment. Besides looking smart, ties make you look important.

EMAIL ETIQUETTE!

Don't base your standards on other people's shabby emails. Nowadays, people use text language so often it is rapidly seeping into emails. Is it really easier to write 'u' rather than 'you'? It's outright laziness and the recipient of your email is going to think exactly that. Here are Girl Banker®'s top tips:

Put in a subject, especially if you want that email to actually be read

People are bombarded with a multitude of emails on a daily basis. Putting an appropriate title in the subject box helps them to sort through emails. Emails without a subject just make you look downright sloppy, there's no two ways about it.

Use polite language

It's very easy to come off as rude on an email so be careful you use the appropriate language. If the person you're writing to has irked you, hold off, and send that email when you're calmer; you'll only regret venting via email later.

Sign off using proper words

Following on from the usage of text language, shortcuts like BR for best regards, KR for kind regards, Tx or Tks for thanks just shouldn't happen. Yes you're going to be busy but not so busy that you can't spare an extra millisecond to sign your email off properly.

Do not ever put Xs on client emails

So you get along with the client, they're your friend, but remember they are still a client of the bank and XXXs on your email are just going to look weird. Even if it's your style to do this, it's not appropriate in a client email. It might make the client feel awkward.

Watch out with the email extras

Different people have different standards; some have stricter perceptions than others and if you are an intern or new to a job go for the most formal approach.

Smiley face: personally, I think a smiley face is okay, especially if a client has made a joke at your expense. If they are teasing you, it just confirms that you're cool with the joke, no offence taken; however, do think about whether it's really appropriate.

Informal language: a client once noted a mistake I had made in an analysis and in my response, I started off with an 'oops'. If I'd known better I wouldn't have; my manager came down on me like a ton of bricks – "How can you write *oops* in an email to the treasurer of a FTSE100 company...are you crazy?" and so on and so forth. I thought I had built enough bridges with the client and incidentally, at the end of the year in a third party survey, that client was the one who raved the most about me. So only you can judge whether it is okay to use a little informal language. If a manager berates you for something, even if you think what you've done is not out of line, just apologize. I still think oops is okay as a word but that's just me.

It's okay to ask someone to check an email through for you

When you first start dealing with clients, you might be unsure as to whether your writing has been formulated well enough for the audience; nobody is going to judge you negatively for asking them to check an email. It always helps to get a second opinion.

DEALING WITH TIREDNESS

As an analyst you're going to be working harder than you have ever worked. This is one of the challenges I was actually looking forward to because I wanted to see the extent to which I could be stretched and boy, was I stretched.

Given that their days are longer, the below tips are more relevant for corporate finance analysts than for those who work in the markets.

Lose the siesta mentality

As an intern, I realized that I needed to wean myself off afternoon naps: a routine I had had since high school. I was in the habit of having a 10 to 30 minute rest after lunch because it helped me work better in the afternoon. If you're thinking, "What impact can ten minutes have?" you'd be surprised. Anyway, the whole siesta thing wasn't going to go down in banking so, when I went back for my last year of university, I killed the catnaps and eventually stopped needing them as much.

Einstein, Winston Churchill, Margaret Thatcher, Bill Clinton, Napoleon and a large section of the Chinese population are widely known to be big proponents of the efficiency benefits derived from a few minutes of shuteye after lunch but it's not (currently) banking culture.

Hope your bank has clean toilets

I didn't come up with this one myself. I was telling a friend how I was struggling to stay awake on some days and he told me that every now and again he goes to the toilet, puts the toilet lid down and has a nap. He sets his phone alarm for fifteen minutes for fear that he might over sleep. A fifteen minute disappearance is just about the right amount of time before your colleagues begin to wonder where you are.

If you're thinking there is no way you could get comfortable enough to sleep on a non-domestic toilet, just you wait.

Take a quick walk outside for fresh air

Most office buildings nowadays are air-conditioned environments without windows; a quick walk outside might be all you need to rejuvenate your brain. This is especially useful if you've just had a super-intense couple of hours to complete a presentation or execute a trade.

Join a gym

Nothing works better than a good run on the treadmill when you're feeling tired and stressed. As a new analyst, I would not recommend going to the gym in the middle of the day even if other people on your team do so.

In corporate finance, the MDs and most VPs disappear home around early evening; that's likely to be the best time to go. After your workout, the next few hours of work will just slide by.

If you're in markets, go when your day is through because quite honestly you're not going to be able to go any other time.

Hydrate´

Some research suggests that even small amounts of dehydration reduce cognitive performance significantly and might increase 'stress hormones'. Water, tea, coffee and Coke (that's Coca Cola, just to be clear) all help to wake you up.

One of my VPs who worked analyst hours started his day with a can of coke without fail. I thought that was too early and so did his wife, so he told me not to bring it up when I met her.

Most people keep a bottle of water at their desk and drink a bit throughout the day. I used to fill the same bottle of water up at the water fountain every day to save the environment (and a buck).

Strange but true: I found that if I had two to three glasses of warm water in one go as soon as I woke up I felt more alert and awake. If you're going to try this, I recommend you have the water an hour before you leave the house or else you could be faced with quite an embarrassing accident en route.

Avoid large, hot lunches

They will make you feel sleepy. In fact, whilst we're on the issue of food, I strongly recommend that upon embarking on an investment banking career you slash your food consumption by at least 25%. As part and parcel of working, you will find that you don't do as much physical activity as before.

Track your weight from the moment you start investment banking so that you catch weight gain in the early stages. You can use my Fat Creep™ weight tracker app on iPhone and Android to help you keep on track (fatcreep.com).

Finally...don't do drugs

I have heard some rumors that bankers are known to take drugs to help them cope with the stress and the hours, but that must have been back in the day. Hand on heart, I have seen zero evidence of this in my time. I can't even pinpoint one person that I would suspect as being a drug user. It's not worth it.

10

GIRL BANKER®'S INSIGHTS

ON HANDLING MONEY

Just because you're an investment banker, it doesn't mean you're astute at managing your own money. I would go as far as saying that the vast majority of bankers I know either don't care or haven't got a clue about such mundane things as saving. Your expenditure has a very funny way of expanding at the rate of your income, if not faster. One minute, a good meal out involves consuming a sandwich you didn't have to make yourself; the next, you upgrade yourself to Nando's (£10/$15 all-in) and before you know it, it takes a couple of Michelin stars before you're excited about a meal out and all your meals are at the likes of L'Atelier de Joël Robuchon.

Between graduation and starting my full time analyst job, I had three to four weeks to kill. I made a conscious decision to find out more about money management. I perused the local bookstore and happened upon:

- *The Richest Man in Babylon* by George S. Clason
- *A Girl's Best Friend is Her Money* by Jasmine Birtles and Jane Mack
- *The Millionaire Next Door* by Thomas J. Stanley, Ph.D and William D. Danko, Ph.D

I found a soft patch of grass under a large tree and enjoyed the May Bumps (a bunch of ripped guys rowing) as I read my books. These three books shaped a lot of my initial views on the best way to look after money. I've reread *The Richest Man in Babylon* a couple of times since.

By the time my first pay check arrived, I had less than £100 to my name but zero debt: a fantastic position to be in considering how much student debt many of my friends carried (a full scholarship paid for my university education). From day one, I saved every month; by the end of the first year I was still sitting on a third of the disposable income I had earned in that year. Mortgages of 95% to 110% LTV were being thrown at people so I took advantage of this cheap credit and went property shopping. I added the savings to my bonus, bought my first property and started a small equity portfolio.

Chatting to friends and colleagues, I learnt that most were not saving and all of them were not even thinking about buying property. Tons of people live like they are going to earn at an exponential rate forever. For some, by the time the annual bonus arrives, all their accounts are in arrears and their credit cards are maxed out. I couldn't live with that pressure.

Amongst the reasons people gave for not saving or investing were:

- "Property's overvalued so I'm waiting for the market to crash."
  - o I decided that I wanted to buy something for the long-term so short-term falls in value didn't worry me. To date, the value of my first property is still up 30% from when I bought it in 2006. Even if it was down, I would be happy with the investment because I bought in a fabulous area where the rental market is buoyant.
- "I don't earn enough to save. By the time my bonus arrived I had £10,000 in debt."
  - o Say what?
- "I can't afford to buy anywhere."

- o Your first property investment doesn't have to be in the 'poshest' neighborhood there is. The most expensive areas aren't necessarily going to give you the hottest return. Importantly, liquidity could be lower for high-end properties because fewer people can afford them.

I have one friend whose only memorable purchase from her first bonus of £40,000 (£24,000 after UK tax) is a £6,000 couch and a big holiday in Miami. Another friend spent £7,000 at a club in one night (!) because he needed to make himself feel happy – I cannot confirm if happiness was forthcoming following the splurge.

What's the point of all these stories? If you don't want your own actions to be overly influenced by the views of others, do your own research, set your views and stick to them. Don't be ashamed to suggest going Dutch (i.e. only paying for what you have consumed[20]). If you don't, prepare to be splitting the bill for bottles of Dom Perignon that you don't even want to drink.

---

[20] Note that although many people nowadays use the term "Going Dutch" to mean splitting the bill equally, in strict usage it actually means paying your *own* expenses. I learnt this on a trip to the Netherlands.

ON BEING FROM AN ETHNIC MINORITY

One of the things that helped me to blend in: I didn't realize being black was really that different.

I'll explain. My sister went to an American university after having been born and bred in Malawi, Africa. She says that for the first month there she went through an emotional process that she believes many African Americans go through all their lives and it was "traumatizing." What happened? She says that she felt as though a lot of the white people were tip-toeing around her and behaving as though they weren't sure how to act. Her perception was that they had grown up in parts of the States where they had never had to interact with people who looked different from themselves and they plain simply did not *know* how to act. It was then that she realized, "Oh my God; when people look at me the first thing they see is the fact that I am black and with that comes a whole host of prejudices and preconceptions that they will associate with me before they know anything about me."

I am lucky to have not had to go through this. Cambridge University in Great Britain is sub divided into 31 colleges and each college has students reading different subjects. In my college, in my year there were 12 Economists: seven boys, five girls. The boys: three English, three first generation English Indians, one first generation English Bangladeshi; the girls: one English, one first generation English German, one Malawian, one mixed race (English/Sudanese). It's very difficult to feel different in such a multi racial group. I think my year was a bit of a cultural experiment but it worked well. We were all very cliquey with each other and, post graduating, we still meet up two or three times a year. If I had joined in a previous year, I may have had problems integrating because they were not that multiracial or multicultural.

At Goldman Sachs, I interviewed with many different teams but ended up working on a team where the one time we did a tally we totaled 21 people from 18 different countries. I joined the team because I thought it was the most challenging of all the teams I had gotten to know. Subconsciously, I may have gelled better with this team because of its diversity.

Final point: The worst thought to hold in your head is that the world is against you because you're in some way different: it's you against the world. If you do, you'll see opposition to your progress even where there is none. Your default assumption should be that no one is racist. Develop the mentality that there are opportunities everywhere and, even when someone is blatantly trying to pull you down, ignore it. Smile, wink and work harder; make it impossible to get a rise out of you; trust me, people will try.

ON BEING A GIRL

This is just my opinion so you don't need to agree with it.

A senior female banker once told me that when she first started out in banking, she felt as though all the women were trying their utmost to act like men so that they could be accepted in the male-dominated environment. She found that a little off-putting and she thinks it's perfectly acceptable to be feminine. I agree, especially nowadays when the corporate world has officially accepted that women do have a role to play in business. However, if you are trying to create a reputation for yourself as being equal to or better than the boys, don't let them treat you differently just because you're a girl. At the same time, let's not discourage gentlemanly behavior if the situation befits it.

Stuck in a rut? You may be able to draw inspiration from the following:

The Glass Hammer (theglasshammer.com)

The Glass Hammer is an award-winning blog and online community created for women executives in finance, law, technology and big business.

Women in Banking and Finance (wibf.org.uk)

WIBF is a not-for-profit organization that works towards empowering women to progress in finance-related careers by holding seminars on issues of interest and by providing access to coaching.

The Female Capitalist™ (christinebrown-quinn.com)

Christine is author of *Step Aside Super Woman: Career and Family is for Any Woman*. With two decades in finance, she knows what she's talking about.

Success Strategies for Professional Women (jacquelinefrost.com)

I have attended a talk hosted by Jacqueline Frost and she definitely has a unique point of view that you could benefit from.

308

There remain many teams in investment banks that do not have a single woman; this is especially true amongst client-facing teams where the only woman will be the desk assistant, if that. Many people do not realize this because the reality is blurred by statistics that include back and middle office staff who are frequently women. Some women are turned off by guys-only teams; they don't want to have to deal with the situation. DO NOT be intimidated; this may have happened by default rather than by design. A team you want to join may well be open to recruiting women.

I have met the odd person that thinks women shouldn't working in banking but these types are few and far between and they are most definitely in decline.

ON LAWSUITS

Okay, what I'm about to say is going to be controversial. I think suing your company for wrongdoing should be the very, *very* last resort. It should not be used as a get-rich-quick scheme. Yes, I just said that. If you are having problems speak to Human Resources or your manager. If that doesn't work out, leave; there are plenty of other jobs out there, although it currently doesn't seem that way.

There's been a lot of press on high profile lawsuits and I think this has negatively impacted the future of women in banking. In fact, I know it has. For instance, I heard a senior banker talking about how a senior female banker wanted to change teams and the head of the team she wanted to join had told him that he's scared of landing himself with a libel suit so he didn't want any women on his team. I am not joking. This was actually the first time I paused to think about how bad all these lawsuits are going to be for women.

Importantly, it really does spoil the reputation of your bank. When I was applying for internships in late 2004, there were several stories about women bankers suing a 'Big Bank'. As a consequence, I did not submit an application to the bank. I didn't even look into applying there; I just thought to myself, *I can't be dealing with all of that.*

ON RESIGNING

So you've decided to progress your career elsewhere. If you have a good relationship with your manager and know he wants to keep you, resigning will be painful, very painful. If you can't wait to see the back of him, it will be substantially less so. A few rules to follow:

Before you hand in your notice, be clear about whether you are really resigning

- Many people use the threat of leaving in order to up their benefits through a counter-offer to their new package. Ideally, such people really do have a new job lined up, otherwise it's a high-risk strategy. Your manager could call your bluff and accept the resignation without resistance.

- If you are open to staying under better conditions, *negotiate objectively*. If you definitely want to leave, graciously state that your mind is set and don't even go into that sort of discussion.

Be polite

- Whether or not you're best friends with your manager, you might need him in the future so being rude is simply not worth it.

- Your manager will have some influence outside your bank; people are very likely to ask him about you even after you leave. You don't want to negatively influence his feedback with a rude resignation.

Be brief

- Your resignation letter will be on file for eternity. Don't write anything you could later regret. Be straightforward and professional.

- It's possible that in the future you will want to return to the bank in a new capacity and you could reduce your chances with a tasteless resignation on file.

Set up a meeting, desk pre-cleared, letter in hand

- It's most likely that after you resign you will be asked to vacate the building immediately: investment banks don't want any insider information leaking and they want you to forget as much as possible about their processes before you start your new job.
- If there are any personal items in and around your desk that you don't want to leave, make sure they have already been removed.
- It's illegal to take bank property so leave that.
- The best place to resign is in a private meeting room: set up a meeting with your manager, book a room and resign face-to-face.
- It's much better to have your resignation letter written and printed. If you don't, your resignation could be twisted to appear as if you were fired. It's shocking how things can be distorted.

Write and print your resignation letter at home!

- A colleague of mine printed his resignation letter at work and I found it on the printer. We were the only ones on the team working that Saturday.
- I tried to keep it to myself, but it was too juicy a secret to keep, so on the Monday I told one of my friends on the team.
- He kept it to himself for a while but the moment the guy resigning told him he was leaving he could not resist smugly telling him he already knew because I had told him. "How?" the colleague asked. "I made sure I removed every paper the moment I printed it!" Obviously not quickly enough.
- If news of your resignation leaks, the chances are you might not be able to execute your departure in the way you planned. In my above example, the person I told didn't do anything perverse with the knowledge but some people would.
- Print resignation letters off on neutral ground: your house, your local library or a close friend or relative's house.

Don't tell more people than you need to tell

- If you haven't signed your new contract yet, you shouldn't reveal where you are intending to go. The fewer the people that know, the better.

- If you *have* signed your new contract, the job is written in stone but it will be a month, three months or maybe even more, before you start. By telling people who your new employer will be, there is a chance they could speak to people on your new team before you join, thereby creating a first impression of you, *for you*.

- You've heard the saying: 'It's a small world,' right? The world of banking is even smaller – tiny, in fact. My recommendation: no one needs to know where you're going until you actually start the new job. This will give you a chance to build up your own reputation.

RESOURCES

The resources below are your friends:

Investopedia.com

- For financial definitions.
- They have a couple of paperback definition books out. If you want a physical copy of a financial dictionary get one.

Bloomberg Markets Magazine

- Has a very good range of stories; most slant towards a business-related theme. This is one of my favorite magazines and because it's only published once a month, it is feasible to go through every one, cover to cover. I am a huge Bloomberg fan, if there ever was one!
- If you're debating between this and The Economist, get this.

Bloomberg's iPhone app

- Is free and has most of the free data you would need in preparing for interviews.
- My only qualms are that there is no swap data at all and historical data is only provided for equity indices. Not a problem: there are plenty of historical charts online for currency, commodities, rates etc.

The Economist

- My favorite section is the Politics and Business summary right at the front. It gives a rundown of the entire week's important news.

Newspapers and news sites

- The Financial Times (The FT).
- The Wall Street Journal.

- City A.M. (in London). It's free and it tends to have a very good summary of financial and political news.
- New York Times Deal Book (dealbook.nytimes.com): a formal source of information on current investment banking deals.
- Dealbreaker.com – provides news and commentary on current trends in investment banking. They apparently get tipped by insiders. I wouldn't quote dealbreaker.com in an interview though; some bankers love it others hate it and you won't know whether your interviewer is for or against.

Sign up to daily newsletters. Personally, I almost never buy newspapers. What's the point when there's so much free news available online and elsewhere?

Wikipedia.org

- Is actually not bad at all as a starting point for many concepts.
- I might be criticized for recommending a site that anyone can update but frankly, with the knowledge I already have, I read through a lot of Wiki pages to check whether the site is worth recommending and came out happy that a lot of the information was accurate.
- If in doubt, cross-check the information with other sources; lots of Wiki articles are well-sourced with citations noted so you can check out where they're getting the information from.
- Some information is dated, so check it's current.

Tweeters

Get on to Twitter and follow one or more of the following:

- @BloombergNews
- @dealbook
- @Reuters
- @WSJ
- @zerohedge
- Of course, I strongly recommend you follow **@GirlBanker**

I suggest you follow all of them to begin with and 'unfollow' the ones that you don't find that useful.

You may also want to look at the following:

Adkins Matchett & Toy (AMT) – renowned for teaching modeling skills. Some banks will hire them to train their analysts. If you want to learn a little modeling before you join corporate finance, this is a good place to start. Personally, I didn't know much about modeling and I was taught all I needed to know on Goldman Sachs' Analyst Program. Having no prior knowledge means you don't need to unlearn bad habits.

Breaking Into Wall Street – provide training similar to Adkins Matchett & Toy (AMT).

Recommended Books

The books listed below will help to give you a feel for the investment banking industry and its culture – although allow for artistic license. I have read all of these myself. I review each book (and more) on my blog at girlbanker.com.

- Without fail read *How To Win Friends and Influence People* by Dale Carnegie.
- *The Big Short: Inside the Doomsday Machine* by Michael Lewis
  - This is an account of the 2007-2009 credit crunch but by someone with some knowledge of working in the industry.
- *Too Big to Fail: Inside the Battle to Save Wall Street* by Andrew Ross Sorkin
  - Journalistic account of the events surrounding the downfall of Lehman and the 2007-2009 credit crunch.
  - Whether you prefer this or *The Big Short* is a matter of taste and preferred style. They are both good.
- *Liar's Poker* by Michael Lewis
  - Written with subtly caustic humor, this is an account of Wall Street culture in the 1980s; you'll probably enjoy reading this.
- *When Genius Failed, the Rise and Fall of LTCM* by Roger Lowenstein
  - This covers the same sort of period as *Liar's Poker*; it's very informative and very much worth a read, especially if you would like to work in the Debt Capital Markets.
- *Monkey Business* by John Rolfe and Peter Troob
  - You must read this if you're going into IBD. Things are slightly different nowadays but there is a lot of truth in the book. Quite funny.
- *Barbarians at the Gate* by Bryan Burrough and John Helyar
  - Written by two journalists. I'll admit, I only got half-way through this one; it was too detailed for my liking but many bankers have read it.

HEADHUNTERS

Firms sometimes use headhunters (recruitment agents) to fill vacant positions. A few months into your job you'll start receiving calls from them asking to meet up. You're going to be feeling pretty smart: *I've only been in the industry a few months and already my reputation precedes me.* News alert: he might not even be interested in you!

A headhunter is as good as his contacts and his knowledge of who does what, where and how. If you agree to meet up, you'll be mined for all the information you can give:

- Who works on your team and how long have they been there?
- Who's *good* on your team?
- Who's your manager?
- What exactly do you do and how do you fit in to your team?
- How does your team fit into the rest of the bank?

And so on. It's not a problem to talk to headhunters but don't reveal anything that could later compromise you.

Don't be rude to them just because you're currently happy with your job. It is well worth maintaining a relationship with good headhunters because:

- They may be able to help you find a new job when you need a new experience.
- They can give you market 'intel' on what other people at your level are earning at different firms.

~ That's all folks! ~

Hit me back with your comments @GirlBanker or coach@girlbanker.com

Appendix 1: Currency Codes

BRL	Brazilian Real
CAD	Canadian Dollar
CHF	Swiss Franc
CNY	Chinese Yuan
EUR	Euro
GBP	British Pound (Sterling)
HKD	Hong Kong Dollar
INR	Indian Rupee
JPY	Japanese Yen
KWD	Kuwaiti Dinar
MWK	Malawian Kwacha
RMB	Chinese Renminbi
RUB	Russian Ruble
TRY	Turkish Lira
USD	United States Dollar
ZAR	South African Rand

Appendix 2: Banking Lingo and Acronyms

A buck	A million US dollars (USD)
A quid	A million British pounds (GBP)
A yard	A billion
BBA	British Bankers' Association
BBU	Blissful Books United (a fictional chain of bookshops)
CAPM	Capital Asset Pricing Model
CCS	Cross-currency swap
CDS	Credit Default Swap
CFA	Chartered Financial Analyst
CMO	Collateralized Mortgage Obligation
COGS	Cost of Goods Sold
DCF	Discounted Cash Flow
EBITDA	Earnings Before Interest, Tax, Depreciation and Amortization
ECA	Export Credit Agency
EPS	Earnings Per Share
EV	Enterprise Value
FRA	Forward Rate Agreement
FRN	Floating Rate Note
FX	Foreign Exchange
GDP	Gross Domestic Product
IPO	Initial Public Offering
IRS	Interest rate swap
LIBOR	London Inter Bank Offered Rate
M&A	Mergers and Acquisitions
MBA	Masters of Business Administration
Mio	Million
P&L (or P'n'L)	Profit and Loss. Refers to revenue made.
PP&E	Property, Plant and Equipment
PPM	Private Placement Memorandum
SEO	Sponsors for Educational Opportunity

Index

Give yourself the best chance. Subscribe, like and follow Girl Banker® on:

Get coaching from Girl Banker®; see girlbanker.com for details

Avoid weight gain with a weight tracker designed by Girl Banker®

You're competing against hundreds of people. If you prepare adequately, **"Even if they only wanted one person, it should definitely be you!"**

Malawi-born Londoner, Heather Katsonga-Woodward, founded girlbanker.com. She is Girl Banker®.

In 2002, she received a full scholarship to read Economics at the University of Cambridge (ranked the best university in the world by QS for two years in a row, 2010 and 2011). Her eyes were opened to many things she didn't know anything about, including the world of Investment Banking.

After an internship at Goldman Sachs in the summer of 2004, she began full-time in 2005.

She joined the Structured Finance Team within the Investment Banking Division (IBD). Their main function was securitization and corporate debt advisory to infrastructure funds and assets.

During her two years in IBD, Heather developed an interest in derivatives. When she heard there was an opening on the Corporate Risk Advisory Team at HSBC, she applied and was offered the job about two weeks later. She spent the next five years in the capital markets, focused on interest rate derivatives initially then all of rates, FX and commodity derivatives later on.

Heather is also creator of the Fat Creep™ weight tracker app on iPhone and android. She lives in London with her husband and their hive of happy bees.

12686157R00180

Made in the USA
Charleston, SC
20 May 2012